'What Natalie Burt has done here is remarkable.

She has written a luminously honest, very funny, often very touching voyage of what it is actually like to be afflicted with the unquenchable desire to dedicate oneself to being a professional actor. It's not only an aide-memoire for any young person about to enter the business, but is also an amazing and fascinating insight into the realities and monstrous vicissitudes of what it takes to survive what is more often than not a pretty cruel and humiliating vocation. I've now been at it for thirty-five years; I'm one of the lucky ones but I've still had my bad patches, so I can vouch for the book's unquestionable veracity.

Natalie is a very talented young actress and has now proven herself to be an equally talented writer, truth-teller, and guardian angel.'
Timothy Spall O.B.E(ese)

'A refreshing and entertaining take on the challenges facing actors and how best to surmount them.'
Ben Seale
Managing Partner, Spotlight

'Natalie's book is like her acting: playful, irreverent, and accomplished. This is an honest and practical guide to what it's really like to be a working actor today and will be an invaluable resource
to training actors or drama school leavers.'
Laurie Sansom
Artistic Director National Theatre of Scotland

'At last! The book all aspiring actors have been waiting for. A truthful, comprehensive, funny guide to life as a jobbing and sometimes not jobbing actor. Nowadays more than ever show business is a brutal business. This book gives young actors a very real idea of what lies ahead – the good, the bad and the downright bloody hilarious. I only wish it had been around when I started out… I'd have made fewer mistakes and had even more fun.'
Caroline Quentin

'The best book ever written'
Natalie's Mum

ACTING: CUT THE CRAP, CUE THE TRUTH

Natalie Burt

ACTING:
CUT THE CRAP, CUE THE TRUTH
LIVING THE LIFE AND DOING THE JOB

OBERON BOOKS
LONDON

WWW.OBERONBOOKS.COM

First published in 2013 by Oberon Books Ltd

521 Caledonian Road, London N7 9RH

Tel: +44 (0) 20 7607 3637 / Fax: +44 (0) 20 7607 3629

e-mail: info@oberonbooks.com

www.oberonbooks.com

A catalogue record for this book is available from the British Library.

PB ISBN: 9781849434799
E ISBN: 9781849434959

Illustrations by Sam Davies

Printed, bound and converted
by CPI Group (UK) Ltd, Croydon, CR0 4YY.

Visit www.oberonbooks.com to read more about all our books and to buy them. You will also find features, author interviews and news of any author events, and you can sign up for e-newsletters so that you're always first to hear about our new releases.

Let's take a moment to discuss what the hell is actually inside
YET ANOTHER 'ACTING' BOOK.

Firstly the content has jack shit to do with learning how to act, I assume you can
do that? If not and you wish to be an actor, step number one would be learning
to act (well if possible). Secondly this book won't 'get you work' how could it?
It's a book not a wishbone. So, that's what it's not. What it is however is the most
thorough source of ball-achingly honest chat regarding the industry written
by someone who still has all their own teeth – it's seven years' worth of lessons
I've learned with the odd STI joke thrown in to lighten the mood, the overall
effect being a pragmatic, informative, thought-provoking tool laced with timely
helpings of comic vulgarity; a conversation not an instruction manual that I hope
may inspire, motivate and support anyone who can be arsed to read it.

At the very least it'll make a fabulous coaster and/or door stop.

Contents

'Let's not dwell on the struggle, let's deal with the fight'

1. AN INTRODUCTION

Why, oh why another bloody 'How to be an Actor' book?

Hello.

Ooh, suddenly I'm feeling incredibly self-aware writing this introduction… The introduction is meant to be the 'pull' isn't it, the bit that determines whether you buy the book or get distracted by a nearby volume of 'DIY for idiots'? …

Wow, ok… Well, here's a new sales technique – I have nothing to sell you. The information I present here is an offering, no more and no less, and as with everything else in this book you have the choice whether to take it or leave it. I'm merely suggesting not instructing.

For those of you who already find my approach less than mildly entertaining and/or borderline peculiar, goodbye (and good luck with the DIY). For those still with me, look back to the shelf. What do you see? An array of 'how to get work'- and 'ticket to success'-type titles, promising the undeliverable and seducing the venerable? Gimmicks and formulas will of course seem attractive to an actor whose agent can't pick them out of a line up, or whose last job was a devised adaptation of *Macbeth* in a barn in Holyhead – (It was great by the way, I saw it; the use of polyfiller and puppets was, erm, interesting.) And who exactly writes these books that litter the artsy sections of bookshops? Teachers? Ex-actors? Milkmen? Probably not milkmen. Hey, look, I'm no author, I don't claim to be anything but an actress, and I certainly don't claim to know much else outside of being one; which is why you'll be relieved to hear that I won't be attempting to explain the history of British Economics (maybe next year)… Nope, instead I'll be sticking to what I know. I am in fact doing what every writer is told to do; to write what they know, and if there is one thing that I certainly do know about, one thing that I can claim is 'my area', it's what it's like and what it takes to be an actor today, this very day. I didn't leave RADA in the 70s hayday, nor do I profess to have a glittering display of achievements and accolades behind me; but I do know what I'm talking about simply because I do it; I did it yesterday, I'm doing it today and I'll do it tomorrow; I live and breathe it and if that doesn't qualify me to write a book about it, I'm not sure what does. What better author is there than one who is also the target audience?

This is getting a bit 'selly'. Let me try and guess what you're thinking… Out of all the scores of actors, why me? Why bother? Why now? Well, it's certainly not because I'm famous and because my face and name will sell books is it? (It's Natalie by the way, in case you've forgotten.) You'll not recognise my face; other than thinking perhaps that I slightly resemble (to quote a drunken holidaymaker in Ibiza in 2001) a 'Poor man's Rene

Zellweger'… Outside of that flattering label however, I am simply a jobbing actor, like most actors, not a famous one, not a pretend one, just one who sometimes works and sometimes doesn't.

Why have I bothered to write this? 'Cause it beats temping in a call centre? I jest. I'm not saying that writing a book doesn't beat temping in a call centre, because it absolutely does – wiping arses at a daycare centre beats that. Marginally. However, the real reason I bothered to write this was because as a young graduate I was absolutely stunned, I think is the best way to put it, by the lack of reliable support available for actors new and old, whether that be professional, financial or emotional. After our showcase I watched my friends and colleagues crash from elation to devastation as reality hit, and felt powerless to help. It seemed that the bottom simply fell out of drama school, and we were all left to sink, swim or float aimlessly, with nothing but bewilderment for company. Drama schools cannot continue to cradle forever, of course not, there has to be a point when the chicks leave the nest; I've come to realise that the reason it felt so harsh, so abrupt, so disarming was because there was, and is, a distinct lack of pragmatic information available to aid us when it happens; as we attempt to live the life, as well as do the job. Those two things are not detached by the way, they are inextricably linked because as an actor you are your work, and your work is your life. Wearing that 24 hours a day, 365 days a year takes a hell of a lot, and I know I would have been pleased to receive any unbiased, constructive assistance that was offered to me. It is my hope that a reliable source of advice, written by someone with no other agenda than to reassure and encourage, might go some way to providing what I feel is so desperately needed. A little understanding and an ounce of guidance can be the difference between survival and demise.

The question of 'why now' is rather simple; it's an itch I've been meaning to scratch since graduating, but one that I knew I couldn't and shouldn't attempt before I was ready. I've been mulling the idea over since then and feel now that I can offer what is needed, both in terms of experience and objectivity. After seven years in the business I have formed my own strategies and philosophies and, perhaps rather arrogantly, have decided that putting a bunch of words in the right order might be of some use to each new batch of graduates who arrive at the playground only to be bewildered by the game the big kids are already playing.

So that's enough about me, this isn't a sodding autobiography. Let's get down to you shall we? If you have picked up this book and are considering buying it, borrowing or perhaps stealing it, then the likelihood is that you are an actor? Or a criminal with artistic aspirations… If you are the former, which I rather hope you are, then congratulations, you are (undeniably) cool as fuck. We all are, did nobody tell you?! You are part of a tiny percentage of the human race that are following their dreams against all odds, striving to realise them, daring to hope and willing to try. You are dodging the vacuum of normality, refusing to feel indifferent about a nine to five job; you do this, not because of something you want, but because of something you are, and instead of burying it or ignoring it you have embraced it, and that is both courageous and commendable. However, what you also '*are*', is buggered if you don't give yourself the best possible head start in a race where the finish line moves, the rules change and the other competitors sometimes quite blatantly cheat. Cue a bit of Bond theme tune? It's my book, why not; in the words of Chris Cornell:

'Arm yourself because no one else here will save you'

… *Casino Royale*, what a film.

In its simplest form this is what my book is for, to arm you. Arm you with knowledge you can use, strategies you can enforce, examples you can learn from and questions you can answer, freely and honestly. The idea is to make you stronger too, (we want to make sure that there is no H at the start of Mr Cornell's lyric!)… In fact, it isn't to make you stronger at all, it is to enable you to access the strength you already have; to add to the tenacity it's taken for you to get this far. All I can do though is offer things to you; it is up to you to be receptive and open and realistic throughout this process, if this is to be anything more than some crappy handbook. You have to want to make this work; you have to want to make sense of things and be prepared to work your arse off to do so. There is nothing terribly unique about an actor who can act, but there is something electric about an actor who will move heaven and earth to work and to learn; who is assertive enough to hear the truth, realistic enough to process it and savvy enough to use it to their advantage. That's what gets results and what makes people stand out from the crowd. Now is the time to tap into your entrepreneurial skills, to merge them with your knowledge and use them both alongside your practical abilities.

Within the business there are simple mistakes to be avoided, vague areas that I can clarify, and so many things swept under the carpet that the carpet is more or less brushing the bloody ceiling. I will be exposing these and discussing them with you openly. I will not be polite and I will not be censored, as you may have already grasped, but I will be honest and always constructive; my honesty coming from the reality I encounter every day as a jobbing actor and my constructiveness born from a belief that using such honesty should always serve you instead of me.

There may be stuff included here that some of you already know, of course there will be, we're not starting at the very beginning; when this happens please know that I am covering bases rather than trying to patronise you, and if there are jokes and witticisms that you don't get/consider amusing, please assume that they sounded funnier in my head; most things do. Apart from 'You didn't get the job', and 'You should've used protection'… Neither of those are funny in or outside of my head.

I'm sure that other actors similar to me, either in age or 'level', might have a slightly different take on a few points or angles, but the main principles of surviving and progressing will be mutually understood and practised by the vast majority. These are the principles I am loyal to here; everything else is about judgement calls, instincts and luck. The information I present to you is an offer of advice, not an instruction and not a formula. As I've said, it's a joint effort; I give this information, these tools to you gladly, but it is up to you to use your intelligence to assimilate what I'm saying and your gut to guide you through how much of it you choose to utilise. I've used the word *choose* there and would like to mark its first appearance. This is a word you will hear SO much in this book you will feel as if you should use it to name your first child… Don't, 'Choose Smith' just sounds weird…but it'd be a fab name for a future little politician though eh? I digress (which will also happen a lot, but stay with me). There are a variety of things I'll say that you will agree and disagree with, and I very much hope there is a healthy helping of both; opinion and initiative (with a dash of shrewd rebellion) will serve you well in this industry, and will not only make you more interesting to work with but also far more fascinating to watch.

I probably should mention before we go any further, that this is not a 'how to act' book. First of all, I do not believe that one can learn such an indefinable, empirical skill solely from a book (even if I did, I wouldn't be the one to write it – we'll leave that to Stella and Stan). Secondly, I am assuming, rightly or wrongly, that by now training will have done its best to nurture and discipline the craft within any person who shows interest in this book. The practical skills and the passion to fuel those skills are no doubt fired up and ready to fly. However, for every five minutes in front of the camera in a casting suite, or in some wooden-floored, drafty loft with a director, there are weeks and months of 'coping' required in order to ensure that when those five minutes do present themselves, you shine; instead of fading, cracking or quitting. This book is less about acting and more about being ready to act.

I'm going to be completely honest with you from the off and admit that probably 92% of the time I've spent writing this book I've felt like a bit of a fraud. In no way have I got it sorted, far from it; I know no secret codes to success or quick fixes for fame and fortune, (evidently not, just last night I coloured in some scuffs on my boots with a permanent marker pen). I don't have it made; but I'm still going strong, making progress every day and loving every minute, even the shit minutes (in a way). There aren't that many actors who can put their hand on their heart and say that after ten years. I think the only reason this is the case for me, is because I have almost faultlessly kept the faith; I have fought to maintain positivity, sustain my enthusiasm and determination in the face of adversity, and sought to improve with every passing lesson. And most importantly, I have used all the shit that I've endured over the last ten years to make me stronger.

The life of an actor is a complex tapestry of bollocks and brilliance, a rollercoaster that truly does both exhilarate and nauseate; it caresses with one hand and slaps with the other. Your love will be tested, continuously, and unless you are sufficiently prepared, thoroughly informed and utterly grounded, those tests may get the better of you.

Ideal timing, Mr Jovi would like to add a pearl of wisdom to that:

'Success is falling down nine times and getting up ten'
Jon Bon Jovi

Cue 'Blaze of Glory'…

2. YOUR 3rd YEAR OF TRAINING

Countdown to the release date.

First of all let's annihilate that chapter title. From now on refer to your '3rd year of training' as your '1st year as a professional actor'. Ooh, I hear you say. Yup, and so it begins. Adopting this **attitude** is crucial when it comes to many things, including the image you portray to the industry, the continuous **development** you will undergo and the **product** you are now beginning to shape. It also has a profound influence on the **decisions** that you will make, both in your immediate future and beyond.

Though there is some debate around the 'necessity' of conventional training where acting is concerned, there is no doubt that drama training is hugely beneficial for any 'wannabe' actor, and a path that should be considered if a career in the arts is sought; it is a safe and trustworthy incubation tank and a first step that is recognized and well respected by the masses. Though the location and type of training required may be up for discussion, there is no question in my mind that training of some sort, whether educational or vocational, is a requirement; whether 'lessons' are learnt in a studio or out on location, the lessons must be learnt, and the correct muscles should be discovered, exercised and understood. It is an essential process whereby potential is nurtured by those whose experience qualifies them to do so. Though the setting for this chapter is drama school, the specific phase I dissect here is relevant to anyone hoping to make the transition from amateur to professional.

Talent is a peculiar word; it's frequently suggested that someone either 'has it or they haven't'. I won't deny that there is an innate flair in most actors and that they tend to show signs of it very early on; it may seem that a child possesses some personality traits, and hints at having some key skills that are widely recognized as attributes intrinsic to the 'performer'. Whether they understand at that stage what a future channelling those attributes entails is a completely different story. But talent is a word that most actors shy away from. Maybe because it carries with it 'god-given' type connotations, as if a mystical gift has been bestowed, readying us to fulfil a prophecy of some sort… (Romanticism and Crap are always only a gnat's fart from each other in my opinion, especially in this business!) That train of thought also suggests that a fully formed skill simply sits there; that it is somehow effortless to execute and sustain, which in my mind diminishes the work, hours, blood, sweat and tears that go into the learning of the craft. I believe in giving credit where credit is due! Surely we as actors do ourselves a huge injustice if we support such uninformed assumptions?

I believe in natural ability, sure, but I also know that a diamond can be shaped and polished to increase its appeal and value. It is ability that provides the possibility for brilliance, but practice that delivers it; they go hand in hand. There is a world between having a skill and having a career and only you are truly in control of using the former to build the latter.

You may notice that some of the 'front runners' in the first year of drama school are floundering towards the end, either because panic is setting in as the realities of the industry lose their soft hypothetical edge, or as their ability peaks, their development stalling at the height of its potential. It is within the process of development that ability, application and ambition need to join forces, each dependent on the other and all vital. All we have in the beginning is potential; our ability must be coupled with a willingness and capacity to assimilate information and then apply it. What's more, we must have an unequivocal love of the practice, a need to do it, a need way beyond simple desire. Is this you? If you are reading on, I think there's a good probability that it is.

Any drama course, whether it be at a drama school or university is a peculiar, possibly even unstable mix of funny farm, playground, intensive care unit and party bus. I found it hilarious that for the first few years of my career the most common question between actors, a question that rolls from the tongue and is universally understood by the acting community, was 'How long have you been out?'… Drama school (or Uni) can seem like a jail sentence and therefore similar terminology is adopted! One can become quite unknowingly institutionalised within the 'system' and too reliant on the structure and guidance provided (not dissimilar from Brooks in *The Shawshank Redemption*)…

IF YOU HAVEN'T SEEN *THE SHAWSHANK REDEMPTION* PUT THIS BOOK DOWN, SLAP YOURSELF, BUY IT, WATCH IT, PAT YOURSELF ON THE BACK AND PICK THE BOOK BACK UP AGAIN.

… As you will now know, having obediently followed my instructions and watched *The Shawshank Redemption*, Brooks had been waiting for freedom for so long, idealising and fantasising about what he would do once his chains were cut, that unintentionally he had become reliant on the system, a slave to authority and content with routine, meaning that when the point of transition came he was unable to function independently of it all, unable to cope. I'm not saying that you talk to crows or that you will hang yourself, but simply that the education system can encourage an over-dependence that is hard to undo. Shit, I just ruined the end for you… Well, let that be a lesson to you to obey my instructions, when I say put down the book and watch a film, I mean it! (Haven't ruined it really.) It is for this reason that the weaning process must start at the end of the second year and throughout the third year of training, to prevent any shocks and false starts. Or conversations with crows.

So how do we actually prepare ourselves for a notoriously harsh world we've only heard, hoped and read about? The four words I mentioned in the first paragraph – attitude, development, product and decisions – might assist you in doing so.

ATTITUDE

Definition: A settled way of thinking or feeling, typically reflected in a person's behaviour.

As an actor your attitude is everything, not only during training but throughout your career. Having a professional attitude, a generous attitude, a positive attitude and a realistic attitude all come under the umbrella title of a 'good attitude'. If you think like a professional you will look, act and sound like a professional. If you are considerate to those around you both on and off 'stage', you will be known as having a generous attitude. If you rise above disappointment it will be because of a positive attitude. If you assess your progression and carefully choose your career path you will be doing yourself a favour by having a realistic attitude. All of this is a good idea. A bad attitude will not only make you unemployable (or certainly not re-employable), it will also make you unhappy, which can, has and continues to lead actors into a debilitating, alienating and unconstructive realm of bitterness and ultimately – unemployment! You must be sure to create, develop and sustain a good attitude; it will provide you with the gumption to continue and the positivity to overcome obstacles of all shapes and sizes.

Sadly you can't purchase good attitudes from Primark or order them on Amazon; they are a direct result of your thought process and take time and effort not only to obtain and maintain but also to apply. This is one of the most important skills for you to master throughout the last stretch of training ensuring that you hit the 'real world' as an energized, enthusiastic, likeable, grounded and above all, happy actor. Nobody wants to employ

a) A miserable git
b) An arrogant git
c) An unreliable git

Gits in general – not good. In finding your 'good attitude' though, there is a danger you will fall into the world of trying to 'please'. Don't; it's disgusting to watch, not beneficial to anyone (especially you) and worst of all, you may run the risk of becoming and/or being known as a 'kiss ass' – not cool. More on ass-kissing later under 'Networking' (there's a common misconception that they mean the same thing…)

At the start of drama school you had potential, but by now you should have blossomed into a young professional in possession of a firm set of core skills; skills that are enigmatic, and intriguing to almost everyone whether inside or outside of the business. Have confidence in what you do and let that create confidence within those you encounter, but never, ever assume that you are the only one possessing such qualities. Complacency or arrogance will dissolve that talent in the eyes of everyone around you at an alarming speed, and without admiring eyes you have no career.

DEVELOPMENT

Definition: The process of developing or being developed. A specified state of growth.

Two of the biggest enemies at this phase of training are distraction and intimidation. Focus on your own energy and artistic development instead of everyone else's and get used to the fact that competition is always going to be a part of your life, certainly for as long as you are an actor. Every second that you are preoccupied with how 'good' someone else is, every minute that you are paying attention to how 'well' everyone else is doing is precious time wasted, time that will be better spent focusing on yourself, on your own unique assets and attributes and on your individual personal progression. I am not saying have tunnel vision, of course take note of the lessons being learnt and the mistakes being made around you, but ultimately keep your eye on the prize; in doing so you will gradually become so self-assured in your work that any lessons you take from others can be nothing but constructive. Oh it's so easy to say eh?! We're human, we're vulnerable, we trip over and we fuck up, but one's self-assurance is obtainable and sustainable, in my opinion, as long as you are sure that you are being the best that you can be at all times. If you can honestly say that then you deserve to be good and will continue to blossom.

You are entering a life-long state of progression; therefore never assume that you know it all, or that you are ever likely to; relish the process and feel invigorated by the fact that it is ongoing. It is one of the most beautiful elements of the job and one that entices us to stick with it. No matter how old or experienced you are, the learning, the developing and the discovering should never cease, and if you find that it does, you will probably realise that you have either lost interest or gotten too big for your boots! To develop is to grow and you must continuously go over and beyond what is asked and expected of you in order to do so; you cannot afford to switch off at 6pm and you can never allow yourself to rest on your laurels. Keep thinking, keep challenging and keep questioning throughout your third year and never stop. Even talking with your mates/colleagues about what you have seen and heard in class or at the theatre or on telly is hugely beneficial; unknowingly you will be forming opinions and tastes, creating aims and goals, feeding off of one another's energies – and best of all, you can do most of that at the pub. Please note that in between my drill sergeant-type antics and dictator-style speeches I do acknowledge the importance of being young and having fun! Socialising, forging friendships and relaxing are all very important *in addition* to your professional dedication and as you will notice over the next few years, as you branch out into this wonderfully social vocation of ours, the two things are massively intertwined! Chats in the pub can become plans for a devised show and meeting a new person at a party can lead to an audition for something you didn't know was casting. There is a barely visible border between work and play for us; just be wary of the pitfalls whilst you're taking advantage of the perks!

Everyday you have the ability to be better than yesterday and worse than tomorrow.

PRODUCT

Definition: An article or substance that is manufactured or refined for sale.

You are the product. You may not be a substance but you have been refined (through the process of training) and you will be sold. Hopefully repeatedly! You have packaging, you have USPs (unique selling points), you have marketing materials and you have competition. This does not differ from any other item within a marketplace, other than the fact that in your case the personal and professional elements of the product are so interlinked that separating them, or better still, differentiating between them is no easy task and doing so can be fraught with danger, especially in the early days when you are still finding your feet. The same emotional investment that makes actors brilliant can also be their downfall; we personally feel the peaks, so naturally we do the same with the troughs. The stakes are high and the lines are blurred, but the pay-off is larger than any other I've encountered; the pay-off of doing what you love.

Being a performer is emotionally exposing, on stage and off, both when you're acting and when you are living the life of an actor. But nevertheless it is essential that you start thinking of it and yourself as the product within your own business. You are no longer treading the boards in the local am dram, revelling in the uncomplicated frivolity of it all; you are now aiming to make a living from it too. Sure, you will be emotionally engaged in the choices you make and the knocks you receive but you must learn to be objective too, in equal measure, knowing when to hear your heart and when to listen to your head.

Make friends with the fact that when we discuss 'business' we mean an environment where money is made, and also make friends with the fact that money will be made using you; your skill, your smile, your arse, your voice – you. Art doesn't exist in some purist dimension, it is like everything else out there; it may have a 'deeper meaning' running through it than most things you can buy or sell but at the end of the day art cannot be made and would cease to exist without finance; as would you! Nurture your product, know your product, sell your product, protect your product and think strategically about the future of your product. Which brings me nicely onto…

DECISIONS

Definition: A conclusion or resolution reached after consideration.

This is a vast and vital subject, one that is difficult to explain in a generic sense but one that I feel is neglected and in need of discussion. First, I will speak about decisions you will be faced with beyond graduation and later I will address the decisions you may make at school. Both contribute to and form your strategy as a professional.

You will find, as I have, that your career as an actor is a decision-making minefield. Now, before I start breaking down those decisions for you, outlining the choices you may face, I want to emphasise to you that *you do always have a choice!* In my opinion (and it has been challenged) you never *have* to take a job, you never *have* to sign with a particular agent, you never *have* to go to an audition and you certainly never *have* to 'take whatever you can' – this train of thought disgusts me if I'm completely honest and I once had a very heated discussion with an older actor about it; his opinion, (which in hindsight smacked of a massive generational gap, a contaminated, embittered view of the profession caused by many years of enduring it, plus a large amount of red wine), was that as actors we are designed to act, and therefore (considering how many of us there are and how little work there is) we should be overjoyed with whatever scraps we are thrown and grateful to be in work at all; whatever that work may be. When all is said and done, we just want to act, right? But surely one of the perks (and there are few) of being an actor, being self-employed, is that you are your own boss and therefore master of your own destiny, no? In my view the more we disempower our role within the industry the more bleak a future we paint for ourselves and for future generations. We are not beggars, prostitutes or court jesters, we are skilled and ambitious and worth more than 'whatever we can get'.

Of course experience is gained through doing, through practicing, but it concerns me when actors passively accept whatever job comes their way without questioning its value. There seems to be little to no guidance for dealing with such choices (outside of a good agent's advice) and I hate to think that actors are taking jobs that don't pay, encourage bad habits and may even close doors and limit future opportunities. This does not mean turning down every job unless the director is Sam Mendes, nor does it mean that we should all suddenly be artless buck-chasers, it means that we are being considered and business-like in our approach to our careers. Each job will have pros and cons and you must learn to identify them, assess them and then be brave enough to make decisions based upon your findings.

Now, please know that sharing my view on this means that your professional (and therefore personal) life becomes a casino, and you the gambler. As we all know gamblers sometimes win and gamblers sometimes lose and both skill and luck are usually at play. It is neither my right nor my aim to tell you to be a gambler, but I feel it is my duty to reassure you that you do absolutely have the option to be one. It's a game of luck so people say. I say that it's a game of risk and unless you are prepared to risk high, how can you hope to win high? This is not something that you necessarily need to decide upon now. There are so many different stages of development, the decisions flying at you will vary and your reactions to them will alter, sometimes at an unnerving rate. Over the next few years you will notice where you sit within this debate by assessing your own aims and observing how the choices of others impact their careers. This is an evolving state of mind, so try not to make generalised sweeping statements or write a list of Wills and Wont's in permanent ink; for now, at least acknowledge that there is choice and that the decisions you make have a domino effect. (More on that later.)

How do I make decisions? I am a huge believer in gut instinct. Of course I will always do the leg work, gather the evidence for and against any decision, assess it all calmly and strategically; but at the end of the day my instincts usually win no matter what the evidence suggests as the answer! Reckless? Not really, my knowledge and professional objectivity inform my instincts, it's not like I'm ever whimsical. Listening to my gut has and does serve me well and though doing so takes balls, a slither of arrogance (or as I like to call it, blind faith) and a gambling nature, if you're gonna reach for the stars you can't be afraid of heights, can you?

Your ATTITUDE will aid your DEVELOPMENT, your DEVELOPMENT will improve your PRODUCT and your PRODUCT will determine what DECISIONS you will be required to make.

See what's happening here, we've only gone and got a little pattern! I know you must be thrilled that there appears to be some logic to all the chatting I'm doing. So, what 'decisions' am I banging on about?! Let's get back to the phase we're talking about in this chapter and start with examples of questions that should be considered during the transition from amateur to professional. You will soon see how the answers to these questions will inform the decisions you face, both now and later on:

Generic Questions:
- What do you like best about acting?
- Do you still think acting is something you'd like to do forever?
- Do you see yourself in a specific area of casting or not?
- What kind of work do you enjoy watching and why?
- What classes are you really good at?
- What classes are you not so good at?

By asking yourself these questions you are shaping the actor you want to be. There are no right or wrong answers, only information to glean; information that you must assimilate and use to your advantage.

Strategic Questions:
- What plays are being planned for your 3rd year shows?
- What parts are available within them?
- Considering your answers to the last set of questions, are there any parts that will let you practise skills in a specific area of interest?

By asking these questions you are ensuring that you get the best opportunity to nurture the actor you want to be.

Though the subjects I'm lobbing at you (for want of a better phrase) are perhaps a tad scary, they are pivotal to your development as an actor and to you as a product. Your knowledge of these things and use of that knowledge is vital.

I will go into more detail on decisions and self-assessment as we move through the book, but for now remember…

You are not an Actor in a year's time, when you are handed a certificate or when you sign your first contract. You are an Actor now. It starts now.

With that in mind, let's tackle your first stage as a professional.

IN-HOUSE SHOWS DURING TRAINING

There are many important things to glean from drama school, but I would like to discuss here two of the most important things, certainly in your third year. Firstly, benefitting from the experience of **practising your craft in a safe environment** and secondly **utilising the opportunity from a sales point of view**, one being as equally important as the other.

The next decade will be a string of opportunities for you, in fact the rest of your career will be, but specifically, the next year or so (from second year to graduation) is the foundation from which it will all grow. This time will never be repeated, so I cannot stress enough how important it is to get all that you can from it. This year is about process not result and learning (as well as enjoying) to walk before you run.

What do I mean by practising in a safe environment?
Though drama courses attempt to function as some sort of simulator for the life you're going to live as an actor, it is important that whilst you embrace the similarities you also recognise the differences; using them to your advantage to aid your advancement. Enjoy the fact that you can and should make mistakes, that it is safe to do so without lasting judgments or widespread acknowledgements; this is an integral part of improvement. Allow yourself to fail and fuck up – as long as you learn from it! You must play. Play throughout your career but especially play now whilst there is no fear of consequence. Make this part of your method this early. To play is to risk, experiment, challenge, dare; you will never be in this environment again with absolute license to do so; now's the time to play, guilt- and pressure-free. To play is to discover and to fail is to learn. Take full advantage.

How can you take full advantage?
- Veer away from your comfort zone, experiment with playing parts that aren't obvious.
- Question your own choices and play with alternatives (in rehearsals).
- Be unpredictable but not selfish (in rehearsals).
- Never rest on your laurels and assume you're doing it 'right', there is no such thing; there's good but there's also different, and different can be better. PLAY.
- Ask questions of your director/teacher, start debates and discussions and listen to everyone.
- Stay later if you're on a roll, stay later if you're not (in rehearsals).

PUSH, PLAY AND PERSEVERE.

Third-year shows will probably be your first proper taste of the casting world and whilst casting decisions made about you and by you right now are important, they are not deal-breakers, they're learning curves – you will gain experience throughout no matter what as long as you are open, able and determined. This isn't to say that you should be passive about casting and simply 'get what you're given' though! No, no, the go-getter attitude from earlier on in this section should start to come into play now, just be ready for things to not always go your way and start practising how you cope when it doesn't. It's a good muscle to stretch!

If you answered the questions I put to you in the intro of this chapter you will be hopefully starting to grasp not only where your preferences lie but also where your skills are strongest (and weakest – also very important to know)! Use this information to…

Make interesting choices when it comes to casting and take that style of decision-making into showcase and beyond.

Choose to go for something – conviction will be admired, celebrated and possibly even rewarded. You can make any choice using the knowledge you're gaining from questioning yourself and from the information acquired by challenging and assessing your own abilities. Be demonstrative and assertive. It is likely that you will be aware of most of the scheduled shows at the beginning of the year, and if you're not then the staff will be, so probe them! (I found that alcoholic bribes work most effectively.) Suggest that you want to carefully map your casting for the year – if nothing else they will admire your tenacity. If you have very specific cast-ability and there is a part that you think is just right – go for it. On the flip side, you could dare to work against type and audition for the part that no one expects you to which may challenge you further, expand your cast-ability and prove that you are versatile. There is plenty of time once you're 'out' to be pigeon holed…

A beautiful, rather peculiar example, which is absolutely true, is the casting of the Beacon Players' 1998 pantomime *Cinderella* in the village of Woodhouse Eaves. The previous year I had played Maid Marion in *The Babes in the Wood* (to ENORMOUS critical acclaim). I did the whole romantic female lead thing; softened my voice, dropped any hint of feminism or teenage angst, tricked the village into thinking I was sweet *and* successfully pretended to be in love with the villager playing Robin; who happened to be a middle aged woman named Hilary. Who couldn't sing for shit. It was a box and I had ticked it. So, the following year when they offered me Cinderella, I paused to consider their offer – thoroughly, seriously. What was I going to learn by playing another romantic lead? Would I be bored with a similar task to the previous year? Would all of the film directors in the village (of which there were loads I'm sure) consider me a one-trick pony if I took this role? Aged twelve I assessed my ability, strategised about my development and followed my gut. And what was my gut saying? That I wanted to be funnier than Cinderella. So I said no thank you and voiced my interest in playing Buttons, the (usually male) comic turn. This was the beginning of my comedy career. It was a gamble, but it paid off. I know what you're thinking… 'What a pretentious little shit'. Well, yeah, you're probably right, but she knew what she wanted, knew what she needed and made damn sure she utilised the opportunities available to her. So…I mean, yeah, she got beaten up quite a bit at school, but she's doing alright now… Despite the nightmares.

You what? You want pictorial evidence that this story is true? Fine. Seriously, the personal sacrifices that I make in order to inspire you lot.

Here it is…

Is the anticipation killing you? Get ready…

Ok, seriously, empty your diary so you can spend the week laughing...

I still wear those tights.

So, back to decision making; if by some miracle you can erase the previous image from your memory and concentrate again.

Never let the risk of it not panning out stop you aiming for things. If the choice backfires (you don't get the part, don't enjoy the part or suck at the part) then choose to make the best of the situation anyway, embracing the opportunity you have been given and finding the lessons within it. It may even turn out better than the original plan. Adopting this attitude is far more interesting than wallowing in self-pity. Now's the time to carve into your heart and mind that choices matter and that you should be making them intelligently.

1. Be clever and focused when it comes to internal casting. Let your choices be both informed and instinctual.

2. Challenge yourself and don't be afraid to fuck up.

3. Don't fuck up continuously though; IMPROVE!

The way that you train your mind now will stick, so trust your instincts (you will hear me say that a zillion more times than I have already), dare to be a little cocky and use the experience of this year, whether it be a good or bad one to enrich both your acting ability and your capacity to cope. Good habits start here.

What are good habits?

- Maybe don't eat in your costume… I learnt that the hard way – and no, I didn't spill tomato soup down a Georgian dress or anything, but I nearly bloody did when Stacy Gollier (teacher) screamed at me for taking the risk in the first place. Hashtagoverreaction… I can't find the hashtag on my Mac… Hashtagtechnoignoramus.

- Try not to dick around (too much) in tech. You will be bored, but only as bored as all of the tech team are whilst you're 'acting' over and over and over again. They endure weeks of you doing your thing, so give them a few hours. However, if you feel the need to be entertaining intermittently because you sense that some morale lifting is required, I say chance it. (Hashtaggaugeit)… I should really stop using the hashtag, having to write it is defeating the object and making me look like a tosser.

- Be careful of not playing up to the audience. Considering that the 'audience' will consist mostly of your mates, peers and family members in your 3rd year, this can be tempting. A girl in our year did just this and though the audience found her erratic behaviour mildly humorous, she completely screwed over her scene partner. She hasn't ever worked professionally… In fact I think she sells diamonds. Probably illegally.

- You will be sharing dressing rooms, so always try to be sensitive to the wants and needs of others, whether that be sharing a section of the mirror or honouring a bit of quiet time. Also, take the opportunity in a communal space to subtly perve on your peers. (Subtle is the word.) On one of our 3rd-year shows we had a great corset-doing-up foreplay session before every curtain up, and whether the lead male knew it or not, we enjoyed it, hey Lil?!… Wink! P.S. He knew.

- If something goes wrong or as I prefer to phrase it, 'awry', don't blame. It is live theatre; this can and does happen. If there is something that needs raising in the notes session that the director doesn't acknowledge then by all means be vocal, but for god sake don't finger point, whisper behind backs or lay on guilt where it is not needed. This is amateur behaviour and you are not an amateur.

- Warm up – you are not above it or exempt from needing it. (But don't be obsessive; apart from the fact that it's just not cool, the anxiety that you end up inflicting on yourself and others will counteract everything you're trying to achieve through being 'warm').

- Don't be late. Just don't. Learn to timekeep or your 3rd-year shows may be your last.

- Try not to fight notes. It's sometimes hard but remember that the point of doing shows whilst still training is not that you are perfect (never) but that you improve. Notes are always to try and make something better. This doesn't end at drama school. I worked with a girl once who simply would not hear the note, write it down, assess it and then try it; she had to comment further and fight it, like it was a personal attack the director was making (a highly skilled director I might add).

On the notes subject, I don't mean never speak up; if you don't understand the note, if the note seems highly unfair or if there's a stagecraft problem that needs to be resolved, by all means communicate with your team, it is your job to do so. Likewise, if an element of your performance needs further discussion feel free to raise it. When I was given a note in a 3rd-year show that I looked slightly distracted and was late for a song cue, I felt that I had every right to point out (through stifled laughter) that my dress had in fact started to catch fire from one of the stage lamps and that I didn't think my flaming arse would have added to the essence of the number I was about to sing, ergo I was late whilst my leading man had selflessly patted my behind *thoroughly* until the smoke subsided (cheers Marc)…that note was worth justifying I felt. Where notes are concerned, use your common sense and you (hopefully) won't go far wrong. Be aware that this is a lesson in being able to receive constructive suggestion in order to enhance your performance. Get used to it.

- Always, always, always go to the pub after a show! Celebrate what you just created and achieved together and wind down from the stress you've just been through. (Maybe decline the last three tequilas though if you have a matinee the next day…)

- Make plans, set aims and have goals but never think that because things aren't going exactly to plan, they are therefore going badly. You must find the positive in every turn, the lesson in every curve and keep working hard in the face of adversity. Believe and it may just happen (and is far more likely to if you do).

- Let everyone speak in rehearsal. Listen and don't be self-important. Unless you are doing a one-man show…

- If someone wishes to try something in rehearsal, don't block it! How do you know whether it'll work or not without giving it a go? Without the constraints of time and budget you are allowed to try things for trying's sake.

- Never boast or gloat that you know your lines before others. We all know this is not what makes a good actor. Plus, you'll sound like a tit.

So, whilst some of these are slightly tongue-in-cheek, there is truth to be noted and a lesson to be learnt in all of them. Start practising good habits now. To be honest, most of them are simply about being a thoughtful and generous performer/human being, which I am SURE (or I hope) you all are anyway.

So as I mentioned at the beginning of this chapter, the 3rd year is a two-pronged lesson. As well as wading through all of the 3rd year obstacles, concentrating tirelessly on your artistic growth, there is also the business end of things to contend with. You now work in sales as well as the arts. Let's get tactical.

How do you utilise opportunities from a sales point of view?
'Sales point of view' sounds desperately clinical I know, but the more you start to think in these terms the more it will benefit your state of mind and work ethic. By focusing on it being business you will learn to take rejection less personally, evaluating situations and outcomes with both your head and your heart (in equal measure), culminating in you being, and being seen as, a centred and reliable professional by the rest of the industry – and that's what it is, an industry.

As you move through the year, playing whatever roles you end up playing, start to identify where your strengths lie. i.e. If everyone seems to agree that you have a period look, if you seem to have a flair for comedy, if you are an actor-muso etc. – by embracing these you are creating your unique selling points. These points will assist you when trying to capture the attention of agents and casting directors later down the line; they are a marketing tool and will be what differentiates you from everyone else. It's worth bearing in mind that whilst playing to your strengths is clever, challenging yourself is a must (and as we've discussed, this safe environment is the place in which to do this – or to at least make a start). As much as is possible, avoid putting yourself, or allowing others to put you into a 'type', 'category' or 'box'. Through experimentation new, exciting and unexpected USPs may be found – the more you have the more versatile you are and the easier you are to sell!

If you're repeatedly being compared to a well-known actor, log it and take an objective look at their careers. Who is their agent? What were their first three jobs? How has their career progressed? Is it a career you would be content with? If not why? If so, why? In no way am I saying, right, I'm a Renée Zellweger mini-me so I therefore have the license to eat lots of doughnuts and must work in films with Colin Firth… Though that does sound like a pretty good plan… (Not the point I was going for!) You know what I mean, the point is not to copy or reconstruct, it is to use others who have gone before you as a template; noticing their USPs and their use of said USPs may better prepare you for your own journey.

So what might your selling points include?

- Your experience before, during and after training.
- Your drama school or place of training.
- Your look, 'distinctive' or not.
- Whatever glaringly obvious strengths you have.
- Extra skills you possess.
  (Neither juggling nor sarcasm have been useful for me yet, but you never know.)
- Your accent.

Get to know your assets, attributes and castability (what roles others immediately see you playing). Doing this will enable you to use it and to challenge it, making you confident of the product you are presenting to the business and sure of the potential it has. Remember that nothing is written in stone! As we've discussed you will change and improve, alter and develop – but for now, at this moment in time, you are selling an idea, a plan. To do this you need to have a tongue in your head, some conviction in your temperament and absolute knowledge of your product or else no one will buy.

I'm sure talking about yourself and your abilities is not something that many of you struggle with too much… But, in a desperate attempt to dodge stereotype, I am aware that the idea of self-promotion does not come naturally to all. In fact most who truly possess skill as actors are rubbish at this bit. Whichever you happen to be, Modest Mary or Blah Barry, explaining and showing your product can only be done once your foot is in the damn door. This is no easy task and one that is and continues to be…fun.

Let's get knocking on those doors and jamming our feet into them before they can be slammed again! Cue the next section…

PHOTOGRAPHS

These are your calling cards, your invitations, and a very important marketing tool. They're a big deal, but they're not the most important part of life as we know it. So my first piece of advice is chill out. The hysteria and hype around this second/third-year activity is ridiculous; students swarming around each other's contact sheets… I mean iPads… What? When I graduated seven years ago an ipad was part of a first aid kit. Friends choosing the one with the eyebrow raised, a tutor choosing the softer one, mum wanting the one that most resembles your first school photo and Bob down the road not giving a flying fuck. It should be exciting and fun as well as important. You may have gathered (from my subtle sarcasm) that I am suggesting that you don't show the entire world and his ferret the options that the photographer sends to you. Everyone will have an opinion (mostly based upon crap rather than knowledge) and it will only confuse the task of choosing for you.

By all means use the staff; they've been around headshots for years and will look at the photograph and not at 'you', meaning that they will not focus on how 'nice' you look or what a good angle your face is at; their opinion won't be clouded by sentimentality or vanity, they will be professionally critical and this is useful. Do ask friends/peers if you must, but select a few that you trust and respect. They will probably like the ones that look most 'like you' which is also useful – I know, they're all you right? The camera's weird and can be a little bit deceptive at times so be careful not to choose a photo that best represents how you'd like to look! However, whilst avoiding airbrush central remember that this is not a new profile picture; comedy gestures captured on an iPhone might not be appropriate – quality is imperative, this is an advert for the product you're offering.

So firstly, how the hell to…

CHOOSE A PHOTOGRAPHER

PRICE – Do not be rail-roaded into thinking that the most expensive photographer equals the best pictures. This is simply untrue and I am giving you license to feel ok about starting to think 'on budget'. Not splashing the cash does not mean that you love acting any less or that you are not prepared to do what it takes to give yourself the best start that you can; it simply means you are operating within your means (something you will get very good at very quickly). Make the decision based on the following three points: **reputation, evidence and comfort**, whilst allowing yourself to be aware of cost. The likelihood is that you will be aware of cost for the next god-knows-how-many years anyway, so you may as well start here!

You may be up against people whose family shit money at them, you may be up against people who have had to ask to have their photographs done instead of having Christmas and birthday presents for the next two years; like I've said, it doesn't matter what everyone else is doing, focus on your own circumstances and make choices according to them and them alone. Whilst allowing yourself to consider price however, you must of course invest in your future, and accept that this is a cost you must cover. Bear in mind that you may want to have new photos done once you've worked a bit, or your new agent might suggest that you have new ones; once they take you on they have a say in your calling card (it is after all their calling card for you). My point is that these first photographs may have a short shelf life, which is another reason not to spend your entire life savings on them. It's best to start researching and saving ahead of schedule; that way you will be making the decision that is right for you and your career instead of cost being a worry.

Most photographers do drama school discounts, and in my opinion they damn well should! *Remember that they need you as much as you need them* (a theme we'll keep returning to) – there are almost as many bloody photographers as there are actors! (And a fair few seem to be both!)…

REPUTATION – Get onto Spotlight (using a casting director password – every drama school has 'illegal' access to one – ask around) and start to look up actors that you like, actors that you've seen etc. Not only will you start to build a mental list of photographs you like and styles that you don't, but you'll also be able to make a note of each of the photographers who took them, creating a list of potentials.

If you have friends in the years above you, ask them or look them up – I guarantee that most actors who've graduated within the last year (and depressingly many who've graduated ages before that) will have their headshot on Facebook, probably as their profile pic (VOM). Have a scroll through and ask around; ask how much a session was, what was included in the package and how they felt about the experience overall.

If you do seek another actor's advice, maybe also ask:

- Did you feel you had long enough?
- Did you have inside and outside shots?
- Was the photographer personable and did they put your mind at ease?
- How efficient were they in getting the images to you?
- Do they do retouches?
- Was the photographer's cat forever rubbing itself up against you as you were trying to not 'smile'?

That last one's optional…

Whilst recommendations are useful, don't fall into the trap of going with the photographer that *everyone's* going with! Dare to be different, you want your photograph to stand out; a line-up of headshots at showcase that looks more like one photographer's gallery is not great for you lot – Remember the U in USP!

By chatting to peers and staff you will begin to form opinions about the array of photographers at your disposal but make sure that your research has the strongest voting power as secondary opinions can be inaccurate and misleading and usually lack objectivity…that's across the board actually not just when it comes to photographs!

I hate myself for even saying this, and please will the majority of you forgive me, but it has to be mentioned…

DO NOT LET A FRIEND TAKE A PHOTO OF YOU AND TRY AND PASS IT OFF AS A HEADSHOT. YOU WILL NOT BE EMPLOYED. AND PEOPLE WILL ASSUME THAT YOU ARE SHIT.

I'm sorry, but you'd be surprised. I am, constantly.

EVIDENCE – As I've said, ask around, look at others' shots, get online and research the photographers whose work you like the look of. For anyone who is not at drama school or university I would advise to look at *Contacts*. This book contains all of the photographers available and will provide website addresses so you can go straight to their portfolio.

Things you might want to consider/notice?

- Whether you prefer outdoor or indoor shots? Outdoor ones will use natural light and give less of a studio feel, but having indoor ones will enable you to change hairstyles and clothes more easily and maintain a more 'prepared' look. Some shoots incorporate both.

- What are your feelings on black and white shots Vs colour? It is a lot more popular now to have a colour shot, certainly as an option. It has been the case in the States for some years and now we are following suit, which makes perfect sense – I think colour humanizes the person in the shot and shows off features that would be missed otherwise. The downside to this (especially for us girls) is that make-up is more noticeable, so be sparing. Also, badly coloured, faded or unhealthy hair will be much more obvious!! So budget in a trip to the hairdressers and a deep conditioning treatment alongside the price of your shots! Being a girl sucks.

- What kind of tops are people wearing in the shots? Which ones enhance the overall picture and which ones distract or ruin?

- If a picture gives off a mood – why? Is it the facial expression, the background, the lighting or the whole composition of the photograph? Notice elements that appeal to you and try to communicate this to your photographer, or show them examples of the headshots you like.

After a while of looking and noticing and noting and deciding you will have a good idea of what you want from your own pictures. Take ideas and elements from the research that you do, but also remember that these are YOUR pictures, no one has ever used the same business card as you, you are creating something new and fresh. Enjoy and experiment!

COMFORT – This is an important point when it comes to having your photographs taken and one that I have first-hand experience of nearly getting wrong. I decided to pay over and above what I had planned to for my third-year headshots and badgered the very busy and in-demand photographer in question to arrange an appointment. Finally (and luckily), we spoke on the phone…

ALWAYS DO THIS, DON'T ARRANGE AN APPOINTMENT OVER EMAIL. YOU CAN TELL SO MUCH FROM A CONVERSATION.

I say luckily because immediately I knew that we weren't suited to each other. Half an hour later when she was still waffling on about her garden gnomes or some shit I was convinced that it was a really bad idea to work with her. She takes lovely pictures, make no mistake, but I knew that she wasn't going to put me at ease, instead I felt that her manic energy would panic me, her flighty nature would piss me off and her inability to concentrate would almost certainly ensure that ALL of my pictures would be of me looking hacked off, or worse still like I had an attitude problem! So I made up some lies and cancelled the appointment with her. That was a gut instinct I decided to follow; now, hey, she may have been the epitome of professionalism during the shoot, but if that is true it may not be the best plan to come across as some batty bloody hippy over the phone! You have to judge for yourself; those pictures might have been fine, but I wasn't comfortable and for god sake if you're not comfortable do something about it before you waste time and money on shots you're going to hate and that will ultimately not work for you.

So, you've done your research, you've picked your photographer, spoken to them and booked an appointment. They will have ways of working and you may have things you'd like to incorporate, so open the lines of communication and be honest with one another. They are there to get the best from you and vice versa, but they're not mind-readers.

DURING THE SESSION

How stupid would it be to tell you to try and relax? ... So, try and relax. You may love having your picture taken, you may loathe it – there are dangers with both. If you love it you run the risk of looking like a posey twat, and if you loathe it you may unfortunately look like some sort of bewildered infant… With wind… So how the hell can you win? By RELAXING! I try to think of myself as Natalie the actress not Natalie the, me. (If that makes any sense!!) I'm not playing a character as such, but I am remembering that this is work, not a happy snappy session in the park with Aunty Pam.

Hopefully your photographer will make you feel at ease and will have little tricks that they use to get the best from their clients. If they do, go with it (unless they come out with really weird, distracting shit, in which case just tell them to shut up and click)… Try to forget how you look or what the results will be like and just exist, thinking only of how bloody exciting it is that you're at this stage in your new career. Be excited, be confident and play. Try different things and do all you can to forget that the camera is there, that's when the best shots will happen and something intriguing within you will be captured.

Ok, cheese, snap – great, you have your images, possibly all 693 of them (the joys of digital photography) – so, now how the hell to…

CHOOSE A PICTURE

Firstly have a good laugh at all of the ones you look a complete tit in. (There will be many of these as they will snap away whether you are mid-sentence or mid-nose pick). So either send those ones directly to the 'trash can' or straight onto your Facebook profile in order to share the humour with the world. Once you're done, go back to your decent options. If you have a contact sheet with all of the images on instead of the images on computer (unlikely nowadays, but it's a possibility) then go through and cover the shit ones, the funny ones and the questionable ones with post-it notes (whoever invented the post it note deserves a fucking medal). Anyway, where was I? Actually no, while we're here let's find out who actually did invent the wonder that is the post-it note… Sodding LOVE t'interweb:

FYI

Arthur Fry, born August 19th 1931. A retired American inventor and scientist is credited as the co-founder of the post-it note.

IMPORTANT
It was his colleague Spencer Silver who invented the adhesive.

… Joint effort. Guys, well done. I salute you.

Bit of trivia… Slight tangent? What were we on about? Yes, covering the pictures you dislike or that are useless with post-it notes so that you can see clearly which ones show promise. If you have a disc (as most people will) or if the photographer gives you a link to download from, then an easy way to do a similar thing is to create three files on your desktop titled, I dunno… Shit, Maybe and Shithot? Then start to sling the images into the relevant files as you look through. That way you're not being so hasty that there's no turning back, you can switch them around at a later time and you will be judging them using gut instincts and first impressions (as the casting directors and agents you send them to will be doing).

A really useful tip that casting director Alice Purser gave me was to try and view your headshots as a casting director will. She showed me how she sorts through submissions for parts on Spotlight – all of the pictures are so tiny! So that she can sift through quickly and effectively she views a page containing about 100 images – would yours stand out? Mine actually didn't and though I really like my headshot, it was very interesting to see how easily it could be missed. FYI you can attach your images to SkyDrive and view them in a similar format.

A quick note on vanity before we move on to the 'piss yourself at me' section… All of us, at one time or another (some more than others) will think about/worry about/obsess about our looks. (This is amplified when you start to work on screen but we'll cover that later). It is no secret and we are all aware that our looks are under continuous scrutiny, and that important decisions are made based on them. For now, try to be as level-headed, sensible and business-like as possible. (Nigh on impossible, especially if you are the age I was when I graduated – a tender 21!) Know your look, use your look, don't be ruled by it and embrace any opportunity to temporarily change it (for performance). Again, you are a product so use what you have tactically, but also allow yourself to be a normal human being at times too! As I mentioned before, the personal and the professional merge in this vocation, you cannot put down your product and go home; you wake and sleep as that product and you must make your peace with that and find a compromise. Vanity and insecurity can be desperately off-putting so make sure you get a healthy balance and start as you mean to go on.

Now here's a paragraph that will make your head ache…

Your pictures should be neutral but not devoid of personality, suggesting casting types but not limiting you to one, accentuating your best features without looking too 'glamorous' and whilst they shouldn't be Cheshire cat smiley they also shouldn't be too 'moody' either…

…Good luck!

On paper this sounds ridiculous, I know, but joking aside, you will end up with lots of options that fit what I've tried to say above. This is about choosing a picture that will intrigue, a picture that will ultimately get you through that bastard door we spoke about earlier. No one photograph says 'I can play all of the parts ever written in all the plays that have ever existed better than anyone else alive. Ever.' All we can hope for is that our photograph is interesting enough to suggest that it's a possibility!

MY PICTURES

Within the next few pages you will find my collection of headshots taken so far throughout my career, from my 'getting into drama school' shot to the new photographs I had done last summer. I have included these in order to display a range of styles to you, but also to demonstrate how your taste, attitude and outlook will inevitably evolve, as you grow older and gain experience.

I might just add that (despite the following self-deprecating humour), I was very happy with all of the shots, and all of the photographers; they were all charming, professional and efficient. (Apart from the first one. I have absolutely no recollection of who took that. Some bloke in a studio in Leicester! Sounds dodgy; it probably was.)

Hopefully the progression is a good one… Say what you will! Having the ability to take the piss out of oneself is a lifeline in this industry, so start following my lead!

My opinions as an actress have changed, my tastes as a woman have evolved and my overall style has altered as a result of the work that I've done, the work I want to do and the lessons that I'm learning in between. You too must go through these all-important stages, safe in the knowledge that there is no way for you to judge something today with tomorrow's opinion. All you can do is make informed choices at the time, using your knowledge, your judgment and perhaps some of the points I've highlighted in this section.

THE MARKETING PACKAGE

Obviously the best marketing for any actor is professional exposure, being seen doing what you do. However, before, during and after that exposure (and especially in its absence) an actor needs other tools to attract, intrigue and alert industry professionals.

Headshots, CVs, letters, business cards and showreels are the main tools and **Spotlight,** mail-outs, agents and networking are the main vehicles.

I don't want to bombard you too much, so for now we will look at the elements you will be dealing with in the immediate future. All of the words above in bold we'll deal with now; we'll cover the underlined words in the next chapter ('Graduation').

HEADSHOTS

You've had your session and chosen your first headshot; it's awesome and you feel happy and excited about it – right? Good. Now it's time to get them printed.

Contacts is littered with repro places, so you can shop around, look at their websites and see who offers the best value for money. The quality should be good across the board, but as I said if you can use a recommendation for your first go, that might be a good idea. Your place of training will no doubt have somewhere that they regularly use. You can take your time with this; obviously there is no sense of urgency if you obey the mother of all rules in your 3rd year (1st year as an actor)…

BE ORGANISED AND ALWAYS AIM TO BE ONE STEP AHEAD.

As promised, here are my headshots…

2002…Well.

This is me at 16 having my first 'professional' photograph taken so that when I applied, drama school would know that I was a very serious and dedicated actress. (With a slight pouting problem)…

It's neutral enough. A little bit 'rabbit in the headlights' though and unfortunately it looks as if I may be topless… I WASN'T… Mum, I wasn't… Mum, stop crying, don't blame yourself…

Ah, bless 16-year-old Natalie; determined little dick.

2005… Oh hello Miss Trained Actress.

This was my third-year headshot. It came to showcase with me, got me my agent and my first three jobs.

You will note that the pout has survived drama school and the determination has become somewhat fierce!

It's studio-y but quite striking. Straps was a student-y thing to do but it's an improvement on topless… MUM I WASN'T TOPLESS!

The lipliner was a mistake but I kind of like that I stuck to my guns and did it anyway. (Spielberg loves a bit of liner – fact).

Photograph by Chris Baker.

2007…I'm a theatre actress don't you know.

Now I look back this was an attempt to get away from typecasting. I wanted to do grit as well as period work, plain as well as 'pretty'. I hardly wore any make up and didn't do much with my hair. (Didn't get laid much that year either.)

It perhaps says, 'I'm not going to let you pigeonhole me but in doing so I'm going to look a bit of a tit?' Natural light but an indoor shoot. It helped me get two years' worth of theatre work.

Photograph by Catherine Shakespeare Lane.

2009… Now we're getting somewhere.

I have made friends with the camera… a bit.

Natural light and again taken inside. Hair and make-up nice, natural and not too much. I've gone darker (now trying to get away from the 'blonde' casting. NEVER SATISFIED)!

I'm showing a hint of personality, which is refreshing. (Just a hint though!)

2009... Same shoot.

This was another option from this session. Colour, as you can see. A slight smile and a nice directness. Though I never really used this for casting, I had it as a colour option just before everyone started having colour pics done.

Much less naïve-looking than the one above I think. Hashtag (still can't find the button) shouldhave hadrootsdone...

2012... Today's headshot (and obviously my favourite, or it wouldn't be today's headshot!)

Outdoors, natural light, colour, fresh, very natural make up.

I have made good friends with the camera here and think that there is a nice ease to the picture that says 'I've worked a bit, you can employ me if you like'.

I had my hair coloured a few weeks before but styled it myself so it didn't look too done. I chose many tops but this one complements my colouring. I really enjoyed this shoot.

Photography by Faye Thomas.

2012… Same shoot.

Bit Waterloo Road, but I like it. It's a good contrast to the one above and gives off quite a different vibe. I've only just started using this one, so it'll probably be cropped, but I like the messiness of it actually.

Photography by Faye Thomas.

Quick tips when ordering prints:

- Don't order 80,000 copies. You can replenish your stock as and when you need – most of these places do a very quick turnaround on orders.

- Order some colour images and some black and white – both are useful.

- Pick a few shots that may be suitable for different things. Differentiate by style (i.e. more theatrical or more filmic) or focus on varying character qualities (i.e. more seductive, or more innocent, more regal, more common etc). Have a main headshot and then have a few options that you can send out if needs be. You don't need to order lots and lots of each of the options either, for now I would only order copies of your main headshot and leave the others as backups. Plus you can upload alternative images to Spotlight instead of ordering hard copies and save yourself some cash!

- Whether you have a white border or your name at the bottom etc. is down to personal preference, have a look around and see what you think works. In my opinion (and it is only that) borders and writing can distract from the image and take away from the striking message you are hoping to send with that image.

- Print your name and details onto labels and pop them onto the back of the image instead?

- Be clear with your photographer to go easy on the retouching of the images – you don't want to look like Barbie, or Ken for that matter, and certainly not Cindy (slut)… This is a photograph of YOU, not a tantastic, piercing eyed, blemish free version of you. A very wise, slightly talented actor once said to an immensely skilled friend of mine:

'Your body is a journal. Each mark, scar and blemish, every curve, imperfection or line is your life making entries upon it. Don't hide or deny your story.'

Mr Johnny Depp – we love you. (Even if you are so perfect that this couldn't ever possibly apply to you.)

So, good times, you now have your copies and the most important part of your marketing package. A woohoo! Next…

CV

It will be short! This is to be expected. Your career hasn't properly started yet, no one expects you to have miraculously worked with the RSC in the Easter Holidays or filmed a cheeky episode of *Poirot* in between voice classes. Your drama school/Uni productions will be the bulk of it, and regardless of what happens with casting throughout this last year those projects will pad it out with a nice list of plays and hopefully some fairly well-known characters that will spark interest and intrigue. You may even have a few reputable visiting directors' names on there (if you went to an institution that pulled their finger out of their arse that is)… Cough…hmm…moving on…

You know that funny saying that 'everyone lies on their CV'? Ah…that's a good one…yeah, don't. It is a VERY small world and lies are daft and unwarranted. You can 'fan out' the truth in conversation, if you feel you must, but I'd rather you didn't; I consider it far more endearing when someone has confidence and pride in the little steps they have taken whilst showing enthusiasm for the big ones they intend to take. Resist the temptation to make it look 'more impressive' than it is. Be impressed with what you've done and what you know and don't underestimate experienced agents or casting directors; they will know when something is too good to be true. And I warn you now, when a panel look at your CV they will be quiz you, they will know names and buildings listed, they will detect inconsistencies and you will look stupid. And desperate.

I was going to provide a couple of examples/templates but to be perfectly honest, this is something I've never been that good at or terribly interested in and I think you're perfectly capable of producing it without assistance; especially mine. I have a perfectly good CV on Spotlight that is printable and email-able so I tend to use that. I have no idea whether that is seen as resourceful or lazy (see the chat with Alice Purser in Chapter 11) but either way, it informs them about the work I've done. Mission accomplished.

At your stage though, to show willing, I would create one; I did. Chances are you won't need it for long and I'm sure your attempt will be far superior to anything I could concoct. (Agonizing about font, panicking about white or off-white paper and dicking around with text boxes is not my forte or idea of fun.) It needn't be that complicated, I'm just a technophobe. Put simply? Make it clear, make it attractive, make it truthful and make it ONE PAGE! It's the picture and the content that count. Include your productions, any readings, workshops and in fact anything that shows you've done over and above what is expected of you. They're looking for signs of dedication and initiative and a desire to gain experience, so show them that you have it all as best you can. Most graduate CVs will be crammed with rapier level 2, Scottish accents (including Glaswegian, Edinburgh and Aberdeen), period dance and juggling. Be selective, there is an obvious temptation to try and please and to try and show off. I think I can put my hand on my heart and say that no agent will give a rat's ass whether you can juggle or not. (Until the beeb are casting for some sort of juggling villain in *Doctor Who*… Shit, put it on.) Prioritise is the message. And only put things down that you are really good at. (Baking not applicable.)

LETTER LAYOUT

There's not a lot to say here, you know how to write a bloody letter, I won't insult your intelligence. But just in case…

- Keep it brief.
- Type it.
- Lay it out clearly and keep paragraphs short.
- Spellcheck everything ten times and have someone else proofread if you're not confident with that sort of malarkey.
- I always sign my name in pen at the end. It could be a pointless exercise but I think it makes it a bit more personal.
- Don't put 'with lots of love'… That was a joke. But still don't.

I remember being absolutely livid, livid, that I had completed my letters and my CVs and had sealed them all in their crisp white envelopes ready to send out to the industry, when a lad in my year swanned past me in the library with headed paper. Yep, headed paper. I wanted to kill him, and possibly myself. Within half an hour everyone in that goddamn library had headed paper and you know what I did? Undid all of the sealed STAMPED envelopes and reprinted my letters so that they too were HEADED… Robyn, you have a lot to answer for! You may be gathering that I used to be (am) a bit of a stationary geek. I am sure, no positive, that you are in no way as unstable or irrational as I was (I have chilled with age), but let it be a warning that competitiveness can make you mental. And it really needn't. I am fairly certain if I asked my agent why they signed me, none of the top, ooh, 8 million answers would be because my letters were headed.

THE LETTER CONTENT

My ultimate piece of advice, and this branches out to many different areas you will be encountering over the next few months and years, is try not to be a div. You will hear me say many, many times throughout this book that there is a 'fine line', whether that be between confidence and arrogance, promoting and bragging, informing and over-compensating or showing interest and kissing arse. There is a fine line in your letter between explaining and waffling. They do not need a blow-by-blow account of your damaged childhood or an essay on how you 'found yourself' during drama training. Think of the letter as a flirt; keep it briefly seductive (that's intriguing-seductive rather than whorish-seductive). You knew that.

So, less about what not to do and what not to say, let's look at what you might include…

Before you say anything, do your research. This will change your whole letter, making it easier to write and more personal and relevant to the recipient.

BASIC CONTENT

- Your name is a start. If you've changed your name and your stage name is now different to your real name, make sure you put the right one; we don't want a casting director remembering the wrong one or not being able to find you!

- Contact details, whether on HEADED paper or featured as normal on the upper right hand side of the page. I'd include your email address too.

- Date the letter so they know how many days they've ignored it for when they find it under a pile of crap on their desk.

- Dear <u>an actual name</u>. Find out the contact's name and use it, this will take away the 'mass mail out' feel that graduate letters so often have. Be polite and not too informal (this is business). I am assuming for the purposes of this that you haven't met them. If you have met them call them whatever you did then or whatever they introduced themselves to you as (and reference the meeting!)

- Type the letter; it looks neat, professional and clear. I send handwritten notes to people I've worked with or have met, as I think it adds a nice element of informality, but I type the rest. (Probably a wasted eccentricity of mine that I needn't have admitted to.)

BIT CLEVER

- Mention how you heard of them i.e. if you have friends who are signed with them (agent)/who have worked with them (directors and casting directors), or if you've seen a show with one of their clients in (agents). This again shows that it isn't a generic mail-out letter and that you have a keen interest in them specifically. *THEY NEVER KNOW HOW MANY OTHERS YOU'VE DONE THE SAME WITH!* If you have no connection to them whatsoever you can research them (you should have anyway if you're making contact) and briefly reference a client or project that you admire.

- Always start with the most pressing piece of information i.e. what you're appearing in, the date your programme is being aired or when and where your showcase is etc. (Just in case they don't read on, get the important stuff said quick smart. Harsh but true.)

- Keep paragraphs short and the whole thing as brief as possible, this will make it more likely that they'll read it in its entirety. Think of it as a tweet, with only a specific amount of characters as opposed to a dear diary moment. (Incidentally 'C U @ Showcase, blood' probably won't cut it).

- Always end on a positive. Well, make the whole thing positive but make damn sure that you end on one!

INFORMATIVE

- They need to know who, what, when and where. Your name and drama training, then a brief comment about your last project, swiftly moving onto what the next is, where they can see it and when. As long as they know this and how to reach you then all is gravy baby.

INVENTIVE

This does not mean printing your letter on pink paper or sending a complimentary chocolate... OBVIOUSLY.

- Mention something that's inspired you recently – a film, show or television programme. They may be interested to learn how you view the world you're about to enter. But keep it brief.

Don't ever beg, or indicate a begging nature, both are vile. Know your worth. This is business, and they can't function within their business without you. Whether we're discussing directors, casting directors or agents; all of them, without exception need us. They need actors in general, but you have to get them to want you!

I was going to include a good and bad example of letter writing here and then I paused and had a word with myself. I trust you to know the difference, you had the skill to get into drama school, the ability to survive it and are looking at a bright future as an Actor; in no way do you need to be patronised in the letter-writing department. You will know what to write, just listen to your instinct and keep your heart out of it for now.

Getting no response is normal and to be expected but it doesn't mean that we shouldn't bother in the first place.

SPOTLIGHT & EQUITY

You're on the edge of your new career, with your marketing tools at the ready, but without reliable ways of getting those tools into the right hands, they're worthless; the best and most utilized vehicle for this is Spotlight. I cannot stress enough how important it is that you take the necessary steps to help yourself when it comes to both promotion and protection, and the two places I am about to outline are the best in the business for both of those things.

SPOTLIGHT – PROMOTION

The guys at Spotlight very kindly agreed to offer a mission statement, so that you can hear about what they do first-hand.

Spotlight is how professional performers find work.

Since 1927, we've been promoting actors to casting opportunities via the iconic Spotlight books, and now via our website spotlight.com: the first port of call for all major casting professionals when they need to find actors for stage, TV, film and commercial productions.

Over 60,000 professional actors, actresses, child performers, presenters, dancers and stunt artists have searchable profiles in Spotlight, featuring their headshots, CV information and video footage.

Our core casting service – The Spotlight Link – allows casting professionals to send out their casting briefs to Spotlight performers and their agents, and receive instant suggestions of performers to be shortlisted for auditions. It's the UK's busiest service of its kind, with over a thousand casting briefs posted every month.

At the heart of the industry, Spotlight also nurtures and supports its performer members at every stage of their careers, offering advice, seminars, industry news, podcasts and events designed to help them navigate the tricky 'business of acting' and promote themselves as effectively as possible. Many of our members will be in Spotlight from graduation through to retirement, and we are proud of the part we play in their careers.

Spotlight also publishes the handbook Contacts *which is handbook for anyone working or looking to get started in the UK entertainment industry. It includes listings for over 5,000 companies, services and individuals across all branches of television, stage, film and radio.*

Ben Seale – Managing Partner of Spotlight

You have to be a member of Spotlight. It is entertainment suicide not be, plain and simple. Membership is a wad of money, the thought of which thrusts a chunk of vomit up into one's throat annually, but it has to be done. It is the main resource for agents and casting directors to view all of the actors at their disposal; it is the marketplace, the catalogue, the library of actors and is the place that all of your details are made easily accessible to the people who are able to provide you with work.

Back in the day you'd be in the book. The books still exist of course, but it is all about the internet now, and we have to be so thankful for this! It is immediate, simple to access and mega easy to update. Did I just say mega? Apologies.

Here is the link to my spotlight:

http://www.spotlight.com/9857-4532-6768

Go and have a look as a point of reference when reading the following points:

PICTURES – Now that you have your awesome headshot, get it where everyone can see it. The main shot you choose will be your 'profile picture' and you can add more that will show up as options on your CV. Some people have two or three shots, some have a million, or like 50, it's up to you to choose. I would go easy, certainly at the beginning, put a few other options from your shoot to show off slightly different looks or attitudes and maybe add a few show pictures, but A) only if they were professionally taken and B) not too many, don't go mad. It's boring and no one will look, it'll just look a bit 'try hardy' in my opinion.

CREDITS – Put all of your shows from your training years, as not only are they talking points but they also map the journey of your development. Also include any external courses or competitions such as Carlton Hobbs, The Sam Wannamaker competition etc. – all of this shows enthusiasm, skill and initiative. But don't panic if you don't have any of this, as I mentioned earlier, they will take you on at this stage because of what they see and hear rather than what they read.

SKILLS/ACCENTS – There is the temptation to put EVERYTHING here. You don't need to. The skill you possess, that they are most interested in, is self-explanatory – you can act! Anything else is a bonus; it's trivia. I'm not saying don't include that you are an experienced (*) fisherman, but ask yourself if you really think it's relevant for casting right now? Stage combat, period dance and singing abilities are pretty standard, include them by all means and certainly put down practical things such as a driving license. Just watch out you don't 'list' too much, in my opinion this looks like you don't have complete confidence in the main skill you're meant to be promoting and are trying to overcompensate with 'other attributes'. I could be wrong, it has been known. (Rarely), (never), (ish). Again, trust your own judgment and look at lots of CVs – you will form opinions soon enough!

Accents. A lot of actors have a natural ear for them, a lot of actors study phonetics, both of which result in most actors being able to do accents fairly well. Have your native accent listed as this may turn out to be one of your strongest selling points. Also have RP on there. If you can do General American (General-whatever that is!), then put it. I have made a point of only listing accents that I have executed professionally but this is something I've built up over time. Trust that they'll assume that you can do the accent they require you to do and also trust that they know you have the skill to learn a new accent given the chance. (I'd also assume that they know you 'have an ear for accents' – it's a given I reckon, there's no need to write it, it sounds rubbish.)

HEIGHT/WEIGHT – I think this is ridiculous. Height I get, but weight? Piss off. You choose what information goes onto your Spotlight profile and if you don't want to put something then don't! (My rebellious streak makes an appearance – hello.) I think your picture gives a fair indication of your stature and therefore I haven't added my weight as I don't consider myself to be a piece of meat needing to be weighed over the counter before purchase. Rant over. You may not be bothered by this, if not – put it! Basically all of the 'visual' questions i.e. eyes, hair etc. are to aid the search engine that casting people can use to eliminate what they're not looking for and more importantly, to hone in on what they are. So, the more information you put the more likely you are to pop up in a search? Or the more information you put the more you are increasing your chances of being eliminated? There's possibly too much thought going into this, but I wanted to flag it up.

Certainly put your height (especially if you work in musical theatre) and put your ethnicity, hair colour and playing age. Oh, and absolutely put your eye colour because that is a real deal breaker when acting… NOT. To begin with you might just want to enter it all and then start to refine as you get cranky and stuck-up like me! It's really funny watching age, weight and dates disappear from profiles over the years!

AGENT – If you have an agent, great, they will register themselves with Spotlight as your representative. Make sure they do.

If you don't have an agent Spotlight will put their address in that area on your page and will receive enquiries on your behalf. They will not actively seek employment for you, that is to say that they will not act as your agent, but they will forward onto you any interest that may come in. This filtering system is clever, safe and useful.

TRAINING – Even if you had the worst time of your life (which I hope is unlikely), do list your place of training. It shows that you went; it shows that you stayed and it shows that you survived. And don't let drama school snobbery intimidate you; some schools get more exposure and attention, yes, but the proof is in the pudding guys and if you've trained, be proud of the fact.

CREDITS BOX – It is so important that you keep this little box up to date (as I was reminded by a rather famous comedienne once – I'll work up to that story and share it later in the book; needless to say that the audition was a joy from start to finish…) – are you becoming tuned to my sarcasm? Wunderbar.

Do keep this filled (if there's something to say) and update it as things change. What to put in it? Natalie is appearing at the …… theatre, playing from 8th – 20th April etc. Or Natalie will be appearing on the BBC playing …… Anything that is pressing news, that you need the 'searchers' to see immediately. Currently filming, recently filmed, in rehearsals for – all look good, it shows that you keep on top of self-promotion in a professional manner and that you are busy!

Apart from anything else, Spotlight is really useful for researching (stalking) other actors. It can become a bit obsessive; I may set up a helpline…

PROTECTION

A chat with Equity's Brogan West

Brogan West is a lovely actor I met and worked with back in 2010. Alongside his acting career he campaigns and generates interest for 'Equity' – the trade union for entertainers. Equity take a lot of time and care over educating new performers about the importance of being part of the Union, but I thought that asking a young representative about the ins and outs of it all might be an informal and concise way of letting you know who they are, what they do, why they do it and why joining and making 'them' become 'us' is so important.

I asked Brogan to answer the following questions:

Q. What is Equity?

Equity is a trade union, representing performers and artists in all areas of the industry including: actors, dancers, singers, designers and directors. The union also represents models, presenters, stunt performers and supporting artists amongst others. A trade union is the body through which workers in an industry can collectively negotiate their rates of pay and working conditions with their employers.

Q. Who joins Equity and what are the requirements for doing so?

Anyone working professionally in the UK in one or more areas of the industry can join the union. The requirements for joining vary depending on your circumstances; if you are working professionally then proof of your engagement (a contract, pay-slips etc.) is required. Even if you have worked overseas, as long as you have proof of work, together with membership of a FIA affiliated union, you are eligible. As students and graduates of an accredited drama school you are automatically eligible, and a reduced membership is usually accessible through the institution in which you are learning.

Q. What are the fees to join and how can I pay?

Full Equity

Subscriptions are based on your previous tax year's gross earnings from your professional work, including royalties, repeats and residuals. As well as the annual subscription fee (see below) if you are joining or rejoining the union there is a one-off fee of £27.

Current subscription rates:

Gross Annual Income	Annual Subscription
• Less than £20,000	£116
• Between £20,000 and £35,000	£203
• Between £35,000 and £50,000	£349
• Income of more than £50,000:	Members pay at the rate which is in line with 1% of their gross income: £582 £873 £1,164 £1,455 £1,746 £2,037 £2,328

There is a 5% discount on any of the rates listed above when paying by direct debit.

Student Equity

- Joining costs £17 which includes professional name reservation (if it is not already in use by another Equity member).
- Annual subscription is £17 per year.
- When upgrading to full Equity, student members deduct £10 for each year of student membership from the cost of becoming a full Member. This is capped at a maximum rebate of £27.

Q. What are Equity's main aims/concerns currently?

Most recently Equity has been concerned with government austerity cuts and how they might affect the arts. Equity has successfully lobbied government on a number of occasions with the sound economics of the arts in the UK, often returning over 3 times what is spent on them.

'THEATRE MATTERS' is an ongoing campaign. Equity has also successfully negotiated an agreement with the BBC to show all credits after a programme and slow them down to a speed that is readable – allowing members to be recognised for their work. Equity has many campaigns, broad and specific, foreign and domestic, all running concurrently. You can see specific details and get involved via the Equity website.

Q. What is included in my membership? What do I get?

Again, see the website for official benefits and concessions as they change. £10,000,000 public liability is fantastic and vital as a freelancer. The Equity pension is pretty great too.

Q. What is an Equity pension?

Most unions offer various schemes through affiliated companies; Equity uses Aviva. The Equity pension is a relatively new idea and a great one. In many respects it works like a normal private pension scheme, you pay in to it, it accumulates and once you reach a certain age, you can access it. However, Equity have negotiated deals with certain companies such as the BBC that when you contribute a percentage of your pay check, the producers will match it up to a certain amount based on the length and nature of your contract. The money is governed safely and ethically by AVIVA meaning, it is not invested into high-risk schemes, only ones approved by the union.

Natalie:

I'd just like to add there that I have an Equity pension and it's brilliant. I am only required to pay into it when I am working, and the contribution I make is matched by the theatre or company I am working for at that time. My parents are nearing retirement age and I am seeing now just how important their private pensions are to them, and what a different quality of life they will have because of them. Even if we never have any intention of retiring from acting, the jobs will become few and far between and our ability to scrape by and tolerance of doing so won't be so manageable. Make sure you plan for your future, no matter how many zillions of years away it seems!

Q. Why do you feel so strongly about Equity?

Exploitation occurs in any and every industry. Where there is any kind of transaction, be it monetary, skills, emotional, personal, a service – anything. Unless strict conditions are outlined, there is room for exploitation. Who doesn't want something for less? However, it can be hard for the person at the end of the chain to exact any power over those that are employing them. Only by joining together, with our collective power, can we negotiate fair and proper working conditions for those in our profession. The Union safeguards exactly that, keeping 'it' and 'us' professional. It means so much to me because it makes such absolute and clear sense. If you care about and value your work as an artist, you should care and value its protection. The annual fees of the union are a fraction of the power and help it can bring to bear. Unionism is one of the foremost ideas and protectorates of our civilisation, whose true power lies in the collective.

Q. Can I get legal advice from Equity?

Any member can call the union to seek advice on professional matters; from careers advice, tax advice, self-employment advice as well as, and often most importantly, contractual advice. It is vital that those engaged on a contract read them. They can be lengthy and full of very long words – if there is something you don't understand, get advice!

Q. What does a non-Equity contract mean?

A non-Equity contract is a contract offered outside the terms and working conditions of Equity. It may offer better or worse terms of employment but the key difference is that Equity isn't able to legally protect those using such contracts. Should something go wrong on a non-Equity contract that has been accepted by a member, they are a lot harder to safeguard and represent.

Q. What is Equity Minimum?

The Equity Minimum varies depending on your contract and which sector of the industry you are engaged in. For example, the London West End minimum will be different from a touring theatre minimum and different again from a TV daily minimum. All Equity contracted minimums are accessible through the members' area of the website. It is a vital resource for performers, young and new performers especially and even more so if you haven't got the protection and knowledge of an experienced agent to help you. Look at them and know them so your talents can't be abused.

Q. I can work without an Equity card can't I?

Yes you can. However, if you are engaged in professional work within an ensemble or company and something goes wrong, you may find that those with membership are protected from a great deal that you are not. If you value yourself as a working professional, then protect yourself with the cover union membership offers.

Q. How can I become more involved with Equity?

Firstly, engage with your branch (see later question) to see how the structures within the union work, and gauge to what to degree you would like to be involved. For example, you may just want to attend your local branch every other month; you might even like to stand for the branch committee. Within central Equity there are a number of specialist committees and working parties that may interest you, you can find these in the member's area of the website. Elections for committees are once every 2 years, the committees meet up to 4 times a year and all expenses to and from official meetings are covered. These committees focus on specific parts of the union such as Young Members, Singers, Ethnic and Minority members, or wider industrial committees such as Theatre or Recorded Arts. There are various cross-union events such as TUC-organised marches that any member is welcome to attend; they are well supported and always welcoming. In conclusion, there are lots of ways. It is simply up to you and how much time you have to spare. It is vital that you engage with the union and not simply be a silent member, it is by being part of its work that you can truly see the worth and value of its collective strength.

Q. Do Equity act as Agents? Can I find work through Equity?

Equity aren't agents. They can give advice on professional matters such as contracts (which an agent, if you have one would hopefully know and do on your behalf; sadly this isn't always the case). Equity can't negotiate an individual contract on your behalf with an employer but it can enforce the working conditions it has negotiated with reputable employers who employ members under the structures and agreements of its contracts. In terms of jobs, Equity does have a limited jobs service on its website which can be accessed in the members' area.

Q. Are there networking or social events through Equity?

Networking and socializing within the union is best accessed via the regional branches. When you join, you are allocated to a regional branch depending on your postcode. Most branches meet every other month in a local venue, theatre or arts centre – it's a great way of meeting other practitioners in your area. The meetings usually start informally with a drink at the bar before the official branch business is covered. This is the branch committee's opportunity to pass any information from the council down to the branch members. As long as the branch meeting is quorate then it can submit a motion to the council and once a year to the Annual Representative Conference. This is the most effective way to have your say within the union. Each branch meeting usually has a guest speaker and concludes with another drink in the bar. Effective branches are the lifeblood of the union throughout the country; make the most of them and engage with those who use them. They are very welcoming and are often full of like-minded people who have invariably gone through or are going through similar experiences.

Q. Is there always someone available to help?

You can call the union at Guild House, Covent Garden anytime within office hours, and if you are passing, the door is always open! Email contacts to most departments of the union can be accessed through the website:

http://www.equity.org.uk/home/

Cheers Brogan!

I'd like to conclude this chapter by flagging up BECS to you all. BECS is the British Equity Collecting Society.

> 'The UK's only collective management organisation for audiovisual performers. BECS is involved in the negotiation & administration of performers' remuneration throughout the EU territories; it also administers artists' payments on behalf of Equity and broadcasting companies.'

Which, put in layman's terms, means that they collect money owed to you for replays etc. throughout the EU and pay them into your account providing that they have your details. Would be pretty silly not to use this brilliant service, yes? Get on it.

You can download a form to join BECS at this link:
http://www.equitycollecting.org.uk

BY THIS STAGE YOU NEED TO FEEL LIKE ACTORS, BEHAVE LIKE ACTORS, THINK LIKE ACTORS AND ABOVE ALL, BE TREATED LIKE ACTORS.

The latter will come when the former is achieved.

3. SHOWCASE

D-day, the Nemesis… or just a Tuesday.

So, the time has come, you have survived drama training – let's take a second to applaud that! Pat yourself on the back seriously; for every one person that gets into drama school there are hundreds, thousands that don't, it ends there for them; and every year that starts drama training sees many drop out along the way. You got in and you stayed in; you're here, and more importantly – **you are ready for showcase!**

> This is the most anticipated part of training, the Everest that students cower at the foot of for three years. It is the driving force behind the years of hard graft and the hype surrounding it causes a feral terror that claims many victims. Three minutes that can make or break you, which can ignite dreams or piss all over them.

I've put that in a speech bubble so you can imagine an absolute arsehole saying it. Go on think of the biggest arsehole you've ever met… (I am, and yes Laura, it's one of your exs.)

IT IS THE BIGGEST BUNCH OF CRAP GOING!

If you listen to that, if you think like that, then I can tell you right now – showcase will be a disaster for you.

The approach to showcase is as much about mental attitude as it is about focusing on an evolving skill and engineering the best way to present it. The proof is in the pudding but the pudding is fucked if you forget the eggs…the eggs being some sort of lame euphemism for confidence…you got it, right? No?… Shit. Well, forget the eggs and just be confident… Yeah, possibly not my greatest piece of advice to date…

Moving on, let's unpick that…

Your approach and mental attitude, throughout your whole career but especially leading up to your showcase, are more important than I could hope to articulate. A positive mental attitude will save your life, your bacon, and your ass whilst preventing a lot of unnecessary upset and wasted energy. Fear, nerves, self-doubt, anxiety and stress can be utterly disabling, not to mention destructive and distracting; by succumbing to them, by letting them get the better of you, you run the risk of undoing all of the good and hard work you've achieved. It's a choice. Your choice. Remember those choices I was banging on about in the last chapter? Well, this is a vitally important one. To sink or to swim; you must choose to be in control or allow yourself to be overcome. You are the master of your own destiny, your own boss and the sole driver of the vehicle that is your career; only you have the power to make healthy decisions that will help and enhance your chances instead of making ones that risk wrecking them. That is why I want to avoid, no, banish the kind of talk in the speech bubble at the top of the chapter; it is counterproductive and I need you to be able to recognise when something is, so that you can guard yourself from it, or better still, rise above it. (It may feel a little like I'm writing some sort of happy clappy motivational rally at times but stay with me, secure in the knowledge that everything written here is designed to assist you in making your showcase a success and to ensure that you start your career as you mean to go on.)

In the following pages we are going to tackle the lead-up, execution and aftermath of showcase; all of which are important stages in your new career. I don't have much else to say here if I'm honest, I want to get on with it. So, let's do that, shall we?

First step…

SHAPING SHOWCASE

Cleverly shaping and carefully moulding the whole experience of showcase into the platform you need it to be to launch your career is the job in hand, and again your choices will determine how this happens. The piece, the partner, the image (i.e. the look, and the sound of it) all need careful consideration. But how do you know what shape it should be? You may not be sure; in fact at this stage it is fairly normal that you probably won't have a clue! You must explore and experiment and in doing so the answers (or clues) will appear. If you've approached your third year as I suggested in the last chapter you should now have a penciled outline of the kind of actor you are and the kind of actor you aspire to be. You've used your ability and instinct to guide you through your third year, making informed choices and learning valuable lessons. Now you must trust that the knowledge you've gathered so far will provide the awareness you need to make good decisions for showcase. These decisions should not be rushed; take your time and use the support available to you.

Now, where the hell do we start? As a wise (fairly rubbish) nun once suggested: the very beginning…

Searching for the piece, let's look at that first. There are several ways you can attack this beast, and I'd give all of them a go, in any order that comes about.

(These are suggestions, not a systematic agenda. Use or ignore as you please.) You can:

1. Look for a scene you love, and then hope you have someone in the year who

A) fits the bill

B) is reliable and fits the bill

C) is reliable, fits the bill and hasn't been snapped up by someone else

D) is reliable, fits the bill, hasn't been snapped up and wants to do the scene

So, as you can see there might be a fair few hurdles to get over here, and different eventualities that can and will present themselves! But yeah, ok, in an attempt at a slither of comedy I have perhaps made it sound more complex than it is. In truth, we actors like to think we can play anything, that's why we're actors right, we can 'morph'? So, it should be fairly easy to see ourselves in many roles as long as we haven't become too wedded to a 'type' or 'image' we want to portray. As discussed in the last chapter, knowing your casting parameters is useful but knowing that they're not gospel is important too. Be as open-minded as you can early on; know your strengths and be ready to use them to your advantage but at this stage don't be afraid to challenge them and to think outside of the box; this is playtime (if you have done as I suggested and started this process in good time of course!)

2. You could decide on the partner first and then find a scene together. This is a less lonely way of starting what could be a long and tedious search. Of course, variations of the following are likely to happen repeatedly if you do:

ACTOR 1:   Ah, I've found this excellent scene; it's funny, then it's really serious and it ends with this brilliant twist. Have a read…

ACTOR 2 reads it.

ACTOR 2:   I'm not really feeling it mate.

ACTOR 1:   Oh.

A fairly inevitable chat. Or this…

ACTOR 2:   This scene is amazing, I think it's the one, look... So she's a policewoman and she suspects that he's committed this crime and upon finding him bound to a chair and gagged she starts to question him, it turning into a comedic sex game that ends in disaster when his wife comes home!

Pause.

ACTOR 1:   So, which part are you wanting to play?

ACTOR 2:   The policewoman you plank, you're a guy!

ACTOR 1:   So...so I'm gagged all the way through?

ACTOR 2:   Not... All the way through... *(Trails off into shameful silence.)*

I know this sounds extreme, it is extreme; I'm trying to make you laugh. The scary thing is that I overheard conversations not too dissimilar to this in my third year when I was trawling through the library archives/sipping from my hip flask.

*Heads up that the infamous Natalie Burt hip flask may get sporadic mentions throughout this book. She's sat on my lap right now in fact, staring lovingly at me... Ssh, later... *(Pats said hip flask).*

Throughout the search there will be differences of opinion and an abundance of self-centeredness to contend with but if you at least intend to behave well, hopefully others will follow suit.

3. Whilst trawling through plays looking for inspiration for yourself, be helpful and keep an eye out for scenes that may be suitable for others. If you read a scene and someone springs to mind, tell them. You are in this together. Yes the 'production' of showcase is made up of segregated scenes, but nevertheless you are a cast, a company, and to be honest if we can't look out for one another in this industry it really is a sad state of affairs. Twenty pairs of eyes looking instead of one can be nothing but beneficial.

My advice would be to juggle all of the above points simultaneously, paying close attention to the results that each tactic presents. Look for your own scene in your own time and play the field with a few possible partners whenever possible (there is no judgment on sluttish behavior here – the more partners tried the better! ... We *are* still talking about showcase, right...?) Take the results from all of your findings and play; play wherever you can and whenever you can. You'll know in an instant whether there is potential in the scenes and partners you experiment with.

So, things to consider when:

CHOOSING A SCENE & PARTNER

THE SCENE

As I've said, you will have started to acknowledge (and notice others acknowledging) where your strengths lie and any areas that you as a 'product', as a 'type' seem to excel within. Use this information, it is the reliable blueprint for your style as an actor and will narrow the search for you by eliminating certain styles and/or eras whilst at the same time highlighting the contenders. Your tutors will have pre-conceived ideas of what you should do – take all of their advice on board, whilst taking care not to just blindly follow; this is your career and your decision, so keep the control but be smart with it.

You have three minutes, four tops for this thing. I know, what the fuck? That alone is stressful enough! But remember that not only is everyone in the same boat (both in your specific school and in every other showcase taking place across town), but also that generations of actors have endured the same throughout history and *have been* triumphant. In order for you to follow in their footsteps it is vital that you attack this intelligently, strategically and prematurely! Start letting the idea cross your mind in the second year, start putting POST IT NOTES (stationary geek strikes again) into plays when you come across a speech or a scene that moves or excites you; if you do, it will make the beginning of the real search a lot less agonizing when the time comes! Eventually you will have built up a little catalogue of ideas, not necessarily serious contenders, but certainly ideas to get you started. Be thorough and give yourself time to be so by being ahead of the game. Do not be ruled by the school's agenda, now is the time to access your initiative and get ahead of the schedule. You should be eager to start this process. Bear in mind also that the longer you delay searching for pieces, the more you run the risk of ideal partners being snapped up by other, more organized actors!!

Questions to ask when searching for 'THE PIECE'...
- What do I need to sell?
- Am I going to focus on comedy or tragedy?
- Am I going to present contemporary or classic?
- Am I planning to be seen as hero or villain?

(Of course all texts are hopefully a little more complex and ambiguous than that, but this line of questioning is a helpful way to start the cogs turning and the juices flowing).

- Has the piece got a good rhythm? I.e. does it dip in energy or are there lengthy bits of action without dialogue?
- If it is suitable but there are sections that don't really work out of context, can you splice separate parts of the scene together to make up the ideal content for the time allowed?
- Are the roles equal in quantity and quality?
- Do the roles complement each other and contrast one another well enough?
- Have I someone in mind to share the scene with?
- How might my character look?
- How might my character sound? (Accents are an important USP.)

As I said earlier, you can be looking at potential scenes and possible partners simultaneously, focusing on one can be a luckless activity, so keep your mind open and regularly present ideas to your peers and teachers. I fluttered my eyelashes at the best actor in the year and backhanded him two free beers at the bar I worked in to get him onside for showcase… That's possibly more of a way to win over a Yorkshireman than an actor, but it worked out well enough. More on that later… Speaking of Yorkshiremen, let's move onto choosing…

THE PARTNER

CHEMISTRY – You will already have a good idea who you work well with, and whilst hopefully that includes most of your year (just agree), there may be specific candidates with whom you will have worked well opposite during in-house productions and/or classmates you've clicked with on specific projects. Be careful that this click is a click of the professional variety and nothing else. Your best mates, lovers, fuck buddies or usual partners may not (and actually probably won't) be the best scene partners for Showcase as the focus could be blurred and you may run the risk of being too comfortable and complacent instead of being the electrifying duo you need to be. That is a generic warning that may or may not apply to you – just beware. I did my stage combat exam with my then 'boyfriend'. What an intelligent decision that was! Actually it turned out quite well as we were at that stage in a relationship when you really start to fucking despise each other, so waving a rapier inches from his smug face was rather enjoyable. My point is that it was possibly more of a cathartic choice than a professional one and could have ended badly – It may work for Brad and Ange but certainly in my case we were lucky to escape a) unharmed and b) with good marks. (And yes, I got a higher score than him and I think it's safe to say that as a result the relationship never recovered! There are some things boys just need to be better at… Gutted, ha.) Ok, enough of my childishness…

Try scenes, try loads of scenes and loads of partners; try them in breaks between classes, in car parks, in queues and in intervals of shows; get some beers in and have a scene fest! Feel what works and what doesn't, argue about what could work and toy with what should work. Spend time with your peers on this, watch each other's work and open up discussions when it comes to assessing work. In doing all of this you will be making progress, and even if you don't find any potential pieces straight away you'll be strengthening your aims and objectives by searching, sifting and trying. And let's face it, if nothing else you'll be having a laugh, practising your craft and exercising your favourite muscle… (ok, maybe your second favourite boys)…

You never know, during the early search you may discover a gem! Whether you do or not you will be stretching yourself through trial and error, and by being rigorous with your examination of the options you will allow yourself to feel truly content with the choice you do eventually make.

TRUST – What do we need trust for? All drama students want to be actors so surely this can't be about trusting that a partner will pull their weight? Sadly, this can be an issue. Not everyone will want this as much as you do, not everyone will be as focused and as driven (hopefully the vast majority will be but there are no guarantees).

From the first day, whether we're conscious of it or not, we are forming a professional persona, creating a mould by which we will ultimately be judged. If you are late, or lazy, or hot-headed, or rude, or easily distracted, or selfish, then your peers will remember, and should quite rightly run a million miles from you when it comes to Showcase. And likewise, you should run from any potential partner who presents such flaws. Aside from dodging the negatives, we should be selecting based on positives. Obviously we're looking for talent, reliability, someone who fits the piece, someone generous and fun to work with, but above all we are picking a wingman; the trust needs to be there both on stage and off, not only to make the performance a success, but to prevent the overall experience from being any more stressful than it needs to be.

We had a girl in our year who was certainly skilled, there's not doubt there, but was also unreliable, unpredictable (not in a good way), easily distracted, disruptive and very selfish. I kept my distance from her for the entire three years, and it was interesting to see how even her supposed 'supporters' steered clear of her when push came to shove around showcase time! There was an uneven number in our year – three guesses who the one left with no partner was… In the end someone had to double up and do two scenes so that she had a scene partner to work with. You get my drift? You know what they say, there's always one tosser at the party and if you're not sure who the tosser is then it's probably you. This is a warning not to choose the tosser, and also a warning not to be the tosser!

Reputation is everything; it's everything during training and most certainly once you're out working in the industry. The saying 'It's a small world' has never been truer in any other business more than it is in ours – so make sure your reputation is excellent from the get-go, you cannot afford for it to be anything but.

COMBINATION – The combination of actors within a showcase scene is a tricky one. You can have an idea of what you'd like it to be, or what you think might work but essentially it will be the text and not the 'types' that attract you to the right piece, so you must try and afford yourself the time to ensure that you are happy with both.

The combination of boy/girl, young/old, gay/straight, fat/thin will be worked out in the trying of scenes and can't necessarily be planned too carefully beforehand. Play with combinations to see what fits and what works, and do the same with a range of different scene partners; the most unlikely pairing could end up being magical. I think it's very important to try pairings with people that you've never worked with, with people you're not connected to. Free yourself up to be surprised and challenged and keep an open line of communication with those around you; both staff and colleagues.

It's very difficult to advise on this in a generic way as each of you will be hugely different, with your year containing a myriad of vastly contrasting actors who are capable of demonstrating a whole rainbow of skills and abilities. For this reason it would be daft of me to advise much further or to encourage you to stick to one 'plan' that may be wrong or simply not helpful. The main reason I've mentioned combination is simply to flag it up as something you should be aware of during the choosing process.

MY CHOSEN SCENE, AS AN EXAMPLE

A month or so into the search for my showcase piece I still hadn't selected one (not for want of trying) and admittedly I was beginning to flap a tad. The people I thought might work well with me were being snapped up and time was slipping away. I looked at Coward for the period thing, at Ayckbourn for the comedy thing, and at a zillion other scenes and nothing seemed to fit perfectly (it is worth noting that attempting to seek perfection will gradually make you insane. I was dangerously close there for a while!) It wasn't necessarily perfection I was seeking, but I had a niggling idea of the rough style and structure that I wanted and was quite adamant that I was going to get it. (Looking back it is probably this sodding 'vision' of mine that ruined the chances of all of the perfectly adequate scenes I had found beforehand.) For your possible benefit/certain amusement, here are some factors that featured in my train of thought at the time:

- I wanted a boy/girl combination. Firstly I needed to be able to sell a brassy sexuality, as I'd discovered that this is indeed one of my main USPs (possibly personally as well as professionally?) and I felt it would work best if I had a male to bounce that off (so to speak). Secondly, I didn't want to be compared to other girls in the year during my three minutes, and the only way to make absolutely sure that a scene partner isn't in your casting bracket is to pick a scene partner of the opposite sex! THIS IS NOT A RULE. In fact, it's fairly ridiculous; there are many fabulous scenes for same-sex teams, I just didn't think that it would work well for me.

- Whilst I was confident that the blatant sexuality thing fit and could work, I was aware that I also needed to show evidence of other attributes too (in a desperate attempt to dodge the two tits on a stick persona – an ongoing battle). So, to incorporate some versatility I looked to my USPs and thought I should attempt to be amusing too. I imagined that this could be accomplished by throwing a female with blatant sex appeal up against a nervous/sexually frustrated/naïve male. This decision created the 'type' I needed opposite me:

Male, comedic, can play naïve/young/inexperienced.

- I didn't want the scene to be a ballet of stereotypes, so needed an arc that would reveal several depths within each character... So when the male is presented with a problem within the scene in an area in which he is skilled, he excels, takes control and dominates (if only for a second or two) – this will give us both a chance to swap status within the scene, showing our VAST versatility, whilst giving a dash of drama within a comedy piece and providing that oh so craved sexual tension.

Sounds a tad specific right? Absolutely right! This was the thought process of someone who had searched and searched and searched and obviously had such a clear/limiting view of what she needed that without knowing it she boxed herself into a corner. How the hell would you find a scene that is that specific without having to read all the plays that were ever written? You couldn't and shouldn't try – I cheated and wrote the scene described above because I had exhausted so many options and was running out of time to find what I knew I needed and wanted. A compromise was not going to cut it and my stubbornness took over. I had unknowingly narrowed my search so much that I'd created a scenario in my mind that would tick all of my boxes, but that was so specific I couldn't bloody find it. So I wrote it, knowing the exact partner I was writing it for. This was a HUGE risk and a really arrogant thing to do now I look back. Thank Christ, it worked; but in no way am I suggesting that this is the way to go, actually I'm saying the opposite, because it could have gone badly wrong and it was only my naivety and sheer bloody mindedness that made it possible for me to take such a risk. It was a last resort and a risky gamble that luckily paid off.

CREATING MY SHOWCASE TEXT

My parents were driving me back down to drama school from the Midlands after the Christmas holiday when I wrote the skeleton of the scene in a text message to myself on my phone in the back of the car. With great apprehension I then typed it up and presented it to the actor whom I intended to drag into this insane plan with me. He sat at the end of the bar where I worked and as I served the punters he read it; every time he giggled I nearly weed with excitement. He casually slid the pages over to me and with beer in hand and a full grin he said 'I love it. Let's do it.' Well, as you can imagine, I was elated! Not only had someone I admired professionally liked something I'd written (first time I'd really let any of my writing out), but he was also willing to use it for his showcase. It is worth noting here that he had a big agent already, so the stakes were perhaps not so high for him. It's possibly also worth noting that we ended up in a rather wonderful relationship after Showcase, which may suggest to some that his decision was rather more tactical than artistic? Sneaky little shit.

The next task was getting the DIY scene past the staff. (What a devious cow I was/am.) I knew they wouldn't judge it fairly and their view would be tainted if I waltzed into class and announced that I had written what we considered was, without question, our showcase piece. So, I put it in a pseudonym and acted (lied) my way around their questions…

Iris Farmer Voice & Text (this is always her full title, every time she was and still is addressed or referred to) was in class that day, along with our director. Marc and I stood up and told the room what we would be presenting.

IRIS FARMER VOICE & TEXT: Who's the playwright did you say? Samantha Dickens?

NATALIE: *(Beat.)* Yup.

IRIS FARMER VOICE & TEXT: I'm not sure I know her work.

NATALIE: Oh really? Well I think she's quite new, I found this particular scene in a showcase folder in the library, one of the other years must have looked at it?

IRIS FARMER VOICE & TEXT makes an 'I know everything, why don't I know this playwright' face, but indicates for us to start anyway…

REDMAN & GEDDINGS

By Natalie Burt

First performed by Natalie Burt & Marc Pickering 2006

Copyright © Mark Dean

A wealthy, confident, attractive and manipulative woman in her 20s is trying to divorce her rich, much older husband. This scene is the meeting with a solicitor who is fresh out of law school (unbeknown to her). He is inexperienced and naïve but perhaps there's more to him than meets the eye…

An impressive-looking office. GEDDINGS sits at his desk. There is a buzz.

SECRETARY: Mrs Redman for you Sir.

GEDDINGS: Thank you Janet, send her in.

> *He chuckles at the buzzer as if it's the first time he's used it. (It probably is.) He straightens his tie in the mirror then licks his fingers and smoothes his eyebrows. He hasn't anticipated that the waiting area is only a few feet from his office door and rather sooner than he had thought REDMAN opens the door with purpose.*

GEDDINGS: Good afternoon Mrs/Redman.

REDMAN: Yeah, yeah hi. An espresso wouldn't go amiss.

GEDDINGS: Sorry?

REDMAN: An ESP-RESS-O, whilst I'm waiting for Mr Geddings, I'm parched.

> *She slings her coat and umbrella to him. He pauses, a little unsure what to do. He gives himself time to prepare for the next conversation and hangs her coat. He turns to her, forcing steadiness.*

GEDDINGS: I am Mr Geddings, Mrs Redman.

> *Beat.*

REDMAN: You're Geddings of Tyler & Geddings Solicitors? *(She smiles sarcastically.)* Yeah, you're cute, it's cute, but I think my appointment may have been with Geddings SENIOR.

GEDDINGS: Ah, then we may have a problem.

REDMAN: A problem? What problem?

GEDDINGS: Yes, unfortunately Geddings Senior would be no use to you I'm afraid; apart from the fact that he was a plumber, he's also dead. So…

> *Silence. She scoffs.*

REDMAN: But you can't be a Solicitor, surely? You don't look a day over twelve. *(Beat as it sinks in.)* Well, I feel I should have worn pigtails and brought along my skipping rope. Is it Kiss Chase or Grandmother's Footsteps we're playing? *(She doesn't pause for breath and begins to pace.)* Well, this is cata-bloody-strophic; you're telling me that some, some, fresh-faced juvenile is now my sole, my ONLY hope of winning the biggest divorce settlement in the district for decades? I mean, he'll eat you for breakfast, in fact, you wouldn't even be an appetizer, he'd use you as a toothpick.

He tries to speak, she continues ranting.

I cannot, I actually cannot believe this. 'Fierce and fiery' I was told you were; fierce and fiery? More like Pete's fucking Dragon. Do you have any idea what I have riding on this?

Beat.

And this, this is our 'team' is it?

MR GEDDINGS sits and eventually looks her in the eyes.

GEDDINGS: Seems so Mrs Redman. *(Beat.)* I can assure you that my skills as a solicitor are not only equal to, but quite possibly/ superior to that of other firms in the area and I will ensure…

REDMAN: Oh save me the sales pitch, it really will get you nowhere. I am concerned with one thing and one thing only Sonny, and that's getting what I deserve.

She nears his desk.

And by god am I going to get it, nobody, but nobody is going to get in my way. Oh Christ, look, if this is the situation then so be it, but I need to know one thing from you Geddings and that is are you with me or against me, and if you're with me we're going to win, we're going to bleed that son of a bitch dry and make him wish he'd never been born, we're going to play dirtier than you can imagine.

She leans over the desk.

Can you play dirty Geddings?

He swallows and his voice cracks slightly as he speaks.

GEDDINGS: Well…erm, let's er, have a look at your statement…and see what grounds we're, erm, lying on, playing with.

REDMAN recoils.

REDMAN: Yes. Let's.

GEDDINGS: Ok, let's see. *(He pretends to scan the document.)* It says here that your husband is jealous, possessive and sometimes violent towards you. Is that true?

REDMAN: True? *(She begins the theatricals.)* Do you know what it's like to be totally submerged in love Mr Geddings? To feel so devoted to someone that whatever they do to you couldn't possibly be worse than the thought of being without them? He devoured me with his charisma and then... I can't take it any longer, the manipulation, the dominance, the endless oppression, *(Very theatrical now.)* there comes a time when you have to gather any shred of strength you have left to stand up and say: No more.

GEDDINGS is unaffected.

GEDDINGS: Was that improvised or did you rehearse it especially for me?

She is mock-shocked and then switches instantly.

REDMAN: Don't flatter yourself; I rehearsed it for the jury, not you. Damn good too, don't you think? I'm going to have them inviting me round for cucumber sandwiches after church *(Now she improvises.)*, they'll be weeping in the aisles for the poor young girl whose naivety about an idealistic romance landed her in a loveless marriage, surrounded by ugliness and corruption with no one in the world to turn to.

Beat.

It's fucking brilliant, in fact I have no idea exactly what I need you for.

GEDDINGS: You need me, my dear, because that is the biggest load of Hollywood-ised cobblers I've ever heard; oh they're going to be weeping in the aisles alright, weeping with laughter if you try and feed them the same tired old story that every money-grabbing young sex bomb delivers when they realize that being a trophy wife to a geriatric gangster isn't quite as much fun as it looks.

He finishes, triumphantly. She is quiet.

So. We don't re-enact cliché, we play straight into it, admit the obvious and plead guilty of whatever they accuse.

REDMAN: WHAT?

GEDDINGS: I may be a toothpick, but I'm sharp.

Impressed with himself for a second, he forgets his train of thought and quickly remembers.

Quick response.

They play as if it were a pub quiz game, but a quiz with high stakes; everyone concentrates, hard.

Go! How old are you?

REDMAN: Twenty-three.

GEDDINGS: How long have you been married?

REDMAN: Two years.

GEDDINGS: How old is your husband?

REDMAN: Sixty-three.

GEDDINGS: Approximately how much is he worth?

REDMAN: Over six million in property alone.

GEDDINGS: Do you love him?

REDMAN: No.

GEDDINGS: Did you ever?

REDMAN: No.

GEDDINGS: Do you still copulate together?

REDMAN: What?

GEDDINGS: Do you still make love to him?

REDMAN: No. *(Beat.)* But I fucked him last Tuesday.

GEDDINGS swallows his tongue/coughs. She shrugs.

REDMAN: I wanted a new car.

He moves on quickly.

GEDDINGS: Fine. Did he ever hit you?

REDMAN: No.

GEDDINGS: Bully you?

REDMAN: No.

GEDDINGS: Do you work?

REDMAN: I have a small boutique of ladies lingerie.

GEDDINGS stutters.

GEDDINGS: F,f, funded by him?

REDMAN: Obviously.

GEDDINGS: Have you been unfaithful?

REDMAN: Of course.

On a roll.

GEDDINGS: So, you're attracted to other men?

REDMAN: Very much so.

GEDDINGS: Are you attracted to me?

She is about to answer yes. They are close. She pauses and he dies of embarrassment as he realizes what he's said. He quickly gathers himself in the silence.

You're an attractive woman and a force to be reckoned with Mrs Redman...therefore we should play to your strengths. Let's give them every gritty detail, every ounce of truth and make you seem so open and brassy that it would have been impossible for your husband not to have been in FULL possession of the facts before marrying you, making it a joint decision, splitting the blame straight down the middle...along with his money, estates and possessions.

He sits exhausted by his own brilliance.

REDMAN: You are a genius.

GEDDINGS: *(Casually.)* I'll get a new statement drafted and sent to you then.

Mrs REDMAN rises slowly, attempting to assess her sudden immense attraction to him. He gets her coat, taking a quick 'oh my god' breath at the coat stand.

REDMAN: Good.

He assists her with her coat and leads her to the door. They are close.

It's been a pleasure playing dirty with you Mr Geddings.

She leaves. He begins an elaborate celebration dance that he's obviously been doing for some years. He dances near the coat rack. Mrs REDMAN comes back through the door and stops in her tracks as she sees him mid-flow. He notices her and stops.

REDMAN: I forgot my umbrella.

Feigning nonchalance he picks it up and throws it to her. She catches it with equal slickness.

And I must say, I'm awfully glad I did. *(Beat. She smiles.)* Stay in touch Mr Geddings.

She winks and he breezily salutes her as she turns and leaves. He collapses in a heap on his desk.

Blackout.

Luckily, they loved it. And to our immense amusement, we fooled them into thinking it was a published piece… Well, it was only a temporary seven-year lie – it is now! After the scene finished there was a pause, followed by a rush of comments like: (Put a wanky, voice teacher voice on for this.)

'Oh, the language is just so sumptuous and rich!'

'It fits you both like a glove, it's like the parts were created for you to play them.'

'You MUST do this for your showcase.'

'All agreed?' I asked. It was unanimous. Later on I had a quiet word and fessed up, but by that time there wasn't really any way they could go back on it! Ultimately though they knew that I had worked hard and that fortunately what I'd come up with did seem to work. So (kept under a pseudonym) that was the piece we did for showcase at The Criterion in 2006.

I've included this story not as some sort of self-congratulatory gloat but as an example of how things can pan out; maybe more than anything it's a warning not to be too blinkered when approaching the decision-making process. Make your aims clear but the journey towards them flexible. Without focusing too much on the outcome of my experience I hope that seeing my process has demonstrated the 'tactical' thinking that is needed to support any artistic choice at this vital stage.

So, let's skip back to you – you've chosen a partner and a scene and all feels rosy. As you rehearse, something exciting but potentially quite dangerous will begin to bubble.

THE HYPE

Pressure will affect the people around you in a variety of ways and you may have gathered from your third-year shows how differently this manifests itself in individual friends and peers. Each and every one of you will fit into one of these descriptions when approaching showcase:

- Blatantly terrified and infecting all around them with their lack of control.
- Quietly terrified and seemingly moodier than usual or withdrawn.
- Undeniably terrified but trying to override the terror by being loud and/ or obnoxious.
- Subtly terrified and pretending that the whole thing is insignificant.
- Terrified that they're terrified and overcompensating with arrogance.
- Acknowledging the terror but repackaging it as excitement and adrenaline.

Each of your peers will fit one of these, as will you. I think it's fairly obvious which is the more ideal option! In the run-up to the day you must be focused, and self-serving but at the same time do try to be sensitive to those around you. You've been a year, a team, a family and a unit for three years; don't divide now just when you need each other the most. You'll notice that every one of the instances above includes the person being terrified. (I would be seriously concerned about what acting really meant to a graduate who wasn't the least bit terrified about their showcase.) Pressure affects us all because we care so deeply about the outcome; it is whether one chooses to turn that pressure into panic or adrenaline, into positivity or fear that counts. Here's another one of those choices! Make the right one. Preserve your energy and use it where it matters.

THE 3 MINUTES

The morning of showcase is here...

...Big breath in, big breath out.

Today is gonna be a good day. First port of call (before your breakfast and even before your morning urination) is to put on a song that fills you with joy, confidence and energy... Mine? Undoubtedly it's Dario G's 'Sunchyme'. It reminds me of a simpler time, before the acting virus had properly taken hold, when life was wall-to-wall fun and my main objective was trying to learn what to do with male genitalia... (must revisit that lesson at some point)... Good times. So, yes 'Sunchyme' is my feel-good song – borrow it by all means, it works a bloody treat. Have a bop (can't quite believe I just used the word bop – let it go and move on, I have)... Have a jig (no better,

I know)… Ok, let out some steam and keep this feeling with you all day, it will serve you well. Energy. Fun. Adrenaline.

…I just lost half an hour's writing time because I got overexcited with 90s dance hits on Spotify…

Ok, I'm back – moving away from ancient dance music and back to your showcase day… Get dressed. Eat breakfast, preferably something healthy that will not bloat you or make you feel sluggish… (Saying that, I had a McDonalds breakfast when we reached Piccadilly Circus; think I was trying to rebel… It nearly backfired; my Karen Millen suit was a dangerously tight fit already!) Don't be a div like me, eat or you'll faint but eat something good to avoid feeling shite. Once you've done that –

GET TO THE VENUE WITH PLENTY OF TIME TO SPARE – HOURS IF POSSIBLE!

PREPARATION – Any athlete or performer knows the importance of a good state of mind before attempting a task that will be physically and mentally demanding. Preparation is key here. You already understand this, having spent the last three years warming up and cooling down seventeen times a day; the two things should feel as natural as waking up and going to sleep, which in a way is exactly what they are – You cannot deliver if you have not woken up properly and you cannot sleep unless you relax. (We'll discuss the 'cool down'/'Get bladdered' part of the day in due course.)

When you arrive, make friends with the space. (I know, wanky as hell, but do it.) The more familiar you are with the space and the more you feel at home in it, the more relaxed you will be during performance; plus it's one less thing to stress about beforehand. If you are doing your showcase in-house, bonus, you already know the space – but don't be complacent about it – nerves are peculiar things! Walk around the space and warm up in it. Step through your scene and check your entrances, exits and props. Also check the acoustics if you haven't already had the chance to do so. Make sure you do plenty of 'filling the space' exercises (it'd be bloody tragic if after three years of training you're not heard). Resonation and articulation, breathing exercises for lung capacity, relaxation and concentration are probably the most vital things to include in your warm-up, but you'll know at this stage what your own vocal needs are. Concentrate on voice but don't neglect your body; make sure you are physically warm as well as vocally. I'm not going to delve into this much further as I know you already know your shit and don't need me to tell you how to prepare your instrument for performance.

If a line run helps then do so with your scene partner, but I would try to incorporate it into an exercise rather than just doing cold runs. (In my opinion this can put too much focus on the lines, sucking the meaning from them, making them sound dull and dragging your energy in the wrong direction.) Attaching line runs to a physical exercise or game will keep your energy up and prove to you that you know these lines backwards. Speed runs are fun and useful, but perhaps not hours or minutes before the actual performance, as your head will be so full and your energy so high that any 'manic' exercises might be counterproductive! Instigate and get involved with a company warm-up – As I've said, you are all in this together and need to feed from each other's energy and excitement.

Be warm, dressed and ready in plenty of time but don't then use that time to wind yourself up or begin to panic. Take some music you can listen to on your iPod, or continue with some small vocal or breathing exercises in a quiet corner somewhere. At the half you should be calm, concentrated, energized, excited, ready and steady.

THE NOISE OF THE SHOWCASE AUDIENCE – I just wanted to throw this tip in, as it was something that really nearly wrong-footed me! When I was waiting in the wings for showcase to start I suddenly became quite uneasy and was confused as to why as I'd been rather excited about the whole thing up until that moment. Since then, in subsequent shows I've done, I've realized that I really enjoy and use the buzz of an audience to get me into the 'zone' before a show. (I am always in the wings just after the half and stay there until curtain up.) The noise I was listening to at showcase was somehow different; colder, calmer, more business-like – which scared the shit out of me!! These are industry professionals who have ducked out of the office to observe and 'shop'; they are not families and friends who are having a nice little trip to the theatre having purchased a ticket to do so. As a result, they sound totally different! This doesn't mean that the agents and casting directors aren't going to enjoy your show or that they won't be receptive, it just means that they're different and you should accept how and why without it affecting your focus.

Another tiny tip – Keep hydrated and indeed lubricate your vocal chords/folds (whichever), but don't drown your bloody self. Continually needing the loo just before you go on is not ideal!

You have performed before, you have worked with these actors before, you have rehearsed well and you know what it is to have an audience; the only difference today is the difference you create inside your own mind. All that stands between you and achievement is yourself. Enjoy being the actor you are and take pride in what you have to offer.

BELIEVE IN YOURSELF!!!!!!

THE AFTERMATH

The *very first thing* you should do (following the schmoozy bollocks after the show) is go to the pub with your mates. Do shots, relax, be merry and brag loudly about how you are going to piss all over Laurence Olivier's chips. Enjoy the moment; you've earned it.

Once the mother of all hangovers starts to fade the following day it is then time to face the music, whether that music is sweet and rhythmic or more like listening to a Bonnie Tyler single stuck on repeat. (It can't be that bad.) What that music sounds like for others and what it sounds like for you will be vastly different and will depend hugely not only on how showcase went, but also how the next few days unfold.

Firstly, how do *you* feel it went? Are you 'IN A GLASS CASE OF EMOTION?!' (God bless you Anchorman). No, seriously…

- Did it go: Well? Shit? Dunno?
- Were you pleased with your efforts?
- Did you get some nice feedback?
- How did you partner think it went?
- Did your audience seem pleased?
- Has your opinion of how it went changed since coming off stage?

Nothing will have gone drastically wrong; nobody will have died (hopefully). You are acting to a professional standard now, you made good choices in the run-up to the event and prepared for the day brilliantly, yes? Assessing the situation rationally is useful but I'm totally aware that many of us are cursed/blessed (fine line) with attributes such as ambition and perfectionism, which don't always allow us to be objective and instead result in us existing in a constant state of dissatisfaction! If this applies to you, recognize that you have a tendency to self-berate and make every attempt to keep it in check; it can be both constructive and destructive and taken to extremes these qualities can both make and break actors so you must carefully monitor yourself.) At this stage I would advise you to be as kind to yourself as possible as you'll need masses of strength and self-belief, whatever the next few days (weeks, months, years, decades) bring.

The morning after showcase you are likely to wake up to a really weird sensation (and I don't mean from the tequila that's still burning your oesophagus, and possibly your wee). Regardless of whether you have decided it went well or not, you have now, overnight, catapulted into the first stage of your professional career and will be already realising the frustration of knowing that vital decisions about your life are being made by complete strangers, based upon a only a snippet of your ability. Sounds fun huh?

Welcome to the madhouse! This will be a reoccurring issue for you as an actor and one that you need to get your head around (easier said than done, but perfectly doable and something we'll touch on later in Chapter 9). This horrible limbo will unfortunately become part of your life; the sick feeling, the jittery uncertainty, the leakages of self-doubt will all become familiar to you like a smelly, old friend; a friend you'd quite like to nut. Joking aside, you must learn to cope with this being the norm for you as a professional actor, stomaching this first taste of it as best you can. I think this can be best achieved by remembering your worth, your goals and the tenacity that you demonstrated when getting into drama school in the first place. Remember who you are and what you have to give. Conjure up the fight within yourself, and back it up with the love you have for your job and the hope you have for your future. That, more than anything else, should see you through any amount of turbulence that the industry can throw at you.

Though the feelings that accompany the showcase aftermath will most certainly arise again in your career, the situation itself will never be repeated; at no other time as an actor will you be required to socialise, take classes and exchange pleasantries with the competition immediately after the audition (which is effectively what you are required to do here. And it's weird). Nothing I've experienced since has come close to the confusing state that showcase leaves everyone in. The phases you go through personally and the stages being played out in front of you by your peers are complex, and at times difficult to withstand. It should surely be a comfort that there are others around you in the same boat? Perhaps, but it can also feel as if you have no right to voice what you're feeling in case you gloat, offend or seem self-centered or self-involved, making it a very lonely and tough time to handle. Naturally when someone else's news is announced or leaked there are bound to be comparisons made and injustices sometimes felt – we are after all human! This feeling may regularly arise in your job as you will be in direct competition with others; sometimes the direct competition will be your friends and it's very important that you learn how to be happy for them (especially if you want to keep them), separating your progression from theirs and not making their path about your own journey. In a way I am asking you to be superhuman, but in another I'm warning you of the armour you must become comfortable wearing if you are to survive past today.

But let's chill out a bit and actually deal with today first, shall we?! Really importantly, don't let the elation of reaching this milestone fade into insignificance too quickly, and don't set up camp by the phone (two very important 'don'ts'). The damn thing may ring, and it also may not; let's take the focus off the phone and back onto you. What's next?

- Do you have any more shows at school?

- Do you have a reading of a play you'd like to hold whilst you still have free access to a studio?

- Are there some follow-up letters you can write?

I hate to be the one to break it to you but now, right now, is where the hard work really starts. Regardless of the outcome of showcase you must get on with making your career everything you want it to be, in spite of whatever obstacles may land in your way. So, think ahead, and remain focused and positive whilst we tackle this next very 'fun' subject...

AGENTS

That beautiful U2 song springs to mind; you know the one?

'With or without you, I can't live, with or without you!!!'

We can live without them but it's harder; we can live with them but it's no bed of roses (partly owing to the fact that we blame them when things go badly and credit ourselves when they go well)!

You might get an agent straight away or it might take a bit longer. Whichever outcome is currently relevant to you please be aware that getting one hardly ever means immediate success and not getting one never means certain death. Both paths can present their own set of problems and we must make the most of whatever hand we're dealt if we are set on achieving our goals. (It's worth noting that getting the wrong agent or a shite agent can be way more damaging than not getting one at all!) In all cases you should never take your foot off the gas or eyes off the road; you are still self-employed regardless of your representational status and should be doing everything within your power to forward your own career, either in addition to or in the absence of an agent's efforts. Represented or unrepresented, there is an abundance of hard graft facing you.

Obviously our objective is unanimous – to get one; I'm not denying that. However I think it may be useful to assess that this business and certainly this area of the business is not formulaic, it does not follow a neat pattern or code...

Talent = Agent + Success = World Domination – yeah, sometimes.

Mediocre Talent + Looks = Agent = Success – yeah, sometimes.

No Talent + No Looks + Connections = Agent = Success – yeah, sometimes.

Talent + Determination = No Agent + Luck + Faith = Success
– yeah, sometimes.

A fairly self-explanatory point there, over-complicated by my absolute lack of mathematical intelligence. From where you're sitting there may be no rhyme or reason to the decisions that have been made about you, and though there will always be reasons, the harsh reality is that it is highly unlikely you'll ever know what they are. Feedback is pretty rare and always subjective and you have no power to change the outcome anyway, so actually ignorance, for now, may be bliss (though it won't feel like it). You must begin to develop a very accepting nature; accepting in the sense that you accept a decision and move on, not that you accept defeat! As with the weather, you cannot predict these things; you can look at the evidence, make intelligent assumptions and prepare for a number of outcomes, but if it wants to piss it down it damn well will, and all you can do is not let the rain ruin your plans – Be prepared for it to change them slightly but never ruin them!

There are many scenarios on the cards for you right now and you cannot know which is coming your way. You may be called into meetings with agents and then again, you may not. You may go to meetings with agents and the match not work out. You may get no leads at all. You may sign with one after a few meetings and have left them within the year. I cannot and would not dish out generic advice when so many of you will be experiencing different things. Therefore in an attempt to cater for all, I hope that the following two points will cover most of the information relevant and useful to you at this time.

A) The phone has rung and you have an interview with an agent who is interested in representing you.

Great! They are (I presume) looking for a new, talented professional and a likeable client who they feel has a place within their existing agency; someone they can openly communicate with and ultimately someone who they believe will work. The good news is that they've obviously liked what they've seen of you and think that you may fit the bill. The bad (or less good) news is that a meeting does not mean a contract. This interview is about a marrying of minds, so try not to put all of your eggs into one basket or set your heart too vehemently beforehand.

At this particular point I believe that all in camp B need me more so please forgive me for focusing on them (something drama school won't do you'll notice). We'll focus on your situation shortly As…

B) The phone hasn't rung and you aren't sure what the shittedy fuck to do.

Don't panic. This is by no means as tragic as it feels right now.

You are going to feel like shit; like absolute shit – allow yourself this. Wallow in it for at least a day and a half and then pick yourself up, have a word, and get back on the horse (or whatever it is you're meant to get back on...bike? Whatever it is, get back on it.) Do I sound unsympathetic? I'm not, honestly, I feel your pain, frustration and deflation, I really do; I've had enough of it in my career to allow me to empathise with you a thousand times over. Whilst the 'wallowing' or 'releasing' phase is an important one, let me warn you that there is a dangerous time limit for such dark and destructive feelings and if you allow them to linger for too long it can only lead to further unhappiness and desperation. It's grabbing-the-bull-by-the-horns time; you've come too far to fall at the first hurdle.

Ok, one of you sharp shits may have noticed (especially if you've read the back of this book), that I signed with a great agent after showcase and have therefore not been in this *exact* position myself. So I should shut my mouth and thank my lucky stars, right? I do. Daily. But regardless of my good fortune, I have watched many actors coping without an agent; I've listened to their triumphant stories, their tales of achievement and their messages of gumption and hope. Plus, to be honest I have been (and continue to be) as proactive as anyone without an agent would be so I do know what it takes to be attentive to and in control of one's career and can therefore advise using the strategies that have served me well.

Yeah, that's all very well, but you still feel like shit, yeah?…

STAY POSITIVE – State the fucking obvious Nat. But seriously, your own outlook will massively affect the next sequence of events for you. Nothing good, absolutely NOTHING good will come from self-pity, self-flagellation and self-abuse (whether of the emotional or vice variety). Sure, go on a massive bender if you must, let off some steam and slag off all of the 'lucky' bastards in your year who don't deserve the outcome they got, but do it quietly, do it quickly and then move on. Focus on what *can* happen now not on what isn't happening.

> **'Grant me the serenity to accept the things I cannot change,
> the courage to change the things I can, and wisdom
> to know the difference.'
> The Serenity Prayer**

STAY ACTIVE – I will be waffling on and on and on about this as it has saved my sanity on several occasions, and will always do you more good than harm – so please heed this advice. I'm not saying you need to subscribe to a million-pound-a-month gym or become a health freak; all I am saying is that taking care of yourself will help if you are low. Being active includes simple things like making sure you get out of the house; if you have no classes at school then go for a walk or run or swim, meet up with friends and play a sport or organize a dance class – whatever, the activity doesn't matter, just be aware that those little darling endorphins should be close allies right now so hang out with them, they're great!

STAY INSPIRED – Remember why the hell you do this job; it's all too easy to forget when you've been battered by it. I know it sounds silly but it's so important, in fact the first thing I do when I don't get a job is go to the cinema or theatre because it reminds me of what lies ahead and of the family that I belong to. (It also lets you escape a little without disappearing into a bottle.) It titillates those creative taste buds and re-energizes the passion within you and if you manage that then I guarantee you'll come up fighting.

Practically speaking though, what is the game plan now?

BE PROACTIVE NOT PASSIVE – Instead of pissing and moaning because bad things are happening (or, more accurately, good things aren't), why not concentrate on the things you can control rather than all the things you can't? You must now evaluate your own personal situation and strike whilst the iron is hot. You cannot allow your energy to dip and for doubt to creep in. These questions might be of use…

- What contacts do I have? Directors, teachers, other actors etc?
- Are there visiting directors or a mock agent I can contact for 'advice' (simultaneously making them aware that you need their help and support)?
- Have I looked into co-op agencies?
- Do I have friends who are in the same boat? What are they doing?
- Can I get an appointment with Spotlight for careers advice?
- What groups/subscriptions/classes etc. can I join to?

That last question is important and following through with it can be hugely beneficial for two reasons:

> A) To keep yourself busy and to continue practising your craft.

> B) To 'Network' – I HATE that word, I wish I could ban it – See Chapter 4! What else do you call it? Mingling? That's equally disgusting… Meeting like-minded people?… Sounds like a dating website. Whatever the hell we call it, it's useful.

It's time to rack your brains, it's time for the entrepreneur in you to flourish; they don't call it SELF-employed for nothing. How the next few months and years pan out is down to no one else but you. You must be tough, you must be energized, you must be focused and above all you must remember that 'luck' or 'fate' or whatever it is that you believe makes up the pattern of life, is the easiest thing to blame and the hardest thing to fight. You have only yourself to rely on here, so don't let yourself down.

You are not doomed.
You are not alone.
This is the first hurdle and you can jump it;
but you have to believe that you can.

Back to outcome A

(For those of you who have had some interest following showcase, this section is to help you with the next step. Everyone from Outcome B, this section will be relevant to you *soon*, so don't have a tantrum and rip the following pages out! You can either prematurely prepare yourself by reading on, or skip and return to this when you need to.)

You may have one meeting or several and no one agent needs to know about the others; they may ask and I'm not suggesting you should lie, but this is business remember, and there's nothing wrong with being a little elusive.

I had five interviews and whilst it was important not to be too cocky about it (mainly because I knew that an interview didn't necessarily mean an offer of representation – in fact only three of the five offered) still, I used the knowledge to boost my confidence and it helped me to realise that it was a two-way process and that I was choosing them as much as they were choosing me. And I think what I've just said probably epitomizes a healthy relationship between agent and actor – They do not 'work' for you, they work on your behalf yes, but you do not employ them. Neither do they employ or own you, nor do they call the shots in regards to your career. This balance is a very important one to strike from the word go and it can be really difficult to achieve as there are many factors at play. These people have been the carrots you've been chasing all of this time and as a result I think it can be hard to pull them from the pedestal they've been placed upon (either by yourself, your school or your peers). But do pull 'em down; pull 'em right down to stand on a level with you, by your side where teammates belong. Do this with casting directors too. Have respect for them for god sake, they know more than you and must be listened to but don't let that knowledge or that power intimidate you. Instead, enjoy the fact that suddenly now they know who you are! Keep in the forefront of your mind that they liked what they saw and are flirting with the idea that you are a person that they wish to invest time and effort in. Showcase is a significant gear change in this game of cat and mouse and you have to note the shifts when they happen and keep noting them as your career changes; behaving accordingly at all times.

You may have interest from ten agents and none of them offer you representation. You may have one interview and they are immediately eager to add you to their books. It is a delicate situation and you need to keep your wits about you, your head in gear and your heart on the periphery, if not out of it altogether.

INTERVIEWS

THE MEETING

Holy shit, you've got a meeting. This is going to be an exciting, yet nerve-racking and mentally chaotic affair. Even as I am writing this, my typing has sped up. And breathe... Focus. Smile.

What might they ask?

- How did you find your training?
- What was your favourite show/role of the third year and why?
- What kind of work do you see yourself doing?
- Which actors do you admire and why?
- What films/programmes/plays have you seen recently that you liked and why?
- Have you met with any other agents? If so, who?
- What directors would you most like to work with and why?

I have listed what I think could/should be asked by an agent, but I have also asked these questions because I think that they're important things to know about yourself; topics that an ambitious professional actor should always have on the tip of their tongue. Answering these questions in detail will make you seem clued up, enthusiastic and interesting/interested. It will also help you and those around you to get an idea of what your long-term goals and your short-term preferences might be.

Remember that we're banishing the idea that they are interviewing you. Instead, this is a conversation between two people with a common interest. The motives and aims that go along with that common interest may differ and vary slightly/massively between the two parties, but that's what you're there for, to see if your parties can and should join forces or not, to see if you can complement instead of clash – Just like a date! You may feel immediately that they might be a good prospect and quickly feel excited that you've established a level of trust; or you may stay for a tap water and get the hell out of there as quickly as possible because you know it ain't gonna work!

What should I already know when I go into the interview?

When the agency was formed and who by?
This will give you a good idea of how experienced they are and how well known within the business they might be. There's absolutely nothing wrong with signing with a start-up agency, as long as you are aware that is what they are and prepared for the experience to perhaps be more of a joint learning curve to begin with than it would be with a more established agency. There are positives and negatives with most decisions, whether you go for an established agent who may ignore you or a new one who sends you up for all types of crap. This will be the first of many gambles and the only thing that will help you, in addition to knowledge, is instinct.

How many agents do they have?
They will have older and newer, less and more experienced agents; assistants move through the ranks and you should make sure you know who is who, who deals with what, and how long they have been doing so. You may be spending a lot of time, especially in the first few years, communicating with assistants – so don't ignore them! Bear in mind that those assistants may one day be the leading agents/partners.

How many clients do they have?
This will indicate whether the agency is a small, medium or large company. But unfortunately it isn't quite as black and white as small meaning less good and big meaning great! The worst agencies will have hundreds of clients, none of whom are working. The best will either have a very exclusive list of gems or a large list of celebs/well-known faces and names. There is a hell of a lot of middle ground in between and you must use all of your intelligence to suss out what it is that you're dealing with before you're sat in front of them!

How many clients in a similar or same casting bracket to you do they have?
If you are a 21-year-old blonde actress and they have sixteen other young-looking, fair haired actresses I would seriously want to know a) whether these actresses are working and b) why exactly they are interested in you if they already have actresses similar to you. Competition within an agency is not good.

What are their current clients working on or in at present?

This will give you a great indication of the contacts that the agent has within the industry. If all of their clients work in musical theatre and you are a straight actor only, then you may want to question their motives; you don't want to be an 'experiment' i.e. for them to try and move into another area of the industry using you. Again, you have to assess your own individual circumstances and make the best of what is presented to you. The work that their clients have on their CVs will tell you whether that agent is able to get you work in theatre and/or television and/or film etc. It will show up where the agent's strengths are within the business and if this marries up with your aims and objectives then great, but if it doesn't then you may have to assess the situation on the whole and evaluate your options before committing.

What is their website like?

I think this is important. It is their main advertising tool and the first thing that will greet any new clients and prospective employers/contacts. If it looks tacky, unprofessional and generally shit, then it makes you look tacky, unprofessional and generally shit. I think you can tell a lot from the way that an agency 'presents' themselves to the rest of the business. Remember they 'represent you'.

Can you access the client list on there? If you can then you can do all of the digging you need to and if you can't, get hold of that 'illegal' Spotlight pin and get stalking!

Where are their offices?

Again, I reckon you can tell quite a lot from this. 'Flat B, Northampton' does not fill me with joy, but 126 Shaftesbury Avenue does. There are a zillion shades in between and you may think this sounds like absolute snobbery bollocks! It kind of is snobbery bollocks, but we're in a snobbery bollocks business where appearance and reputation matter. Again this is not a fixed rule, just another indication of how that agency presents itself to the rest of the industry (and if you sign with them, what you will be presenting to the rest of the industry). Practically speaking if the agents are going to see shows most nights (as they should be) then they need to get to the theatres easily and quickly, ergo their offices should be fairly central (London, not Ilfracombe). Likewise, if they are having regular meetings with industry professionals they need to be somewhere that is easily accessible for people within those circles. Of course any dick can rent an office in Soho, but still that needs to be a dick with money and how do agents make money? By having clients who are in work.

What might **you** *ask?*

Yep, a two-way conversation – not one judge and one in the dock!

- Will I be 'allocated' a specific agent or is it a collaborative office?
- Do you have strong feelings/instincts about what I should be working on?
- If so, what? (Obviously they should, or else why the hell are you there.)
- What percentage do you take for different areas of the industry i.e. TV, theatre etc?
- What are your feelings about actors writing to industry professionals?

When my agent asked me in our second interview if I had any questions I had at that point almost made my mind up that they were the agency for me. The question that I blurted out was 'Why are you an agent? Why do you do it?' (Knowing full well that he had previously been an actor – *research*). I had not planned this question, it quite unexpectedly sprang from somewhere within my subconscious, but it obviously mattered to me why he gets out of bed every morning to do the job that he does. He looked at me for a second, a little taken aback and said 'No one has ever asked me that before.' He then proceeded to give me a genuine and crap-free account of what it is about his job that, basically, turns him on. We knew then that the match would work. I love what I do, and I needed him to love what he does too because after all, their enthusiasm is what sells us on a daily basis!

Another thing that attracted me to my agent was that they were the only one I met with who called me in for two meetings, to meet the two lead agents separately. This told me that they were selective, thorough, and that they have a collaborative but also independent way of working. You certainly don't need an agent who gets overexcited, takes on millions of clients every year and then does nothing with them. An ideal agent will back a horse and bet big – you being the horse and the bet being the amount of work they put into your career – obviously! (You must be getting used to my insane analogies by now?) Putting 5p on all horses at the race is not going to get anyone very far so the more selective and careful they are with their client list, the better the agent, in my humble opinion.

In the meeting, try and be yourself. I know, the very nature of that statement suggests an uneasy level of self-awareness rather than relaxation, but, if you can try and free yourself up, enabling them to see who you are and what makes you tick, it will be beneficial for both parties. Keep your aims near to the surface and by all means voice them, but make sure that you listen too; these people (most of them – we'll deal with charlatans later) know what they're talking about.

INSTINCT INSTINCT INSTINCT INSTINCT

It's so integral, that I had to write it four times. It's important now and will continue to be so throughout your career. Trust your instincts and follow them; and if you don't dare follow them immediately at least make sure that you acknowledge them. Sometimes despite all evidence, regardless of pros and cons, rationale and logic, instinct will be the thing that is most reliable to you; the thing that will guide you towards the right decision.

CHOOSING AN AGENT

As we've discussed, you always have a choice; even when it may seem that you have no alternatives! Never feel that you have to sign with an agent because you have no other options; only sign with one either because you want to or because you won't jeopardize anything by doing so. Sometimes, even if you are weary of them, (as long as they don't ask you to do anything ridiculous like pay them money up front) it may be worth giving it a go as you can still do everything you would do if you were representing yourself and it's an 'in' that could pay off. Nothing ventured and all that. But stand your ground if you think they will hinder your career rather than help it – You would be better off alone in that case.

When you do sign be weary of contracts, making sure that you read them thoroughly. If there's anything that you don't understand or are concerned about then ask Equity.

If you have the luxury of a few offers then fab! Take your time and go for what you think is the right choice for you and your career – how will you know it's the right choice? Because you will be making it based upon everything we've discussed, everything you've researched and all that your instincts are telling you. You'll know what the right answer is, and it'll be the right answer because you'll never know if the other option was! All you'll have are the reasons or gut feelings you listened to when deciding that the other option was wrong. Cling to those.

One agent I interviewed with actually said to me, ACTUALLY SAID OUT LOUD TO ME as I walked into the room…

'Hmm… Good teeth and let me see your nails… yep, good' …

What am I, a fucking show poodle? Even if you are checking them don't be such a twat as to say it, we're not on Broadway in the 60s now love! I fear she was trying to prove a point. She proved it and I left. Ha, she also told me (before I had even removed my coat) that she knew Keira…

'Keira?' I said (as if this was a mutual friend I hadn't realized we had in common).

'Knightly,' she said. 'We've known little Keira for years.'

Great. Why the fuck aren't you her agent then? That same agent called me to ask why I declined their offer of representation and asked (with a slight tone of paranoia) if someone had told me not to go with them!!! I couldn't be bothered to list my twenty reasons, so I faked that I was going through a tunnel and hung up. I know a fair few people who did go with her and have been…fine? Maybe we got off on the wrong foot…or maybe she was a div and my instinct was to run so I did!

Do you think I've worn out the word instinct yet?

To conclude this chapter with an opportunity to smile, here is a wonderful story about an incident that happened when and my mates/peers and I were in a bar some hours after our showcase.

Here's the scene…

There were about twelve or fifteen of us in a bar, adequately merry and enjoying the release and relief of having done our showcase. We were seated on three big tables that were alongside one another; they were red leather and had a lounge feel to them, which is fairly insignificant other than to help you visualize the relaxed, half-cut drama students that were sprawled all over them.

It was quite a large group and a rather open forum where inevitable chats about the showcase pieces arose; compliments flying and tales of near-disasters entertaining all involved and in earshot. Amongst our group there were a few ex-students (mainly from the year above us) who had either come for drinks with friends in the lower years, or who were just coming along to feel superior, who knows. One of these guys was an ex-muso from the year above, and was now an agent, or agent's assistant. Instead of him feeling conscious that someone might wonder why he wasn't doing the thing that he's actually trained to do, acting, he seemed to relish in the fact that he was (technically) part of both camps, and was lapping up the attention he was getting when a few of our party sought his approval and knowledge. He started to (quite loudly) critique the pieces. He was pleasant enough about a few and rudely disregarded others regardless of who was listening/involved in the conversation. I was just behind this guy as they started to discuss mine and Marc's piece. (This is the piece that I had written but was presenting under a pseudonym and no one but the staff, Marc, a few close friends and I knew that this was the case.) His feedback…

ACTOR: What did you think of Nat and Marc's then? It's a wicked piece don't you think?

'AGENT':   Yeah, it was ok.

ACTOR: Ok? Nat's already had a meeting this afternoon.

'AGENT':   Yeah, I mean it was good, but it's quite 'done'.

I pipe up.

ME: Sorry?

'AGENT': No, I liked it, don't get me wrong, you did well with it, but it is quite 'done'.

Inwardly screaming with laughter at what was about to happen I kept repeating the word to attract more attention.

Me: 'Done'? What are you saying it's over 'done'?

'AGENT': Honestly, don't take offence, I really liked it but people are asking for my opinion / and I –

ME: No, please, continue, I really respect your opinion.

The tables have gone fairly quiet now and awkwardness is lapping at the bow.

'AGENT': Well, as I said, I enjoyed it but it is quite done and if I'm honest I've seen it done better.

I giggle blissfully.

ME: Have you now?

I turn back around and my (slightly intoxicated) friend KATIE quite beautifully killed the conversation with…

KATIE: She wrote it you twat.

Simon's face, I mean, the 'AGENT's' face, was a picture. I glanced at him as he squirmed. I playfully shrugged and took a sip of my beer.

Silence and stifled laughter ensues.

'AGENT': I'm sure I've/seen it done before.

ME: You haven't. Its theatrical debut was today, World Premiere was today. But thanks for the crit. Really useful.

He didn't stay long after that and I'm not entirely sure whether he is still an agent or not, who cares?! This story has literally no relevance to the chapter, other than it happened after my showcase, but I felt that it was simply too funny not to share. The moral, if there is one, is don't pretend to be something you're not, or pretend to know more than you know, or to fantasize that you have power over others that you do not. And of course the overall moral is don't be a dick! You will meet SO many of these people over the next few years; not horrible people, not nasty people, what they are actually is a bit pathetic, they're overcompensating or over-egging because they are desperate to prove to the world that they are a success and in doing so they can attempt to convince themselves. The most talented, the most 'successful' people are the discreet ones, the modest ones, the quietly brilliant ones who don't need to prove anything to anyone!

A brilliant aside to this story (that is possibly one of the greatest things anyone has ever said to me) came shortly after this incident. One of my good friends (who was unaware, until this rather public admission, that I was in fact the playwright behind our piece) came up to me later that evening…

CHRIS: You wrote it?

ME: Er, yeah.

CHRIS: What, you wrote that piece from scratch.

ME: Yeah.

CHRIS: But it was funny.

ME: Yeah?

He paused in thought.

CHRIS: You're not funny though.

I paused in thought.

ME: Ta… Another drink?

CHRIS: Yeah.

Three chapters in and you may just agree with Chris…

4. GRADUATION & BEYOND

Escape, grow up, live, shite yourself.

This is a big chapter, because it's a big deal. So I'd grab a beverage of some kind and settle in for this one.

Whatever the outcome of showcase was, is, or seems to be, you are now a trained actor ready for the professional entertainment industry, and this chapter aims to acknowledge, address, celebrate and deal with the transitions you face; the transition from amateur to professional, from student to self-employed, from graduate to actor. And most notably from cradled to dropped.

Though graduation is an important day, which marks the end of your institutional life and the beginning of your professional one, I think it is important that you focus on what lies beyond; excited in the knowledge that this is where the learning really begins – as with driving, you can only truly grasp the technique once you're allowed out onto the road unsupervised. You are now ready to walk the boards and wow the lens; putting all of the theory you've gathered into practice. Though of course take a day off from all of that on your actual graduation day to collect your certificate and get piss-your-pants drunk! (On my graduation day I got so hammered on Lanson that I could have had a conversation with Nelson Mandela and not have had the slightest recollection the morning after. My overdraft took a caning that day – worth it).

Soon after the celebrations have subsided however, you will quickly realise that this is real, and that this is now! There will no longer be rules and deadines, no more mentors at your fingertips and lessons at your disposal; and there is likely to be basically nothing in your diary that you haven't instigated or organised to be there yourself. If you're anything like me you may have been in full time education from the age of 4-18 and then straight to drama school from 18-21 (which we all know is fuller than full time!) Therefore being released from this/deprived of this can be one hell of a culture shock if you don't prepare yourself and start to use initiative throughout your latter educational years; accessing your entrepreneurial abilities and pre-empting your soon-to-be self-employed status are paramount. Of course you may have already been snapped up by an agent and are now auditioning your little heart out (which is absolutely amazing and we will come to that in a bit), but if not, it can feel as if the comfort blanket of institutionalization has not gently slipped off of the bed, but instead is being yanked with great ferocity from your quivering body! (I'm using this imagery with the intention that it will make the actual event seem not so harsh, my theory being that if you are able to see it coming you can prepare for it, stick two fingers up to it and laugh in its face!) You have to welcome this new independence and the challenges heading towards you with tenacity and energy (instead of sitting in a darkened room you have no rent to pay for, quivering, thinking SHHHHHHIIIIIIIIIITE! Before phoning the parent bank and counseling service)…

Joking aside, this can be a really difficult and daunting time, and depending on your personal make-up and the progression of your professional development it may be harder for you than it is for others. Whether things are going swimmingly, or whether you find yourself in dire straits you must already be aware that no one phase for an actor is permanent, they are ever-changing and you must arm yourself with the attitude and knowledge to cope with whichever you find yourself in at any given time whilst being careful to dodge both complacency and hopelessness.

So, with that in mind, I hope that the things I've included here go some way to guiding you through this period, whatever this period means for you, and I want to remind you, above all else, that this is a really exciting and fun time (anxiety of the unknown aside), and one you'll never get back – Embrace it!

(If you trained a while ago or haven't 'trained' in the conventional sense this section is still very much for you and I hope that you can align what I'm saying to your own personal circumstances; hopefully it's all useful information, whatever your path.)

Number one on the list? Let's find the right place to live…

A HOME

In my opinion this is something that should dominate the least amount of your time and money, but I am so aware that this is still one of the most important parts of our overall well-being. What you require and desire are unique to you, and what you are able to have is dictated by your personal circumstances – attempt to obey them both.

> **'He is the happiest, be he king or peasant,**
> **who finds peace in his home'**
> **Johann Wolfgang Von Goethe**

RENTING TIPS

You may already live in London or you may be considering moving here. You live where? Goatham? Lovely… I would move though, you're an actor you plank. There are a few who disagree but I think that really, London is where you need to be, and certainly at the beginning of your career when last-minute castings, London theatre jobs and basic industry mingling should all be on your agenda. When all's said and done you should want to be in the thick of it and you will be required to live and breathe it if you wish to stay in the loop, keep up with your competitors and basically gain a good understanding of the industry you are now a part of. (I must stress that there's nothing wrong with Goatham…much.)

Obviously all who read this book will have individual circumstances, and it would be impossible for me to cater for every eventuality or attempt to make everything relevant to each individual, certainly on this subject, so please feel free to skip over and/or rip out what doesn't apply to you… but don't rip the renting section if you're either going to resell this book on Amazon or are likely to have your house repossessed… (Probably not a subject to joke about.) Most of the information here is just a collection of stuff that I wish someone had mentioned to me when I was renting for the first time. So here I am, mentioning it to you; I moved into London following graduation and would have loved a few friendly tips to help me do so. My parents had never rented and had only ever visited London once, so I was fairly alone with the task and felt it. You may be the same? Many of you will already be here and settled with friends and peers from drama school; if so that's great and I would strongly recommend staying put for six months at least (just so that your professional affairs are able to take up the quota of turbulence that one is able to cope with, instead of house moving/searching using it all up!) If you are happy in your current student house or flat then I wouldn't rock the boat and if you have to/need to/want to move, then the following information might come in handy.

RENTING CHOICES

Of course, if we're dealing with open choices, tastes and preferences then we would all like to occupy a nice apartment in Chelsea or Pimlico, yeah? Lovely. However, I'm going to go out on a limb and say that few (if any) of us have those kind of options regarding where we live right now! At this present phase in our lives, due to our turbulent financial and professional situation we may be on a fairly low rung of the luxury ladder… (unless you have rich parents or some foreign millionaire who'd like to support you through the early stages of your career – if so, fabulous, congratulations!) For the majority of us though, finding a place to lay our hat is all about priority lists (shortening them), realistic outlooks (swallowing humble pie), and intelligent assessment (read on).

The area you live in does matter (to some more than others, admittedly). It matters that the area is relatively safe (I know, where is?) and that you feel adequately comfortable in your surroundings. The obvious snag is that everyone in the country desires the same, so naturally the places known to be currently accomplishing said 'safety' are the most sought after, and therefore the most expensive. The more sought after the place, the more the rent will increase and the smaller the property will be – Marvellous! The good news is that there are many, many areas of London that feel safe, are vibrant and that offer lots in the way of entertainment that won't break the bank too badly. All of that is obtainable as long as you're ready to sacrifice and be flexible!

One or more of the following statements will probably apply to you:

- I need a nice area; I can't cope with feeling unsafe where I live.
- I'm not too fussed about the area, as I'll either be inside the property itself or in the centre of town most of the time anyway.
- As long as it's close to the centre of town I can put up with a rough area and small/less desirable accommodation.
- I need a clean, well-presented and spacious home; wherever it is situated.
- For now I can sacrifice how nice it is or where it is situated, I just need it to be cheap!

So, did more than one of those apply to you? Or did elements of each? I'll fully admit that about three of them applied to me when I first moved. The unfortunate news is that you will probably have to list them in order of priority, expecting to lose at least three of them, as the chances of getting it all on a budget is nil.

On top of basic location and cost requirements you may then need to contend with other added factors such as:

- I need space for a car.
- We need a specific amount of rooms for the group we've arranged to live with.
- It would be useful if the bedrooms were of a similar size to prevent unfairness.
- It has to be within walking distance of the tube or rail.

After that, there's a ridiculous list (that possibly only applies to me)…

- It must have a bath (they calm me).
- It'd be great if there was room for a dining table (eating on lap – not ideal).
- A garden or terrace would be nice (less claustrophobic).
- Dominic West should be contracted to make regular spot checks. Naked.

Demanding? Me? Perhaps. Trust me, I could and did demand all I liked, but at the end of the day I had to sacrifice like everyone else! As an actor, you will constantly be required to assess your level of 'need'. We'll come across this again in the Finance chapter. Did I need the property to have a bath? No, I wanted one. Could I live without a bath? Yes, but I didn't want to! I had to assess whether it was a big enough issue that it would be a deal breaker. (To this day, no matter how tight things have gotten I have never lived in a flat without a bath!) Moving on from my obsession with being submerged in water – you understand my point? You and your potential flatmates will have these debates amongst you, repeatedly! So be true to your needs but always be ready to consider readjusting them. There are probably very few people in the world who don't want above and beyond what they possess, or what they have the means to one day possess; we are human and 'to want' is one of the first things we contend with as infants. Try if you can to view this process of 'settling for' in a similar way to temp work (we'll discuss this in Chapter 6). The situation you find yourself in now 'will not be forever thus' (a favourite quote in the Burt household). By thinking of rented accommodation as a stopgap, not a life-long sentence you will release yourself from a lot of pressure caused by unrealistic limitations. All you really need is an adequately safe and comfortable base from which you can build your career; a career that will hopefully, in its own sweet time, offer you the opportunities to indulge in what you want.

As well as sorting your main priorities out and sticking to them, you will then have the arduous task of marrying your list with your flatmates' lists! (I can think of better things to be doing with your mates than arguing. I can think of better things to be doing with your mouth than arguing too… Singing, obviously! Filthy minds, the lot of you.) Can I suggest that smaller groups of two or three friends might be a better plan than a houseful? The less of you there are the more likely it is that you'll get a place that both you and your flatmates are happy with. Also, it's worth remembering that you've probably done party house, or you've certainly been through the stage where that should have been done! The more people in the house the less the chance of it being fun when you need it to be and calm when you need it to be. Do I sound boring? All I'm thinking is that for the next few months, even years, you may be working long hours for little money; you will need your sleep and your sanctuary in order to function and apply yourself to the extent that will be required of you when juggling jobs, auditions, unpaid work etc. Mid-week all-night raves with twenty guests (whilst fun) may hinder your ability to cope and to blossom effectively. I'm not saying don't have fun, of course I'm bloody not, but do choose to live with people who are either in a similar position or who are considerate towards your situation or the shit may very well hit the fan, and that's not fun for anyone, least of all you.

FLATMATE/HOUSESHARE

We're all different, and our tolerances, habits and expectations vary hugely. Although we may get on with certain people, living with them is quite different and you may have learnt this lesson during drama training?! My flatmate was a bitch and I lived alone. Terrible gag, apologies. Good friends can be good flatmates, but so can strangers or acquaintances and deciding which makes the best cohabitant for you is a very important part of the next phase of your life. Bickering with the people you live with is exhausting so maybe keep your 'spirited' friends for tequila Tuesdays when you end up drunkenly running through a fountain naked at 2am whilst singing Jellicle cats at a less than considerate volume. (Never happened.) Make sure that you trust the people you live with to be considerate, and make sure that they have a guarantor (explained later) in case they suddenly don't/can't pay their way! (The last thing you want is to be homeless because of someone else's inability to manage money, however nice they are!)

You are entering a new chapter, one of discovery and unpredictability and for this reason alone it might be useful to choose like-minded people to have around you, who care about you, and who have a vested interest in your professional progression. Then again, living with a banker who's out 7am-10pm everyday and who doesn't give a flying fuck who just got Mike Leigh's new film might be a godsend too! It's up to you to make informed choices that are right for you at this moment in time.

CALCULATIONS

When you are on a limited budget it is important to know about and understand the costs you are likely to incur when renting. I did not, and six years on I'm still not quite over the shock! If you are renting through a private landlord then you will be asked for a deposit (usually a month and a half of the rent), which will be required in addition to your first month's rent.

DO NOT HAND OVER CASH TO A LANDLORD

(It sounds obvious but people can be disgustingly deceptive, and the last thing you need is for the little money that you do have to be taken from you by a bastard.) If your landlord is someone you know and trust then ok; in fact if that is the case they may not ask for a deposit – hurrah! If the landlord is acting alone there should be an agency with whom they are affiliated, who will at least deal with the deposit side of the tenancy even if the landlord intends to manage the property themselves. The TDS (Tenancy Deposit Scheme) is a must for tenants. Make sure when you are discussing handing over a deposit to a letting agent or landlord that it will be protected by the

TDS. This involves the landlord or agent registering the money with the TDS and providing a reference number for that deposit within 14 days of the start of your tenancy. This scheme gives a small amount of protection to tenants; a small amount that can prevent a landlord from simply 'taking funds' from your deposit upon your departure from the property without cause, permission or evidence. If when you come to leave your landlord wishes to take money from your deposit for damage or cleaning or because they damn well feel like it, you then have the right and the support of the TDS to file a dispute. If you do this then the landlord will be forced to provide evidence and an adjudicator will decide who is entitled to the disputed amount. I am fighting a complete arsehole for cleaning costs at the minute, even though the flat we vacated was fit for a Queen to have her dinner served on the floor; if it weren't for the TDS we'd have lost £150 and had no support in fighting the landlord who was blatantly 'trying his luck'. Unfortunately there are very few rights for tenants in this country (don't even get me started!) so I cannot stress enough how important it is to take responsibility and be thorough in anticipation of a problem. This means *check your documents*; the tenancy agreement, the check-in report, the inventory, the receipt of deposit – check them, have your flatmates check them and then check again. Main things to check for?

Make sure that:

- The deposit is protected.
- There is a clear indication of days in which the landlord is required by law to return the deposit (usually between 10-20 days).
- You have it in writing that they must give notice to you if they wish to enter the property.
- You take photographs of everything when you move in; floorboards, cracked tiles, dodgy shelves, dirt, rust, limescale, grease, chipped paint – anything that you might be blamed for/charged for when you check out. Make sure that the pictures are dated! Evidence is key.
- You keep all correspondence you have with the landlord, especially if there are any disputes.

(Little tip though, if the landlord doesn't offer to do a check-in report then don't necessarily push for one, just take your own evidence and make sure that the tenancy agreement is all ok; if there is a dispute and there is no check-in report, then the landlord has no evidence of what state the property was in when the tenancy commenced, hence, you cannot be held liable for anything and it was the landlord's own stupid fault for not providing the proper procedures.)

I know it's usually stressful and (these days) rushed but take the time when signing contracts and handing over money to make sure that the tenant is protected by the documents as well as the landlord.

Oh, and make sure that *all* parties sign the documents; landlord and/or agent as well as tenant. Only then are they legally binding.

In addition to the deposit and the first month's rent there will also be 'other' charges if you deal with an agency. These will include admin fees (usually between £50-£150), inventory fees (£70-£150) and possibly a few more small hidden charges thrown in at the last minute. If you are in doubt, ask the agent for a breakdown of costs or for a clear explanation of what and why. I will just say (sorry, I can't help it) based on the experiences I've had with letting agents that they are a species like no other. They can be over-keen to sell and therefore indifferent to what you actually want or need, not to mention forgetful, never prompt and basically a total arse ache. You must be firm, persistent, patient and also assertive with them at all times (and have a good ear for detecting bullshit). I was trying to avoid saying it, but I can't: the majority of them are imbeciles and it seems that incompetence is the core skill required in order to become one. There, I've said it, it's out there… Reckon I'm fairly safe though, I doubt too many letting agents will pick up this book on their lunch hour – they're all far too busy on Facebook anyway… Ooh… True.

Moving on!

When you look at properties the rents may be advertised as PCM or PW (Per Calendar Month and Per Week). If the rent is per calendar month then it is straightforward and you simply pay what the PCM is on an allocated day each month. But if the rent is advertised as per week then it is likely that you will actually pay it out monthly – that make sense? So, in order to find out what you will be paying out monthly when a weekly sum is advertised, you have to do the following calculation;

52 x (£) by the weekly rent / 12 (months) = £000.00 payable per month.
(52 multiplied by PW amount, divided by 12 equals the amount you pay per month).

We made the grave mistake with our first flat of simply multiplying the weekly figure by 4 to get what we'd pay per month. WRONG! This gave us a lower figure than the amount it was actually going to be and it wasn't until we were unpacking tealight holders and the toilet brush that we realised! Schoolboy error. (I'm sure you are neither as stupid nor as naïve as we were, but just in case I thought I'd mention it.)

NOTICE

Our situation as actors is so unpredictable both in terms of finance and work demands, as touring or filming on location is a constant possibility. For this reason you should always try and get a 6 month get-out clause in any rental agreement. This means that although you sign a 12-month contract you will be able (after six months) to either leave, or only give a month's notice before being able to do so throughout the rest of the contract. If you can get a 12-month agreement where you're able to leave at a month's notice at any point during the tenancy – even better! (The chance of that is slim unless you're renting through a friend.) My note to you here is to beware of landlords and letting agents attempting to trap you into a 12-month contract when you cannot be sure of what your immediate future holds. Flexibility on their part may be non-negotiable, and if you must commit to secure the place you want then so be it, but do it with your eyes open to the possibilities that lay before you, and only after you've made damn sure they won't lean a little!

GUARANTORS

The likelihood is that you will be asked to have a guarantor for your tenancy agreement. A guarantor is someone who will sign your agreement on your behalf (in addition to you as the tenant), therefore accepting responsibility should the rent not be paid by you. The obvious choice for this is a parent or family member and as long as the rent is paid, they will not be contacted.

I was mortally offended when I was asked to have one; feeling that I was being deemed 'untrustworthy' simply because I'd got up off of my arse to study, allowing myself to therefore be branded as a lazy, debt-ridden 'student' for all eternity. (I can be touchy like that!) I quickly learnt that being offended was a waste of time, and that I was going to have to get used to companies and businesses assuming that freelance unpredictability equals unreliability! It's all about the money (it's all about the dum dum duh dee dum dum –) (It is likely that won't make sense to anyone not born in the 90s.) People cover their backs; I get it. I don't like it, but I get it.

When you sign your tenancy agreement make sure that each individual tenant has his or her own guarantor. I know this might seem a little paranoid, but at least that way no one parent or guarantor is responsible for other people's conduct and each of your guarantors can be secure in the fact that they will only have to bail you out, should you find yourself up shit creek.

Wherever you do end up living remember that this is more of a means to an end than the ideal place in which to 'settle'. It's unlikely that you'll be nest-making or home-building right now, mainly because both take time, money and emotional investment (time, money and emotion that should, certainly in the early stages, be focused primarily on pursuing your career). It's about finding a happy balance, finding somewhere that allows for your lifestyle and that also offers you a degree of domestic satisfaction.

'Home is any four walls that enclose the right person.'
Helen Rowland

Ah, well said Helen. Who the hell is Helen Rowland? (Quickly googles.) Ah, 'An American journalist and humourist who for many years wrote a column in the New York World newspaper called "Reflections of a Bachelor Girl."' My kinda girl.

So that's a big chunk of the mundane crap out of the way. (The stuff we need to know about but would rather someone else dealt with! I'll split it up as best I can.) But now, back to you and your career.

DEALING WITH 'SUCCESS' AROUND YOU

By 'success around you' I don't only mean the momentary feeling of nausea we sometimes secretly experience when encountering friends and peers whose lives seem to be going well/better than your own, (another taboo subject that is perfectly natural and never addressed), I also mean general success that will be all around you in your everyday life. Televisions blaring out, posters on the tube, film adverts on buses, theatre signs as you walk down the street and newspaper reviews of plays will all be countless reminders that shitloads of other people are doing the thing that you want to be doing, wish to be doing, should be doing, are capable of doing; this, can be hard to swallow, some days more than others. Try to remember that almost every actor you see on a poster or billboard went through quiet times, unpredictable times, low times, times when they were looking on longingly from the sidelines as you might be now. (It's also worth bearing in mind that most of them will be there again at some point!) Avoiding bitterness and resentment can be incredibly challenging, and some days it can feel nigh on impossible to manage, but I promise you that succumbing to it will not only be exhausting for you (and all those around you) but will also be potentially damaging to the professional life you're attempting to build. You must try to put a helpful spin on it, find that silver lining. For example, for every poster and trailer, advert and article there is a production, programme or film that has been invested in and made! This is good news for our industry and, eventually, us! It means that work is being generated, work that will at some point require our services. Your time will come, but be careful not to blame and sneer continuously until that day arrives; if you do you may just find that it never does!

Closer to home there's the success of your friends and peers. This is a tricky subject. Really tricky. I can attempt to rationalize it all I like but ultimately emotions are what they are, at the time in which they're felt, and sometimes there's not much to be done but allow. But know that there's a huge difference between what we feel and how we choose to project those feelings; they need careful consideration and monitoring. Feelings of jealousy and even resentment can and do arise, but without the ability to monitor the degree and frequency of those emotions you run the risk of inadvertently blaming other people for their good fortune and achievements, which is simply not acceptable. Making unfounded comparisons between others' careers and your own is not only damaging for yourself but also for the relationships around you; relationships you need. If you feel it, feel it but you can't make it anyone else's problem. Hopefully you will have chosen friends who are perceptive and sensitive when and where needed and who will not 'rub your nose in it' anyway – if you haven't, you soon will!

It is so important, whether we are the ones flying high or the ones on our knees looking up, that we take a moment to consider the feelings of those around us. I know that sounds like some sort of Sunday sermon, but it is such an important element of living and functioning within a highly competitive world, where most if not all of your friends are your competitors. Bear others' feelings in mind but at the same time remember that business is business and just because there are an immense amount of emotions involved in the job we do, it doesn't negate the fact that it is still a job and we must look after our own interests. If you dwell on shit you will feel like shit; if you choose to rise above it you will still be able to smell the shit but you won't be lying in it… An analogy based around shit; what a highbrow book this is… Ok, how about this instead…

We each have a different path to walk upon and though someone else's journey may look inviting, it is not for you, you have your own path so follow it…. Better? I preferred the shit one.

SHOWREEL / NO SHOWREEL

This seems like a bit of an obsessive topic for graduates so I thought I'd slam straight into it. Showreels are important and can be an excellent marketing tool. I say 'can be' because it depends hugely on the contents of the reel itself – simply having one will do jack. Like any other marketing tool, having it is not the point; it's how effective it is that counts. I feel very strongly that a bad showreel can hinder way more than a good one can help, but the assessment of this is hard. You will (understandably) be proud of any screen work you have achieved and be eager to use it to try and entice industry professionals into noticing you, but the phrase 'there's no such thing as bad exposure' does not apply here! The last thing you want to do is jump the gun and ruin a future relationship with a casting director or agent by giving out a less than professional impression of yourself, something that does not show off your true abilities or an accurate impression of your professionalism.

If you went straight from college to drama school or uni you will not have footage to make up a showreel anyway. This is fine and to be expected. If you had a gap year, the likelihood is that you will not have any footage for a showreel either, unless you did some television/film acting courses or such like in that time, (even then the footage will be dated, possibly questionable and a completely inaccurate representation of the actor you are today, considering how much you will have developed throughout your training). The other option is that you've filmed some stuff during your training – obviously I cannot judge your work with some generic sweeping statement, it is for you to decide whether it is suitable to use or not. Maybe show some friends who are also in the business (and by friends I mean those people who are honest and who care about you and your career, not those flighty fuckers who blow sunshine as a hobby). Watch their reactions and listen to their feedback (though even if they say go for it and you are confident that the footage is useable, I would keep it as a secret weapon for now, and pull it out only if you are asked; it is most likely that you won't be at this stage).

Let's say you have no footage. Should you create some for a showreel? (By this I mean actually filming isolated scenes, out of context to create and edit together a showreel.) There's an opportunity for discussion here as I am aware that many people within, and on the periphery of the industry, may have differing views. In my mind, whichever way you look at it, there is no dispute that a badly shot, lit, edited and written showreel can be damaging to you and to your professional reputation; good for practice, bad for exposure. I'm not saying you'd never be forgiven, but just as you would be judged for a headshot taken by neighbour Fred in the garden, so will you be for a shite and amateurish showreel. By all means write scripts, get together with mates and colleagues and film stuff, but use that as playtime in front of the camera instead of attempting to create something to impress which will probably end up having the opposite effect.

If you do some short films with mates or for one of the film schools (a good thing to look into) and you feel that some of the footage can stand up there with what you see on television and on other reliable showreels then do start to collect it all and start to consider how it might go together. It took me six years to gather what I considered 'good enough' footage to put on a reel and there is still some debate about how well it shows me off! I worked closely with my reel editor to ensure that the right frames, in the right sequence made up a reel that showed me off in a reasonable amount of time. This is harder than it sounds and you will need to select someone with experience and ability to assist you in this. Please refer to my Appendix section for details of where I had my reels edited.

Don't panic about having one, worry about having a shit one.
Marketing is serious, get it right!

AUDITIONS & INTERVIEWS

The nitty gritty. Let's address the thing that is going to get us work! Can I just reiterate that all of the following advice/information is an offering and nothing more, based on my experiences and my careful examination of what seems to work and what perhaps hasn't. There are no secrets revealed here, no promises made and no surefire ways to get jobs!

An audition is the last phase you have to endure before the phone rings with an offer of a job. Training, graduating, agents, photographs, and letters – the whole shebang has been working up to and leading towards auditions. They are not a surprise add-on, a thing you weren't told about or something you weren't expecting, so let's get rid of the idea that 'audition technique' is a new skill that you are now required to develop! Auditions exist for you to show off your acting skills to employers; skills that you already possess. We've baked the pie and it needs sampling so that everyone who takes a bite will rave about it. It's a tasting session.

There is no rigid structure that each audition follows making it possible for you to 'work them out'. You will gradually find your own rhythm within auditions, eventually becoming confident enough not to be fazed when those 'in charge' fuck with the goalposts – and they will! Over time you will also become accustomed to what you personally need to do, both beforehand and during the meetings in order to, not always get the job, but certainly to walk away feeling satisfied with the effort you made. Being able to achieve all of that in every meeting may come quite naturally, or may take a while to master. To help you build a rhythm (or to shake up an existing one if it ain't working) here's a few thoughts…

PREPARATION

This single word is what auditions are all about. It is a process that begins the minute you are notified of the audition and lasts until the moment you leave the audition room. I have always prided myself on the prep that I do for auditions and can say absolutely that this has provided me with the strength I've needed to face the disappointment of not getting jobs; to me, there is no point attending them if I do not leave the room knowing that I've done everything within my power to impress. There are so many other factors that go into giving an actor a part or not, way too many for us to agonise over. All we can do is deliver the goods, which will either make it implausible for them not to give us the part, or should at the very least guarantee us further audition and employment opportunities with them in the future. Making a good impression is what it's all about and it is your responsibility to do so. You are in charge of how much preparation you do, what that preparation is and ultimately how you conduct yourself during the meeting. If you want this life and this career enough then you will soon see that opportunities are not to be wasted and that there is never room for complacency. Who sees you matters, what they think of you matters, who they then talk to about you matters and if they remember you and how matters; it all matters. Every audition is a marketing tool that you must learn to use cleverly, and to me preparation is the key to it all. (Preparation coupled with ability, naturally, but I'm assuming you have heaps of that?!)

As a result of the love you have for your work, preparation will be (should be) no chore; you want the job and you know you need to work for it. Yes, it will piss you off at times, when you have plans to be at a family function or have booked in well-paid temp work that then has to be cancelled in order for you to do that all-important preparation, but remember that regardless of what it buggers up, auditions are your ticket to acting work and work is what we're all chasing. Some people don't even get tickets! We're more on call than a bloody surgeon; being inconvenienced by your work is an occupational hazard you will learn to allow for.

Preparation takes many forms, but basically:

- Who are you meeting?
- What do you need to know about the text/project/venue/production company/role/era?

Always know with whom you are meeting. It's so easy to check the backgrounds of professional people now with a click of a button, that you'd be an absolute fool not to. IMDb will provide all past, present and possibly even pending information for any directors, actors, producers and casting directors who have worked in either television or film. For any other area of interest, the internet has an abundance of information easily accessible to you. It is so vital that you have a basic knowledge of the people who may employ you. Why?

a) They may reference their own work and when you haven't got the foggiest what they're on about, you may look like a bit of an impolite, lazy tit. Know who they are and if you wish, act as if you always did! (Borderline ass-kissing but done well it can be useful.)

b) You may have seen work of theirs that you've loved but didn't bother to check so never made the connection. If you had, you could have possibly understood their vision or style better and would have had a good talking point.

c) You may have worked with the same people. It may seem kiss-assy or a bit petty, but anything you have in common with them may help; the 'webs' within the industry are very important.

The more research you do in regards to the panel or project the better you will understand the job and the role, and the more you will have to offer in terms of performance and conversation.

When it comes to researching a project I will admit that I can, or certainly used to be a bit obsessive about this. Whether it's down to some deep-rooted feeling of inadequacy (shaking my head), or whether quite simply it's because when I want something I will do everything within my power to get it; it's immaterial which, it is the result and effect of going above and beyond that matters. I always do too much rather than not enough and know for a fact, because I've been told, that this has set me apart from others that may have possessed a similar if not superior level of ability. There are loads of good people out there, good will not always deliver results; you need to be good and informed, good and enthusiastic, good and inquisitive, good and connected. Research is the thing that pads out our characters and makes them three-dimensional human beings; show off that you know this and can achieve it; don't just want the job, prove that you want it.

Masses of preparation (no matter how committed you are) can only be done if there's time. Depending on how much notice you are given before your meeting (we'll move onto time in a minute) you must use it as effectively as you can. It shouldn't take you too long to grasp a basic understanding of the main era or themes that surround the piece; then try to pay as much attention to all other relevant information as you are able. Whilst in my view no work done on a script or character is ever a waste, be careful not to neglect the main job, which is to deliver the scenes! Research can obviously enhance this but do not squander time that should be spent on learning lines and working on the text. You must organize your time and prioritise what needs doing within the time frame that you have.

For theatre you may get somewhere in the region of 3-7 days' notice before an audition – may. If so, great and you should be able to get a lot done (even if you are having to juggle audition prep with a full- or part-time job). Television tends to be a little more rushed and you may only get 24 hours' notice, in which case you obviously need to spend your time on the scenes, as that is what they will be focusing on primarily.

For all of the detailed research that you do, for all of the clever things that you discover and plan to discuss, it may turn out that they don't 'chat' and that you never get to show any of it off! (Hate it when that happens.) Remember that the research is for you not them, and regardless of whether the information is formally 'presented' during the meeting, the self-assurance you'll have simply by knowing such information will shine through in your performance and overall behaviour.

**'Give me six hours to chop down a tree
and I will spend the first four sharpening the axe.'
Abraham Lincoln**

THE DAY BEFORE

Everyone differs in their approach and there is no universal right or wrong; only what is right or wrong for you. I am generally very quiet and focused the day before an audition; I remove myself from most people (if possible) and keep my mind on the project. Other actors (usually older or cocky ones) take auditions much more in their stride and slot them into daily life seemingly without a second thought. I approach them in the way that I do because I believe the character that I could end up playing deserves my respect, care and attention from the off and to focus on them completely is the only way I have found to fully achieve that. (Luckily the people I have lived with over the years have been aware of this and I am very lucky that they have respected it and left me alone!)

I don't need to patronize or insult you by stating the obvious that partying/drinking or smoking to excess the night before an audition is not the best plan (but I kind of have by saying that… Sorry). Your body, voice and face are your performance tools and they need to be in top condition for an audition; if you are knackered, hoarse or hung-over it may not go down too well, and in my opinion if you show that amount of disrespect for an audition then you don't deserve to get it. Harsh? I can be. You are lucky to get auditions in the first place, plenty of very good actors don't, so take the chance while you have it and run with it.

Whilst making sure that your research is rigorous, it is also important to know when to stop. You don't want to fall into the trap of seeming 'over-rehearsed' (which undeniably contradicts the whole nature of acting, but it happens), and you also don't want to be so settled into a way of doing the scenes that you are unable to take direction under pressure. You will reach a point in your preparation when you have to adopt the attitude of 'what will be will be' and in my mind the only way of reaching a time when you may feel comfortable saying that is if you have worked hard and worked well in the allotted time you've had.

Practical preparation is important too. I always Google the audition destination (and route I intend to take) the day before, in anticipation of something causing a delay or confusion, or in case doing so flags up any further location or venue-related questions that I need to ask my agent. (Don't make frantic calls to them two minutes before a meeting; it makes you look disorganized, a tad unreliable, and will put you in exactly the wrong state of mind for the meeting… Sorry when I did that James, I will always read the name on the buzzer properly in future.)

The night before I usually have a long bath. In the dark. Weird? I am a bit. Whatever relaxes you, whether it be a walk, or a swim, or some sex – whatever makes you calm, do it (within reason…) I avoid watching films or programmes that require massive amounts of concentration or emotional investment as I think the night before an audition I should be focused on the job in hand, or I should give myself license not to think of much at all! If your sleep is disturbed when you're anxious, then try not to fight it; as we all know, trying to go to sleep and failing is one of the most annoying things on the planet and will wind you up and completely undo any of the calming activities you've done beforehand! Putting some wanky music on might help, and by wanky I mean whale song, waterfalls, that kind of shit; resting is almost as good as sleeping and one will eventually lead to the other if you allow it/encourage it to. Generally I really struggle to switch off from the day; our job has no start and end times and yes, I have found that natural noises like waves or rain do help me … (I know, I probably shouldn't have admitted that in a book, but if it gets me a good night's sleep and enhances my chances of nailing the audition, then I don't give a monkey's uncle who knows it.) Having said all of that though, for god sake don't relax and rest so well that you sleep through or forget to set your alarm!! Error.

THE MORNING OF

No matter how shaky and wound up I am the day before an audition I always seem to wake up on the day of it with a 'Let me at it' type attitude. I believe that this is a direct result of my preparation, and of my day before 'routine'. It is natural to feel stress and to have self-doubt, but it is your job to have exorcised as much of that bad energy as possible before you walk into that room; it will simply screw you over if you don't and then it's a waste of everyone's time. Each audition is an opportunity and opportunities are what we long for; you will find your own way of making sure that nothing as trivial as terror affects you…

You should have already chosen the clothes you want to wear the night before and have them ironed and ready. When considering your clothing for the audition, it can be useful to indicate the character you wish to present.

COMMON SENSE ALERT!

DIRECTOR: Why have you come in a basque and suspender belt?

ACTOR: My character's a stripper.

DIRECTOR: Get out.

Indicate is the word. Enough said.

You need to be as calm and gathered as possible on the morning of your audition and having to choose something as important as the packaging for your character/you with a limited amount of time and a high level of anxiety will only stress you out further (and may result in some questionable choices!) Another little thing I always do is to make sure that I have everything that I need to take with me ready; when packing my little bag I always include a bottle of water, mints, compact powder and a piece of paper with the address/names of the people I'm meeting written on. No one wants to see a shiny, dehydrated, dragon-breathed, disorientated actress turn up late to audition for an upper-class, nonchalant 1920s beauty now do they.

TURN OFF YOUR MOBILE PHONE.

BE PREPARED, LIKE A SCOUT.

… Is that the motto for the Scouts, or the Guides? I wouldn't know if it was the motto for the Guides as I never became one; I wasn't allowed as a result of being thrown out of the Brownies for calling Brown Owl a bitch. What? She was, I stand by it… I only became a goddamn Brownie because I liked the little dresses they wore anyway and then they brought in calottes the year I joined. Calottes. When in the history of the world have calottes ever been an acceptable item of clothing? Brownies suck ass… It's a sore subject.

Here's a slightly better quote that beautifully encapsulates this section…

'By failing to prepare, you are preparing to fail.'
Benjamin Franklin

MUSIC

A bit of a peculiar heading to find in this section, I know. 'What can she mean?' I hear you say. 'Does she mean that I should always take musical accompaniment in case I am asked to sing?' No. Quite simply I mean what music you listen to on the way to the audition (if you choose to at all). This is undeniably quite a strange thing to include here, but it is such an important part of my preparation regime that I felt odd not mentioning it. Music evokes mood and emotion and can inflict a sense of something upon us whether atmosphere, era or emotion. So (if this appeals to you at all) use the time leading up to the audition to get into the mood and headspace of your character using music. It is also the perfect way to remain focused and isolated from the outside world during your journey to the destination. (Again, this is just one of the weird things that I do; it may help you, or it may become something you can whisper, point and laugh about when you see me on the Southbank.)

CLOTHES

I'll discuss this with you more in Chapter 7 and 10, but for now, just know that what you wear matters. Not only does it tell your interviewers something about you and about your perception of the character, it also gives you an opportunity to feel a bit more like that character (if doing so helps you, it may not). Hair and make-up are useful ways of presenting the 'image' of your character, but be subtly indicative and don't over-egg the pudding; doing so could make you feel uncomfortable and confuse or distract your potential employers! Indicate era where possible (i.e. if you are auditioning for a period piece… I'd leave futuristic/space gear to their imagination).

FOOD

Eat before your audition or you will not have the right amount of energy to give it your all. (Plus, there's nothing worse than sitting in an audition competing with the volume of a rumbling tummy!) I can never eat much on the morning of, but a piece of fruit or a bowl of cereal should see you through. Then you can congratulate yourself with something naughty afterwards! (Usually beer for me. About three pints does it – see Cycle of Doom.)

So, that's the lead-up, and now we're nearly there! Seems like a bloody lot of work for a job you might not get eh? It is. But you also might get it…

DURING THE MEETING

There's not much to say here, it's down to you. As I've said you cannot predict what they'll ask or not ask, or what the feeling/atmosphere in the room will be. All you can do is be calm and confident, secure in the knowledge of how well you've prepared; be on time (early), and open to whatever they throw at you. After all they're not going to ask you to do anything that you can't do (it's acting!) but they may ask things that you weren't expecting, so, expect the unexpected, accept the unpredictability of it and be ready to play.

AFTER THE MEETING

It has become a bit of a habit that I make my way to a public house or bar after an audition. Firstly, I feel that I deserve it not only because I (will) have done a good job but also because I won't have had five minutes to myself since finding out about the damn thing. Secondly because it's very important for me to unwind and assimilate the audition fully before I can move on with my life! Plus, thirdly, it's an excuse to drink in the middle of the day and that's always fun. Should you follow my work/drink ethic though, don't drink too much or this may happen…

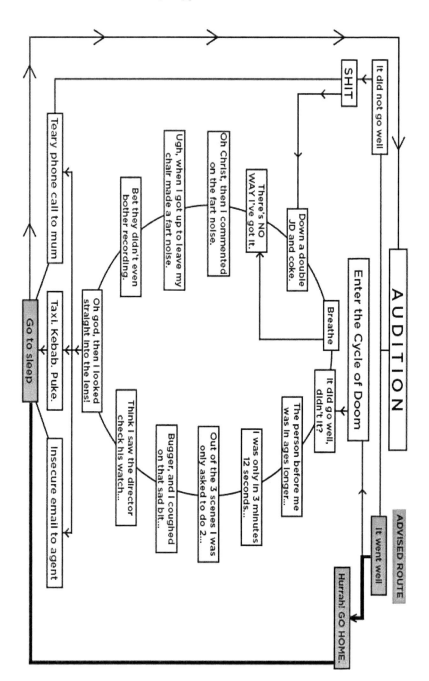

FEEDBACK

The brutal truth here is that you may never get any. You may not even get a definitive answer, and it is highly likely that you'll never learn why. (I think that this is both a technique to spare you from hearing 'someone was better' and a strategy to save them admitting all of the stupid, shallow reasons that one actor was chosen over another! Or, of course it could be because logistically it would be a bloody nightmare and far too time-consuming!) This is why I cannot stress enough how important it is that you do all that is humanly possible to get a part that you want; if you can leave that room pleased with your performance, knowing that you did all you could to impress, then you can move on without regret and without thinking that it was somehow your 'fault' that you didn't get it. You may not look right, you may be too young, you may be too tall or you may be shit, nervous and ill-prepared. The last three are within your control, the rest aren't.

If you do receive feedback it can be great, but it can also be irritating. Sometimes 'notes' that are given to you or your agent can feel whimsical and puzzling, and though you should always be open to criticism and advice, be careful not to harp on an opinion that was formed in ten minutes and may have lost its meaning through translation. And always remember, this is usually one person's opinion; a subjective opinion and one that nine times out of ten is based upon a hell of a lot more than who is best for the job.

Good feedback is nice and of course it can be a comfort to know, even if the job 'hasn't gone your way', that you were being seriously considered for the role and that they'll bear you in mind in the future. Having said that, other 'good feedback' can be tough to take sometimes, like when you are informed that it was between you and 'one other'. This is heart-wrenchingly difficult; so close, yet so fucking far! It's a bittersweet taste that follows and though it feels semi-gratifying it also sort of intensifies the agony! There is no sodding section on your CV that lists the jobs you nearly got! Your skin must be strong enough to withstand whatever they throw at you (or don't throw at you) and if it is, you will perfect the technique of moving on, using all experiences as lessons, all encounters to plant seeds, and all near-successes as rays of hope.

INTERVIEWING

So you're amazing at the performy bit and can nail the scenes you've prepped; but what about the chit chat??!! Shite… A lot of actors get quite wound up about this bit, or they think that they're fine with it and then repeatedly it seems to let them down. In my view it is all, again, down to preparation. The interviewers aren't there to trip you up or humiliate you (however much it may feel like something's a trick question, it won't be). They want to know you and want you to be good, or else their time has been wasted.

As I've said, you can never predict how this bit will go and it really depends on time constraints, the personality of the interviewers, what mood they're in, the size of the part and length of the contract (they'll need to get a good idea of what you may be like to work with, especially if they're planning to spend six intensive months with you in a cave in Siberia!)… (God knows what weird ass show that would be.) Ultimately the extent and content of the 'interview' bit will depend on the style of the director or casting director i.e. how personable they are, whether they're pleased to be involved with the project, whether they like to keep their actors in 'the zone', whether they like actors or not…! You can't know what you're going into until you're faced with it, but try not to be thrown either way; if a director doesn't chat to you assume that they have their eye on the ball, that they have numerous pressures upon them besides casting your part or that they are simply interested in your acting ability and nothing else – in which case, great, sock it to 'em. Every time I think I have a good idea what'll be said, something leaps in and surprises me and keeps me on my toes! All you can do is be friendly, calm and ready, then do your job well and leave. You cannot tell what they're going to do and be careful of over analyzing what they do do (back to the Cycle of Doom and more chat about this in Chapter 9). How it went will become very apparent when and if the phone rings, but winding yourself up by analyzing what's happening *during* the meeting will do nothing but hinder your performance. Take what they give you, react accordingly, and then get back to what you've prepared.

I learnt this the hard way. In one audition years ago my performance was, well, shat all over, because I allowed my interviewer to intimidate me. A popular northern comedienne (who shall remain unnamed as I work in comedy and wish to continue doing so) was the interviewer in question.

When the call that I had an audition with her came through I was beyond ecstatic. She is, yes and still is, one of my all-time faves and the thought of her choosing me to work with her made me feel on top of the world. Now I look back, I wanted it too much (if that's possible) so much so that I not only put myself under an immense amount of pressure but I put her up onto a ridiculously high pedestal. I had learnt the scenes and gone over and over and over them to make sure I could wow her with my comic brilliance. (Should have put brilliant in inverted commas there but didn't. Noted.) I had carefully chosen clothes for the character and had worked on my comic physicality in case she asked me to stand and do it – all bases were covered. I had also been asked to prepare a song (I can sing but my repertoire is fairly limited as it's not an area I'm hugely into anymore). However, I chose one and my voice was more than adequate for what the piece required.

Though I was outwardly very calm in the waiting room, I hadn't quite yet mastered an inward calm (so important to get a handle on). I was 23 and desperate to impress. (Plus, I was really excited about meeting her.) There was my first mistake. This was work and therefore I should have thought of her not as 'OMFG it's that very funny northern comedienne, I have to make her love me', but instead as another director I was meeting for a part that I was capable of playing. It wasn't that I was star-struck (it's not a condition I suffer from) but that I let her profile and therefore the prospect of working with her add unwarranted pressure to the task. Mistake.

Anyway, I enter the room and there she was. I'm not sure what I had expected; some bubbly, laugh-a-minute woman who makes people feel like they're her mate? Regardless of what I expected, the quiet, cold, serious and distant person who greeted me, threw me completely! It didn't end there sadly. She unsettled me with a comment about my CV, lectured me on keeping it up to date (it was a month out) and upon noticing that I hadn't worked in a few months she delicately said 'So, it's August, you haven't worked since May – what have you been doing?' I was young and this had been my longest period of time out of work at that point and I was stumped. But, in true Natalie Burt style I didn't show any venerability or honesty, no, no, instead (safe in the knowledge that she probably hated me and that I had as much chance of flying to the moon as getting the job), I answered straight back, with a tone of joviality, 'Watching Jeremy Kyle and praying'…

She glared at me… I thought it was a rather witty comment and I detected a slight glimmer of agreement from the assistant cowering to her left, but her? Not amused. She paused momentarily and then said in the least enthusiastic tone she could muster 'Fine. Shall we read.' BOOOOOLLLLLLLOOOOOOOCCCCCCKKKKKS I thought.

Well I was devastated, forgot most of the script, screwed up the majority of the punch lines and focused way more on how much she was enjoying her own reading than what the fuck I was doing. The song quickly followed and was as painful, and though I remembered all the lyrics, being made to sing Rizzo's song from Grease in a northern accent is never gonna go well. Try it, it's funny. But not funny enough.

I left and sobbed all the way to the tube.

Did I learn anything from this experience? Yes, I never prayed or watched Jeremy Kyle or attempted to be funny ever again. Seriously though, of course I learnt from it, one can and should always try to identify the lesson within every experience (even if the teacher was perhaps a *little* harsh with the lesson plan). I learnt to keep my Spotlight up to date, to take songs from the right country and to NEVER attempt to make a comedienne laugh.

Every actor has a story or six about auditions; a self-deprecating party piece that they use to entertain both friends and strangers. And yup, you guessed it, I am no exception. In addition to the one I've mentioned I could write a whole separate book. And maybe I will. But for now, I will share this slightly lighter tale of cringe-worthy hilariousness provided by my dear friend Chloe…

She works in musical theatre and was auditioning for some West Endy thing. The meeting had gone extremely well and all eight of the panel (what the fuck all these people need to be in the room for is beyond me) seemed very pleased with what she had delivered and thanked her for coming in. Excited and adrenaline-fuelled she thanked them in return and collected her sheet music. As she backed out of the room during the obligatory sixteen exchanges between her and the panel, 'Thank you', 'Well done', 'Great to see you', 'Many thanks', 'Thanks for having me', 'Bye', 'Bye', she turned to leave the room, opened the door and walked straight into a cupboard…

Er… Ah crap. This is awkward…

She paused in contemplation as she stood in the cupboard (her credibility crashing around her with each passing millisecond). I'm sure she made a fairly instant recovery but for comedy's sake we'll leave the extremely embarrassing, hilarious blunder for a few more seconds until we move on…

Ok, finally she swung around, and giggling desperately she said, pointing at it, 'Cupboard' (just in case they hadn't noticed??) The (now shaking) panel then watched as she located the correct door and made her exit. She didn't get the job. Good party story though.

MAKING YOUR OWN LUCK/WORK/WAY

One year after I graduated, the UK went into recession. Since then the arts have taken some huge financial hits and belts have been tightened throughout the entertainment industry. It's been a time of immense pressure, and theatres in particular have had to seriously pull out the commercial stoppers in a desperate attempt to stay afloat. We, actors (the cogs in a struggling machine) have suffered and go on suffering as a direct result.

There are businesses and industries crumbling all over the country and by no means do I put ours above theirs, however we are important and what we provide should be valued; without morale where the hell would this great country of ours have been during both World Wars? And without culture what would our tourist trade be like? Though the future may seem a bit bleak and the journey even more of a struggle than it usually is for our profession (with fewer and fewer opportunities causing more casualties than possibly ever before), we must fight on; if we love it, we must, and we do and we will. I reckon this means accepting the state of things instead of bitching about them, and being entrepreneurial and inventive with how we exist inside of it. We should be shirking passive and encouraging proactive.

There is no set way of being an actor; fate and clever choices make it up as we go along. Gone are the days when you signed on when unemployed and smoked and drank yourself into oblivion until the (house) phone rang like the guys in *Withnail and I* (for god sake watch it if you haven't, it's absurd for any actor not to have seen that film). The image they create in the film is a dire one (bloody funny – but ha, ha, then slit your wrists kinda funny); one made up of victims and one that demonstrates a time when an actor was at the mercy of everyone else. Though there are many things now that are worse than then, I don't believe that the passive struggling artist should be an acceptable state for any of us today, regardless of how bad things may seem in the country. We as performers can be more empowered now and have far more freedom and opportunity to create outside of 'convention'; we have the ability to form theatre companies, to devise work, to experiment with new writing, to explore site-specific projects and utilize TIE, we have the power to pick up our phones and film with them, to pool together and buy a boom and submit short films to festivals. We have the opportunity to do so much and the self-made actor is a trend that I support – look at Ben Affleck and Matt Damon, and closer to home Paddy Considine and Shane Meadows. These people weren't fazed by challenges nor defeated by the risk of failure and in order to follow in their footsteps we must use every fibre of our being to set aims and then work like a dog to accomplish them.

Ooh, felt a bit like some sort of politician for a moment then…but more caring and honest and realistic and genuine… So not really like a politician at all. Aside from the motivational spiel (really never try to write the word 'spiel' the way it sounds; what I ended up with on the first attempt looked more like the spelling of some German insult) I will acknowledge that many of the things mentioned above take money to achieve. But I do believe that creativity can and will find a way and if you team up with like-minded individuals you can make things happen both for yourselves and for culture. The key is believing that you can. I think that almost anything is possible if you put your mind to it but there's absolutely no point in ideas without actions. There are so many people talking absolute shit in this business; learn to filter, learn to laugh, learn not to get sucked into it. There is also far too much talking and not enough doing, don't be guilty of this. I'm off on one again, watch it Cameron…

I guess my main point (if I drop the attempt to gee up the troupes) is that I don't want you to feel trapped by convention and commercialism just because of the decade you have accidentally graduated into. If you have an idea, make it, if you have something to say sing it or tell it, if you have an opinion show it; you are not a puppet. Neither are you simply a person waiting for a phone call from an overcrowded, underfunded industry that will never ask you to speak out, but might listen if you have the balls and the tenacity to try.

FURTHERING/PRACTISING YOUR CRAFT

As we've said, once you graduate, your conventional 'education' ends and when all of your classes stop you suddenly realise how lucky your were to be waking up everyday facing a full day of practising your craft. This end can be abrupt, miserable and may take a while to compute and rectify. Obviously, I am going to say keep acting, keep singing, keep dancing, keep learning, keep playing – but I know full well that the desire to do so isn't the biggest problem here; cost and lack of time usually are. Well if I'm unemployed I'll have loads of time to take classes and workshops, won't I? No, you'll have loads of time and no dough (unless you get a commercial or big voiceover).

Or you may have a regular income and not much spare time. (More on temp work in Chapter 9). What a fun conundrum huh?! It may be ridiculously hard work, it may be relentlessly exhausting but if you truly want to do it all you will find time and you will find a way, some way to make sure that you are engaged in creative practice of some kind.

There are many companies, schools, clubs, organizations etc. all offering classes, courses, workshops, master classes and the like; so many in fact that it is rather hard to tell the drivers of the bandwagon from the hangers on. In my opinion, anywhere worth attending will allow some sort of taster session, which gives them the opportunity to 'hook' you, and you the opportunity to try before you buy. Just as you were careful about which drama school you went to, also be thorough now in your assessment of any source that offers to 'teach'. You will note a tone of caution in my voice; remember that this area (extra artistic development) is a money-making haven for businesses who can/will prey on a venerable consumer base (without much risk of being proven to be doing so as what they offer is so subjective). You are a professional, and if you seek further learning, or simply somewhere to exercise and practise your profession, then make damn sure that the people 'advising' and 'teaching' are not only qualified to do so (and by that I don't mean degrees and exam results I mean experience and ability) but also make sure that they will be nothing but a healthy and beneficial influence upon your life and work. There is no room in your career for misguidance, bad habits, inaccurate feedback or excessive additional pressure.

I have only attended one workshop with one company and I have mentioned them and one other in the Appendix section near the end of the book as a good place to start when sourcing companies that provide professional practice for actors. Both places mentioned require members to be a professional working in the industry and membership is granted through audition and/or proof of professional experience. Though these are what I'd call 'the main players', there are many places available following the same idea. When searching, a quick way you can sort the wheat from the chaff is by asking:

- Who are the patrons?
- What are the backgrounds/CVs of the 'teachers'?
- Can you find anyone who has been and get a recommendation?
- Are there constrictions on who can attend? (i.e. are you likely to be doing scenes with amateurs or only professional actors who've been vetted.)
- Can you observe a class or take a taster session?

I know it may sound like I'm being a snob, but in all honesty there are a lot of places run by wannabe actors with a BTEC in dressing up or a GNVQ in role-play who seem to be claiming that they can teach and guide professional actors. I would be wary of this and certainly wouldn't pay for it. I respect the skill that you have and want it to be nurtured carefully and correctly. People who are low and down on their luck are venerable and venerable people are not only easy to sell to but also easily manipulated when bombarded with enthusiasm, compliments and attention. Research anywhere you'd like to attend and behave as any consumer would – remember they need you more than you need them. There are a good few places that seem to cater very well for professional actors; so whether you have the funds to sign up to regular classes, or if you just want to attend the odd workshop to reignite your ambition or boost your confidence, then by all means do!

If it's just practising you're after instead of further 'education' (I've purposefully used the word education instead of learning there as you will learn through practice, whether it is supervised or not), then this can be done on a shoestring without you needing to pay anyone for the privilege. Plays are put on using only people and a space! You can gather mates and have play readings in lounges or cafes, you could club together and hire a studio space to devise something or get a mate with a camera to film you all doing scenes and monologues in a park, and in the summer it's great because you can do whatever, wherever! (Calm it, I almost completely meant work-related activities… Almost completely.)

If funds are low but determination, inclination and enthusiasm are there in abundance then things can and will happen.

SUBSCRIPTIONS/EXPOSURE

Exposure is vital for actors. It starts at showcase and never loses its importance, regardless of the levels of achievement that an actor reaches; in fact it could be argued that exposure is *more* important for those actors with high profiles to maintain than it is for the jobbing theatre actor. You can be the most gifted actor ever to walk the earth but if nobody sees or notices you then you're dead in the water, or your potential for progression certainly is.

Whilst the saying 'there's no such thing as bad exposure' may be true for z-list celebrities whose careers exist solely because of public/media perception and attention, there's an amount of debate around whether it can, does and should apply to struggling actors. Making sure that you don't get bad exposure is as much to do with not taking crap work, as it is about being good at acting; it is about managing your product's marketing well. It's a package deal and all facets matter. (For fear of going off on an absolute tangent and running the risk of being generic and misleading, I will leave the assessment of what work is 'worth' taking in your own capable hands and focus for now on the other aspects of exposure.)

If you create a profile on a site that is renowned for being a bit rubbish, or a site that accepts any random onto it whether they're professional or not, then it reflects badly on you and groups you into a mass category that you, as a trained professional, should be distinguished from. Plus no director or casting director worth his or her salt will be browsing such a site, so what is the point in wasting your money and jeopardizing your respectability? Ask yourself:

- What do they offer?
- How much do they cost?
- Is there a trial period available?
- Are you able to cancel your subscription?
- Who else is on there?

Most of them will have a free version that is basically a shite version of the paying one, meaning that you can see castings but can't apply for them – great! Like telling a child to look at the ice cream but to not touch or taste it. Torture. Have a shop around the available sites but be realistic about what you can get from them.

If interest is flared and castings do start coming your way (if you haven't got an agent to manage this for you) then by all means take opportunities to work, but remain focused on generating interest within specific circles that you'd like to work in and filter opportunities you're offered carefully. Remember that for every job you take you are making yourself unavailable for others, so with this in mind you must strike a balance between not always waiting for the next 'biggest thing' but also not just taking any old crap that comes along that may not further you in any way. How do I know if it will further me? You can't always KNOW, but by asking these questions you can at least clearly assess the pros and cons:

'What is this job going to do for me?'

- Is it a dream role?
- Is the director someone I like and respect and have been hoping to work with?
- Will the play or programme get a lot of attention and therefore will I get good exposure?
- Will it fill an empty gap or create a new area on my CV and therefore open some new doors?
- Is it really good pay?
- Will it give me some confidence back?
- Will it give me something to do and make me feel like an actor?

All of these are reasons to consider taking a job and I am not casting judgment at all; it's all too easy to cast aspersions from the outside of a situation. I think that you have to be a very strong/brave/gambling sort of person to always go with the question 'Will the play or programme get a lot of attention' because not only will you be turning your back on jobs that may reward and nurture you artistically, but also you will be limiting your employment opportunities and lessening your income. No easy decisions here. On the other hand I think you'd be a really daft person to always go with 'Will it give me something to do and make me feel like an actor', because you are an actor, whether in or out of work, and (depending on your own personal aspirations) you should try not to succumb to the temptation of just doing it wherever with whoever as this can be hugely limiting not only for you artistically but for your potential progression. Realistically and ideally you will make choices during your career based upon all of the above at differing stages of your life and development. Grab opportunities that you feel will benefit you and have the balls to assess and discard the ones that may not.

I was offered the opportunity to play three parts in a rep season at a regional theatre. I would have been working and earning constantly for six months. The director was nice and I hadn't worked in a while, plus I was pretty poor. However, I turned down that job and went back to office temping for two reasons; firstly because the parts didn't excite me as much as they should have, and secondly because I knew full well that the exposure would be limited. I had done some television work a few months prior and I didn't feel comfortable taking myself out of the loop for parts that I could have lived without playing. Two months later (when I would have been up north rehearsing) I was cast opposite Jennifer Saunders in a ruddy lovely job. It was a gamble and that time it paid off. Many haven't. But regardless of whether they have or haven't I have never regretted giving up a role or job because I know that I made the decision by taking into consideration both my short-term needs and wants as well as my long-term ambitions, thus making all choices informed ones. You must work out your own levels of endurance and draw your own map.

A WORD ON 'NETWORKING'

This is a bloody disgusting word, one that fills actors (especially ones of the more shy variety) with dread. As far as I can see, this is because of the clichéd connotations attached to it that are not only unwarranted and misleading but also inaccurate. In my opinion putting yourself into these situations or opportunities in the first place is the hard bit because of the stigma around networking (the connotations suggesting that we are somehow required and expected to prostitute ourselves to anyone willing to give us a job). I used to dread occasions that might involve it, but I learnt that the best way to get along is just to be myself; my calm, confident, fun and slightly strange self. You don't need to be over-demonstrative; never underestimate the power of being seen and not heard… (Definite wink required.)

The misconception of what this activity actually is is an annoying and costly issue that I would like to shed some light on.

- What does networking actually mean?
- What does it involve?
- How best do I approach it?

Firstly, what it doesn't mean is kissing arse. If you are pushy, arrogant, self-involved, dull and tactless, I can guarantee that the industry professionals surrounding you will make their excuses and leave your presence rather rapidly, probably without trying to disguise why!

What does it involve? Really? Just chatting to people with whom you have a common interest. Just because this common interest happens to be work and this activity happens a lot in environments where it is very much 'expected', does not mean that it is somehow dirty or desperate or sycophantic – not if you execute it well and with the correct intentions. It is no secret in business that we are of use to one another, of course we are, but you must observe that there are ways of doing it and ways of not. In Chapter 9 I discuss 'fine lines', and this is one of the most important lines of all! There's a huge difference between bragging about personal achievements in a vulgar and cringeworthy manner, to being honest about your work and aspirations. I would wait to be asked questions and then delicately leak in a reasonable amount of self-promotion (if it's being sought), but please remember that Miss Modesty is the attractive sister of Miss Self-Inflated full of shit bore hound – choose your sister wisely! Be humble yet proud of what you do and have done, but above all, be inquisitive and ask questions about the person you're speaking to – it'll be useful information for you to know, and will increase the chances of them reciprocating!

Don't dominate someone's time, and always remember who you've spoken to by keeping a record of who you meet. After the meet, look them up (not only is everything and everyone connected but when you meet them again it would be useful to be able to reference something you've spoken about previously; useful and flattering for them that you listened and bothered to remember). This is another reason (apart from your love of it) that you need to watch stuff, whether theatre, telly or film; so that you can comment on it all should the opportunity arise. Doing this will ensure that you come across to possible future colleagues, employers and collaborators as being interested, enthusiastic, knowledgeable and 'in the game', even if you haven't worked in a while.

To be honest it's about common sense and behaving like a decent human being instead of a twat. Maybe it's easier said than done; I've seen so many times what being desperate to be accepted, noticed and respected does to people – it's a powerful repellent! Be interested in people because they're interesting, not because you are trying to get something from them; becoming known as a sycophant is not a great way of engaging people into conversations! Most people (certainly at jobbing actor level) are re-employed because they're pleasant, fun, and down to earth as well as being talented – not because they stalked the director and took CVs and headshots to a cocktail party they weren't even invited to in the first place. Trust that people will find out about you should they wish to and learn that your knowledge of them is as powerful as theirs is of you.

Once you have made some foundations with connections then you have a slight license to get a little (that's a little) cheeky (which means asking for their advice or opinion – not necessarily for a job). Make sure once you have met someone that you keep in touch with them. And no, I do not mean that you send weekly requests on Facebook or that you email them every hour on the hour; just be aware that gentle and well-timed reminders from an acquaintance are useful for all. Know that cleverly timed, occasional reminders of who you are and what you're doing are useful and to be expected. Making connections with industry professionals and staying in touch also means that you have a direct and more personal way of inviting them to see you in things, which creates the all-important platform for you to show what you do instead of just describing it. Some people are really cheeky and are charismatic enough to make it more endearing than annoying. (This is an art form and a rarity, and even then it only works occasionally, so be careful where you 'practise'!)

Business cards can be a good tool. Many other industries exchange cards as frequently as shaking hands, so why I feel like a div doing it is beyond me. A business card is a multifunctional professional etiquette; a confirmation that you are who you say you are, a way for them to know how to contact you (or your agent), something to remind them of you when they next come across it, and a widely recognized invitation for further contact. For me however (and this is a personal thing) the jury's out… If you think you need them, get them, but if you don't think you need them and still get them then won't you end up looking like a bit of a try-hard burk? I am one of those burks, but I keep my cards mainly for collaborators (writers, filmmakers etc.) not employers in the acting world. (I rely upon the human ability to remember and investigate, and if that fails then the power of the internet usually comes up trumps!) But that's got to be your choice.

My last word on it… (I know that the title of this section said 'a word on networking', which was a blatant lie and I promise I'll shut up in a minute.) Though I have said be yourself and have fun, always remember at a press night or at a function that you are technically 'at work' and that you are constantly being noticed, watched and judged. So behave. Or misbehave out of view/with the right people… Did I just? Yes.

Oh, and never stay until the bitter end of a party in the hope that the director you want to talk to will eventually get round to you; they won't and you'll look pathetic. (Says she who stays so late at parties that I'm still there while the next party is being set up.) Do as I say not as I do – a classic mum response.

LEISURE TIME

If you're anything like me, your leisure time will merge almost completely with work. I'm not sure how healthy or not this is and I only half-consciously do it, but as long as time-out (completely out) is taken when needed, then you loving your work and all that encompasses it can be no bad thing. If I am supposedly 'relaxing' or having 'fun' then I will usually be at the theatre, the cinema, writing or reading anyway. (Of course I spend time eating, drinking and talking too, but even then it's probably with people from the industry so is technically 'networking' anyway) – It's a hobby job.

You might be different and may have many different interests that involve weekends away, outdoor pursuits and a whole myriad of activities that have no connection to 'work' whatsoever, and if this works for you, then great! Apart from the all-too familiar obstacle of cost, nothing should stand in the way of you taking time to yourself to do the things that you enjoy and that remind you that you're a human as well as an actor. (More in Chapter 9).

Cost is a familiar obstacle because when you are unable to predict incomings and struggling to meet outgoings, it can be all too easy to fall into a trap of never doing anything (not a healthy option, or a fast-track ticket to fulfillment). In an attempt to combat this do try, when budgeting (Chapter 5), to make sure that you have a small amount of 'play money'. Being able to schedule things that you enjoy into a busy week and/or have things to look forward to can do wonders for your self-esteem, morale and your general outlook. If most of your friends are actors then you will collectively find ways of having fun on the cheap, letting loose occasionally when all are in agreement. And let's face it; two of the best things in life – sex and conversation, cost nothing (or shouldn't…)

You'll find that spending leisure time with like-minded people will combine a number of the sections I've mentioned here. Discussing work and your aspirations with other creative, determined people will inevitably result in knowledge and collaboration ('Networking' & 'Making your own work') and all under the umbrella title of fun!

YOUR 1ST JOB

Amongst the trials and tribulations of graduating you will, at some point, land your first job!! HOW EXCITING IS THAT?! I've had some lovely things happen in my career so far but honestly, none of them can quite compare to the phone call I received informing me that I had my first acting job. It was immense; a confirmation that I could actually do it and the start of a very exciting adventure that I'm pleased to say I'm still in the middle of. You may have already had the pleasure of this experience or you may be eagerly awaiting it; either way, I hope that the next few chapters take you through what to expect, whether your first and subsequent jobs are on screen or in the theatre.

You should pretty much have the tone of the book by now and will therefore know that anything I've included is honest, to the point and always an offering, never an instruction.

So with that in mind, let's get all professional about it and get to work…

5. WORK IN THE THEATRE

Hard work! (and hurrah)

You know, in the second draft of this book I started this chapter with a wildly poetic, almost lyrical ode to the theatre and the life of a thespian. Then I realized that the brilliance of theatre, what it's been, what it is and what it will continue to be, forever I think, needs no jumped-up, half-ass introduction from me. We love the theatre; there's absolutely nothing quite like it, no one way to describe it, and nothing that any of us actors can do about the fact that it runs through our veins and will do until the day we die. (Ok, well that sort of was an ode, but it was better than the last draft's attempt trust me, this one was at least honest instead of an attempt to be intellectual).

This innate sense of theatricality we all have is present in most actors from a very early age, our ambition and passion having blossomed from a first role in a school play or from evidence of us being 'the entertainer' at family functions. These signs and 'symptoms', if you like, will then gather momentum for many years leading to a point when that once feral theatricality, having been trained or tuned, now sits like a coiled spring until the phone rings and some angel whispers, 'You got it.' And from that moment on we are never the same; we are no longer dreaming, we're doing.

Your first paid theatre job is a milestone, a rite of passage and a very special time in your personal and professional life, whatever age and stage it happens to arrive at. As you tread the boards, radiating the very essence of contentment and oozing with the pleasure that it brings, you will feel as if the mother ship has called you home! It's a wonderful feeling, and one that should be celebrated and cherished. (I did! My hangover lasted for about three days after finding out I'd bagged my first gig at the Northcott Theatre in Exeter in 2006 – thought I'd won the fricking lottery!)

Once the elation has settled (and every single family member has been informed), the reality of what you now face will kick in. This chapter is not here to discuss acting or practitioners, nor does it offer advice about text or methods; I am assuming that by this point you know your shit (and if you don't, there are probably six million books on the shelf next to this one that cover all that jazz). What we are concerned with now is your first professional job in the theatre, the realities of living it and the practicalities behind getting the very best from it.

YOU GOT THE JOB

Well bloody done! I'll let your head swell for a moment by pointing out just how high the pile of odds stacked against you were; it's a humbling thought and when you're on the right side of those odds it's good for the soul to acknowledge them (but for god sake don't linger on those statistics for too long as the realization of it might just bite you on the ass seconds before your next audition!) You've been fighting odds as a wannabe actor since the idea was hatched, and getting your first job confirms that you can handle that pressure, so well done. But now what?

A contract will be offered to you, either through your agent or directly to you, depending on whether you have representation or not. You will be required to sign it and it will be a legally binding document, so please do read it thoroughly (regardless of whether an agent is involved). It may be lengthy and will most certainly be rather boring, but it is imperative that you properly understand the pay they've offered, the hours of labour they've proposed and the duties they required you to undertake throughout the duration of the job – all should be clearly stipulated; never sign if it isn't. Also be careful (if you are representing yourself) not to be bamboozled by contract lingo and assume that all is fine. Never assume. If you are a member of Equity they can offer you any contractual advice that you require (so make sure you're a member). Although I do read my contracts, I am completely unqualified to advise you any further (as my agent takes care of everything else), and feel that any generic drivel could go on for an unhelpful amount of time. Most of what you need to know will either be in Chapter 2 ('A conversation with Equity') or on their website.

Leaving contracts aside (flaps her hands like a nonsensical Southern belle), the next step following a contract will (should) be a phone call or email from your new Company Manager. On a personal level this will be to say 'hello, and welcome aboard', and on a professional level it will be to organize the logistics of you getting there, being there and doing the job for the duration stated in your contract.

Maybe it's important at this point to separate the most likely kinds of theatre work that you may encounter:

Regional – At a theatre outside of London in the regions of the UK. Rehearsals will usually be based at the theatre instead of London. This can vary, but it rarely does as all of the rest of the crew will be in-house staff based at the theatre's location. The standard rehearsal period is about 4 weeks and a show usually runs from 2.5 weeks to 7 weeks. Equity Minimum pay or above is to be expected.

West End – A show at a theatre in the main commercialised theatreland in London. Rehearsals will be in London and transfers are possible, though never set in stone!

Tour – A production that moves from venue to venue either nationally or internationally, usually spending a week (Mon-Sat) in each venue. You may either rehearse in London or (sometimes) at the venue that is producing the show.

T.I.E. – Theatre in Education. A production that travels to schools either nationally or internationally (or more often than not, regionally). Additional skills like driving and set building/erecting are required as cast often double up as stage managers etc.

Fringe or Off-WestEnd – This may be a production actually taking place at the Fringe Festival in Edinburgh throughout July/August, or it could be a production staged at an unsubsidized venue such as a studio theatre, pub, or site-specific venue.

Broadway (transfer) – Like our West End but in the US. Some West End shows transfer to Broadway.

Off Broadway – Like our Off-WestEnd/Fringe but in the US.

I know that you know that I knew that you knew all that. Just sayin'…

Money paid in the theatre varies hugely, and whilst there is a minimum wage set by Equity that all reputable theatres obey, work can be put on by anyone, anywhere with any financial agreement.

Hopefully you will receive sustenance pay if working away from London (i.e. on tour or in the regions). Sustenance is given in addition to your performance fee and is a contribution towards your accommodation and living costs.

The Company Manager will not talk money with you at all, it is not their job to do so, but do feel free to query things with them, it is their job to assist and advise you wherever possible (though I would seek monetary advice from Equity and leave your company manager to attend to matters that are within their control). Hopefully contracts and pay etc. will all be sorted and fairly self-explanatory – it certainly will be if this is a reputable theatre or company you're dealing with, and if it's not, check everything twice and seek advice.

A good company manager will make sure that you have an up-to-date draft of the text (if applicable), they will give you the overall dates and timings of things (if they have them) and they may also send you a welcome pack from the theatre/company including all information about the job you are about to begin. They may wish to discuss costume fittings with you, but depending how far in advance you are contacted this will most likely be left until nearer the time, or be done when rehearsals begin. They will be your first point of contact during the gig and will be responsible for letting you know call times, and any other notices. (They also complete the show reports so don't piss them off or let them see you arsing about too much in the wings!)

Amongst the masses of information the company manager will pummel you with (if the gig is out of London or a Tour) will be this delight…

DIGS LIST

This magical document is a list of accommodation options that have been 'vetted' by the theatre. As always, there are varying degrees of most things, and 'vetted' is no exception. You will find that the definition of 'vetted' (hence the inverted commas) varies from theatre to theatre. I have faith that most theatres will make it a priority to have an extensive list of clean, accessible and pleasant abodes for their actors to choose from, but be aware that the ideal scenario is not always the one that will be presented to you! On my first job I was booked into some digs only to be informed on my first day at the theatre (before having visited the digs) that the crew's nickname for my new landlord was in fact 'the man of death'. At the tender age of 22 I laughed along (whilst crapping myself) and politely enquired why…

> 'He keeps bats and there's cobwebs everywhere. There are some skulls around the flat, he seems to like death; we're not quite sure what the deal is with him' …

I laughed along with them until a tear welled in my eye; I quickly skipped off to the ladies to wipe it and immediately after, cancelled my booking. Why was he on the digs list? Good question. He has since been taken off it (or so I am assured).

Of course there are differing levels of tolerance when it comes to cleanliness, space, location, price and general living requirements, so a list will naturally have variations to supposedly 'cater for all'. The game here, is that any money from the sustenance that you do not spend on digs, is yours and can 'bump up' or 'pad out' your wages. (An appalling reality that theatre wages do need padding out and bumping up – but there it is.) A lot of actors are happy to live in squalor (or what I would say is squalor – again, differing opinions) in order to pocket the money left over. Whilst this suits some, others think about their comfort, and tend to reward the sacrifice of being away from home with choosing something as close to whatever that is as possible. Which one are you? Probably somewhere in between.

It takes a certain sort of person to sublet their homes to thesps. The way I figure it, those types of people fall into one or a combination of these categories:

Lonely – Kids have flown the nest, spouse has scarpered, they're old or they're just, well, alone.

Weird – Some of the same reasons as above, but here it is more noticeable why they are alone.

Wannabe – Someone who has an interest in the theatre and is excited by the prospect of being involved in some way and 'knowing' the actors. These ones are quite endearing actually, although they sound annoying. (It's all about striking a good balance and outlining the ground rules early on!)

Hard up – It's possible that they need a lodger, more than desire one and they aren't altogether happy with that. Though most will hide it beautifully, a bad landlord will not be terribly subtle about this and will make you feel as if you are a massive inconvenience. Not ideal.

Genuine – Lovely people that for some reason have a spare room and decide that it's a nice thing to do, whether 'nice' means some extra company, or a little look into a world that intrigues them; or whether a little extra income wouldn't go amiss. This is what most of the list will (should) contain (hopefully).

This half-comic, half-dead-serious breakdown isn't meant to terrify you, honestly. Even though there may be an element of the first four categories within the landlords that you encounter the majority will be genuine. However, there are exceptions and my god are there some stories that reflect this when you get a bunch of actors together!

My story? Oh, go on then… This isn't about a landlord, it's more about their property…

I was staying in some perfectly lovely digs in Chichester whilst on tour in 2010, with a lovely couple who were in the 'autumn' of their life (nicely put eh mum?)… Anyway, it was only my second or third day there, and though I had met them both and had a brief chat, I was only aware of where the spare key was, how to work the television and that they would be going out early on the morning in question as they were going Christmas shopping.

So, when I finally awoke that morning I merrily lounged around, prepared my breakfast and took it back to bed. Whilst enjoying my honey on toast I felt an almighty rumble; the ground shook, everything shook, and a huge crash filled my ears, quickly followed by a cloud of thick grey dust, which filled my eyes. I managed to make out that the dust was bellowing through the open door that led to the landing. My first thought was an earthquake (dramatic), but the impact seemed isolated so I assumed (within split seconds) that a vehicle must have crashed into the property (again, dramatic, but it was a really loud bang!) I covered my face and cautiously made my way out into the corridor. The dust was thicker there and I could just see that it was coming from the 'lovely couple's' bedroom. Being terribly British about it I stalled for a few seconds as I contemplated whether it was polite to look into their bedroom (twat). A voice in my head very abruptly said, 'look you idiot, the building could be unstable or someone might be hurt'. So, coughing and spluttering I peered around the door to be greeted by a pile of rubble and a room that no longer seemed to have a ceiling… Yep, the entire centre of the ceiling had collapsed into the room and there were huge chunks of plaster and wood and crap everywhere; right on top of the lovely couple's bed. My first thought was of course, could they be in there? No, no, I remembered them saying they were going out, and besides it was far too late for them to be lounging around as I was. My second thought was what the fuck do I do now???!!!! So, I flapped… Paced… Then talked out loud to myself for a few minutes, and eventually made my way downstairs where I flapped some more.

To my relief the room directly beneath was intact but had a huge crack in the ceiling where the impact of the collapse above had weakened it, and I won't lie, the alarming creaking sounds it was belching out weren't filling me with confidence.

There I was, in an unfamiliar, unstable building with no fucking idea what to do. I didn't even know the lovely couple's Christian names! Whilst flapping I noticed an address book, and proceeded to make one of the most surreal, ridiculous and horrible phone calls of my life…

ME: Oh hello, is that Mr Kendle?

HIM: Yes.

ME: Er, good, ok… I take it you're a relation of Mr & Mrs Kendle, who live in, er

(Thinking where I was – occupational hazard when touring.)

    Chichester?

HIM: Yes, Maggie and Cliff?

ME: Maggie and Cliff, yes, Maggie and Cliff Kendle. Erm…

A pause the size of the Mersey tunnel.

ME: I've got some…

(Suddenly realizing that's a 'someone's died' way of starting a sentence.)

Everyone's ok, no one's hurt. But…

HIM: Yes?

ME: My name's Natalie, I'm working at the theatre and staying with Mr & Mrs Kendle and…their ceiling has collapsed from loft through to bedroom…it scared the living crap out of me and I don't know who to call or what to do, so I looked in their address book and you were the first person I came across with the same surname, I know they have a daughter but she's *(Getting more and more high pitched.)* married I think and I have no idea what her name is now and I don't know what to do!

HIM: Are you hurt?

ME: *(Crying.)* No, no, just…pathetic. *(Beat.)* The bloody ceiling collapsed though! This is ridiculous, my life is sodding ridiculous.

My life is no less ridiculous now. However, it all turned out ok; it seemed that the couple's daughter lived up the road and fairly soon after that phone call she arrived to deal with everything/calm me down. Later I turned up to work and presented a rather shaky version of Caroline Bingley to 1,300 people. The show must go on and all that. (Don't even get me started on that bloody saying.)

So that's my best digs story, but then there's the equally bizarre, way more creepy story that happened to my friend Graeme, which involves him waking in the middle of the night to find his landlady standing naked at the end of his bed… Maybe I'll leave that one for him to include in his book…

Ultimately these anecdotes are here for your amusement but there can be no harm in taking a hint of a warning! Obviously some things cannot be prevented or predicted (like ceiling collapses and nympho landladies) but if nothing else you will always have a ridiculous story to regale guests with at dinner parties.

Just remember, when you are choosing your digs, that you are not picking a new home, or a new family; you are simply selecting where to 'crash' whilst you temporarily wow audiences with your brilliance. Look at the evidence on the digs list and assess that evidence using the following information.

Here's a rough idea of what a digs list will look like…

SAMPLE DIGS LIST

Accommodation:	1 x Double, 1x Twin bedroom available
Facilities:	Beautiful Victorian terrace where owner lives with his dog. Full use of property; living room, dining room, kitchen & garden. Non-smoking guest preferred. Wireless Internet and guests are permitted.
Price:	Double £90 p/w, Twin room £90 p/w
Location:	20 mins walk to theatre
Contact:	Mr Jackson. (0000) 000000
Comments:	Lovely house, nice area. Landlord works at home. Checked by Stage Management.
Accommodation:	6 x Bedrooms/5 x Bathrooms or Loft Flat. Five-storey Georgian house.
Facilities:	All rooms contain TV, tea & coffee making facilities, microwaves & fridges. Street parking.
Price:	*£100 p/w Loft, £90 p/w En suites, £80 p/w Double room*
Location:	On same street as theatre – 30 seconds.
Contact:	Mr Scott (0000) 0000000
Comments:	Fantastic house. Easy-going landlord.
Accommodation:	2 x Single rooms.
Facilities:	Clean and spacious. Towels provided. 3 small children in the house. No use of main lounge.
Price:	*£60 p/w*
Location:	10 minutes by bus to theatre. Buses regular.
Contact:	Mr Spielberg (0000) 0000000
Comments:	New to digs list but checked by Stage Management.

I believe that knowledge is the foundation of all good decision-making, so by providing you with information I am hoping that you will be informed enough to know that:

> *'Single man, works from home, has sixteen cats and enjoys evenings of karaoke'*

… Probably ain't a winner… (Depending on your preferences of course – whatever floats your boat!)

If you are organised and get onto this arduous task early then you will hopefully be able to secure the best and most suitable digs (without being left with the 'man of death' and his skulls). You may want to bear some of this in mind:

- A well-lit walk home/not too long a walk home?
- A double or single bed?

If you expect 'visitors', you may need to check what the deal is with that. Many digs people are funny about overnight guests, mainly because all of you live wire panto dancers shag like rabbits throughout the silly season and we are all therefore tarred with the same brush! I'm half-joking. No, actually probably only a quarter joking… (We all know it's true, and credit to ya; whatever gets you through panto!) My point (hang on in there, I'll get to it) is that landlords can be a little funny about randoms rocking up in their bathrooms in the early hours half-naked; understandable. So to prevent it, they usually put a 'ban' on it. Some landlords are way cooler than that; they remember what it was like to be young and attractive and therefore don't give a shit. However, in all seriousness, if you plan to have boyfriends/girlfriends visit then you may want to check if they allow/charge extra for this before booking with them. And if you plan to put it about to all and sundry either clear this with them or work out where the creaks on the staircase are.

- You will have your days free once the show is 'up', so if your landlords have toddlers or work from home you will all be at home 'together'. How nice. Though most actors get out and about and you may find that you're one of them, it's worth a thought. It would be a deal-breaker for me, toddlers and I don't gel.

All actors utilize working away from home and touring differently. Some see it as a bit of a break from family life (sorry families, but I have witnessed this) – which involves heavy nights out with the cast and hang-over laziness that lasts until the next day's evening call (this is also relevant to young actors/rebellious actors/dissatisfied actors and 'fun' actors). Some others see it as an opportunity to explore a new part of the countryside and an opportunity to make the most of the empty 'guilt-free' time (having 'free days' away from life and work is a license to do what you want and know that you're being paid for it!) Other actors, like myself, may intend to 'get stuff done' in the day – I have written whilst on tour but my god do you need to pick the right digs to do so!!! (And if you don't manage to, then cafes, museums, parks and the countryside are the touring actor's best friend!)

Also consider:

- Animals. If you're allergic, don't even consider it. A puffy-eyed Benedict isn't ideal for anyone.

- Unless you intend to survive solely on microwave meals (and you probably will, certainly in tech week), make sure that you are entitled to use the kitchen in your digs. Hopefully you will be operating on very different hours to the inhabitants of the house, so this could work quite nicely – but always check!

If you have a recommendation for digs from another actor, listen to it, if you can stay with someone you know or a friend of a friend then do. If you tour a lot you will probably return to people you've stayed with before (which is lovely) but make sure if this happens that you pass on the information to your fellow actors! Share the love.

So, the long and the short of it is that booking digs will probably make you want to vom. But don't delay; study the list as soon as you get it and book as soon as you have made a shortlist. I cannot stress enough how important it is for your sanity and professional wellbeing that you have digs in which you are comfortable and happy.

Look at the options on the digs list and assess them with what I've mentioned here. Remember, no booking is set in stone; you can always cancel or move. Embrace the experience, it's a little like being on a weird holiday, and if nothing else it is kind of cool/odd opportunity to see into people's houses and to go through their stuff, dressing up in their… Not that I've… Mr Gilbert I put the Wonder woman costume back where I found it and no harm was done. (Apart from to your reputation because I posted it on Facebook)…

FIRST DAY OF REHEARSAL

This will feel like first day of school, Christmas day and a first date all rolled into one. It's such a strange mix of apprehension and excitement that can be coped with but certainly not eradicated unfortunately, you just have to ride it – and you will.

You will be a bundle of enthusiasm and creativity, itching for the clock to count down to show time. However, before 'show time', there is a load of first day stuff to get through, which can be daunting. I think the main reason it's daunting, is fear of the unknown; it can be perturbing not to know what to expect. So I hope this 'typical first day' breakdown will put you at ease, leaving you to focus all of your attention on the excitement of it all.

MEET & GREET

Tea and biscuits, possibly cakes will be had – not since the recession actually, maybe just tea, or just hot water bring your own tea bag? (I'd wink but it wasn't a joke.)

Refreshments (of some sort) will accompany the many polite handshakes, raucous reunions and utterances of who's seen whom in what. The introductions bit is where you will meet not only your new creative family, but where you will also be formally introduced to the other members of the company, including the crew; stage managers, designers, lighting and sound technicians, costume department, and of course your director and their assistant (if applicable). You may possibly get the marketing team; box office, press etc. thrown in for good measure too – the more the merrier.

Do try and remember people's names. It'll take time but for god sake be on top of it by the closing night party! Being warm and friendly to all is a given, I don't know why I've mentioned it, and it is always good to remember from the off that these are the people who will assist you in your quest to do a good job. Make some friends and have a giggle – this is your new temporary family, the people with whom you are going to make some fabulous art!

THE DIRECTOR & DESIGNER'S VISION

The model box. (I love this bit and most actors get fairly giddy at this point, so allow yourself to!) The director may make some sort of 'welcome speech' and will then, probably fairly swiftly, move on to discussing the project (time is always of the essence). In amongst the discussion they are likely to introduce the designer, which will lead nicely into the model box. This is a scaled-down version of the stage/set, a design of the world inside which your characters are to exist. I think at this point in proceedings, when actors see how much work has gone into the project way before they were even cast, we all truly realise how much we are the icing on the cake of any production. Pretty damn important icing, but icing all the same!

The director and designer, with the use of the model box, will explain their vision of the production, the surroundings for your creativity and the flavour of the piece as a whole. It's a really exciting time and a lovely collaborative moment for any company; actors touching and feeling the world they're about to inhabit and the team meeting the humans who will bring all of their hard work to life.

If you have a burning question during this introduction/chat then by all means ask it, but do be aware that this time (where all collaborators gather in one room) is precious and if it can wait, or be aimed at a particular individual rather than to the collective then it is probably better to hold onto it.

THE READ THROUGH

Right, let's get down to business (everyone enjoys this bit/shits themselves a little!) The actors get to flex their muscles and interact with their new onstage wives and pals and the rest of the team get to see the project leap from the page and come to life – it's fab, and the first read is always an exhilarating part of the day. It is also one that will ignite many questions, quandaries and conundrums for everyone, and the next month or so will be dedicated to answering, discovering and exploring all of the answers. I am now making myself miss the theatre in a big way – Take me back!

THE CHAT

Depending on time constraints, and on the way in which the director works, the post-read discussion can be lengthy, brief or somewhere in between. Be prepared to chat about the text, about your character's journey within it and to listen to the opinions and offerings of your colleagues. You obviously showed signs that you knew what to do with the character in the audition (or wouldn't have been offered the job), so celebrate what you've found and what you intend to find, but also be open and willing to take on brand new angles and ideas. This is, after all, where the fun of it all lies!

THE SCHEDULE

Again, depending on your director (their efficiency and method of preference), you may be informed of a schedule that will outline working hours, aims for the dates of first runs etc. and the technical rehearsal times and dates leading to a dress rehearsal. You may then be given calls for the first week (and then again you may not – you may never know your calls until the night before!) It is your job to be available whenever you are needed, to be punctual and sensitive to the time constraints you face as a team, whilst being thorough with the job in hand.

THE PUB

(This fully deserves its own section ESPECIALLY if the gig is out of London.)
Actors away from home – A woo hoo! It is likely you will have a real mixture of colleagues, depending on the size of the company. Within the assortment there may be, for example…

a)   Actors who drink like fish (the majority).

b)   Actors who drink nothing because they did too much of the fish thing.

c)   Actors who are being obsessively 'studious' because their parts are (or they consider their parts to be) more demanding than other people's.

d)   Actors who will happily have drinks if someone else is buying them. These same actors may scab fags too (probably because they still feel like a twenty-year-old party animal but they have mortgage arrears, six kids and a partner at home who is bending their ear about cash flow). And a word of warning, that when you are working in the theatre and go out every night you are more or less working for the 'love of it'; don't expect to have much change from payday!

e)   The preoccupied or antisocial actors who have lives going on outside of work that need over and above a normal amount of attention (details of which won't come out until press night, if at all). Or preoccupied and antisocial actors who are trying to seem like they're deeper than everyone else. (You can have a great laugh with these ones. Sorry, I mean at, you can have a great laugh *at* these ones.)

You may have an eclectic mix of young and old, funny and emotional, happy and bitter, talented and deluded – it's a fascinatingly fucked-up pick and mix, and whatever wonderful concoction of characters you end up with, there is one thing that is certain, one thing above all else, and that is that the foundations of that company, however diverse its members, will be made during the first day's visit to the local Public House. Fact. So go!!

Sitting in the pub is the first time that everyone can actually relax, and with a pint in your hand (preferably not of sambuca), you can behave in a 'normal' way together and just chat. Actors will always have something to say to one another (try shutting them up!), and once alcohol is added to the mix everyone will be wrestling one another to deliver anecdotes and drop names. Within an hour you will have discovered that at least three of you have friends in common, and within half an hour you will have sussed out who has worked with the same actors, directors and shitheads. It really is a small world, and I would be lying if I denied that these conversations provide us with a sense of belonging; they remind us that we have membership to an exclusive club and yeah, we should take pride in our own version of tribalism.

A few hours in (depending on the nature of the text you're working on), the conversations will unintentionally get quite deep, quite quickly and you will learn things about these relative strangers that you don't even know about your own brother or mother. As a breed we are 'open', as a type we are honest, and at the end of the day it is our job to deal with emotions of all kinds, so a few comparisons to real life are bound to creep in (especially by the time the sixth pint has been ordered).

…Now. Let's be serious for a second. Stop smirking, this is me being responsible… Though I have encouraged a visit to the local with the cast, I have not suggested that you go out tanking it all night, puke in a bus stop, forget where the hell your digs are and turn up late to rehearsals the next day! I HAVE NEVER DONE THAT. (Alright maybe the bus stop thing but I was NOT late to work because of it. I just smelt of sick.) You are, when all's said and done, at work and believe me every black mark against you is made in permanent ink and noticed by everyone. Enjoy all things in moderation, keep your mind on the job and your eye on the prize, and remember how much hard work it's taken to get this opportunity; for god sake don't fuck it up.

REVIEWS

Bloody reviews. Make friends with the fact that they are now part of your job and hopefully this may prevent you from living in fear of them. Critics of anything whether it is food, theatre or fashion are there to provide an opinion. It is one opinion; they are entitled to it and are equally entitled to express it, whether doing so dents egos or seriously inflates them. Apart from all of the ego crap, what reviews can also do is sell tickets! I think the key to not being too affected by them is to not put too much emphasis on them, if any. They are a marketing tool; as are you! In my opinion the people who deal best with any kind of fame, or attention (whether good or bad) are the ones who take it with a pinch of salt and go home at the end of the day and laugh about it all. The same approach should be adopted when dealing with reviews, if at all possible. If you are happy with your performance, if your director is happy with your performance then you can ask for no more. Let the critics do their job and don't let them doing theirs affect yours; if we allow them to then we are making directors of critics and that is a terrifying prospect – Like making popstars into actors... Oh no, wait, we do that in this country, don't we? Sorry I forgot.

(High fiving myself for getting that dig in!)

Very early on in my career I decided that I was too vulnerable, when opening myself up in performance, to handle the hype and bollocks that come with reviews. It wasn't that I couldn't take criticism, it was that I was terrified that whatever was said might contaminate my performance, bringing a level of self-awareness into my work that I was uncomfortable with and that I had worked my ass off to eradicate over the years! So, I made a rule that I would not read them, possibly at all, but certainly not before the job I was on had finished. This is a personal decision, one that I have stuck to rigidly and that has worked for me. I always subtly let my company know that I would appreciate it if they didn't go out of their way to tell me about reviews as I find it distracting, to which most actors are completely empathetic and obliging (others can please themselves). This works for me, but may not for others, it totally depends on the individual and you must do what works best for you, whilst respecting the decisions of others.

I always thought that reading a good review of oneself was the epitome of egotism; which is daft really because it's good to be praised and we should enjoy recognition for a job well done, and if not for ourselves then for our production. Now I know that reading one's own reviews isn't necessarily about ego; it's a tenth about curiosity and nine tenths about reassurance; something that most actors desperately seek and need (whether they are conscious of it or not); and no wonder really, what we do is incredibly self-revealing. I feel though, that there should be one rule for all, i.e. you can't ignore the bad ones and read the good ones! So, instead I ignore them all! I tow the line of confidence and creative satisfaction, I trust my own abilities and that of my director and as a result being praised or slammed by the press is immaterial to me. Well, that's what I try to abide by!

You'll find your own way with this, and in time you will learn to laugh whether you read them or not (crying will eventually finish you, so laughing is the only option really). Invariably, whether you've stated your intended ignorance of reviews or not, someone will blurt something out anyway, and you must then use the same mantra of indifference to block it out!

Of course, now we're not just in a world of newspaper reviews, we also have to contend with internet reviews, forums, tweets and Facebook comments too. Nowadays Barry from Enniskillen can tell me how much he enjoyed watching my arse on the television moments after it has appeared. It's insanely magical/disturbing. But, we are completely in control of whether we buy a paper or not, as we are also in control of whether we submerge ourselves into the weird world of Twitter and Facebook. One is also very much in control of not 'Googling' oneself! Come on, admit it, you know you have/do it every night before bed. If we go looking for comments we cannot complain when we find the little fuckers. People say the most absurd, distasteful and outrageous things online; it allows thoughts to become public knowledge with the click of a button – terrifying. Realise that you can limit your exposure to it by maxing your privacy settings on social networking sites, and by not trawling the internet for shit posted by idiots! Some people really take this kind of attention to heart, and for others it's water off a duck's back; you will gradually assess how much it all seems to affect you, and then (if needs be) do what you can to protect yourself against it. The last thing we need or want is for our confidence to be unnecessarily knocked, and certainly not by people who haven't got an elephant's wanger what they're talking about. My advice would be to use exposure and learn to manipulate it to benefit you, whilst always protecting your heart first and foremost.

A few funny things that have been said about some friends of mine; a few, picked from the MANY possibilities:

'I hope you get cat AIDS' …was written on a forum about an actor friend of mine after he featured in a commercial for a product that was seemingly not to this delightful internet user's fancy.

'You look as if you've been face raped.'… Was a lovely comment left on Facebook before a colleague of mine had worked out the privacy settings on their account. (Schoolboy error.)

'The only thing worse than the first act of Mr Denham's Othello was the prospect of sitting through the second.' Harsh. No further comment.

The unique thing about our business is that it's all about opinion; it floats on taste and preference and thrives on the conflict caused by them. There isn't a tick or cross or a right or a wrong, there is only ever the possibility of it/you being liked or disliked for a myriad of reasons that are uniquely experienced by each spectator.

UTILISING THE EXPERIENCE

Contrary to naïve opinion, acting is not simply about the sheer fun of it! Once it is a career and not a hobby, each acting job (as well as being an artistic lesson and professional credit) becomes a strategy for securing the next one. We do this through exposure and networking (covered in Chapter 4) which, combined and used alongside a strong performance, create something invaluable, infallible; that thing is a faultless professional reputation. If we are achieving that, we will be steadily gaining an audience of admirers who are intrigued by, impressed with and eager to work alongside us.

Let's get building the rep then…

LETTERS

This is an important part of being an actor and you should do it. Some agents may sneer at it, some actors may be defeatist about it, but the way I see it you are *self-employed* and one of your main objectives should be to introduce yourself, as a product, to influential people within the industry. For the sake of a stamp, some spit and a dollop of patience, why would you not? You need to be putting yourself out there and letter/email writing is a huge part of this.

By 'utilising the experience' I mean taking full advantage of the fact that when working in the theatre you are exposing your talent in a known location, at specific times, for a set duration. Invite casting directors (and agents) along to see you and use the opportunity to say something other than 'Hi, I'm an actor, I like acting and I want to work'. You have a *reason* to write to them and must run with the chance to announce and promote yourself whilst you have the opportunity. Casting directors go to the theatre, it is part of their job! They need to know who is out there and in what – so tell them. Hopefully, if you have an agent, they will bring someone along to see your show and a nice connection will be made when you impress them. We can only 'talk' about our abilities so much; the very nature of our business is that it is practical, it's about the doing, and I'm afraid that there are so many people all claiming to be able to do what we do to such a *phenomenal* standard that it is almost impossible to differentiate oneself without proof. This is your proof, your trailer, your advert and your opportunity to show what you can do instead of trying to describe it. You must seize the moment and be confident when doing so.

I mentioned this in Chapter 2, but I will reiterate that it is doubtful that you will receive replies, so don't expect to. Take a second to imagine how many letters they receive and always, always remember that this is business; it is not personal. By writing a letter you are putting an advert on a noticeboard, a noticeboard that the people with the power to further your career walk past (and possibly even read!) The replies will come in the form of auditions, and these auditions may arrive weeks, months, even years after you've written, but I promise you that each letter is a seed that you are planting and an important one, regardless of the return.

If/when you don't hear back, instead of assuming they didn't even open it or that they took one look at your small CV, laughed and threw it in the bin, I suggest that you pat yourself on the back for having taken care of some of the 'business' that a lot of actors neglect, and skip to my conversation with casting director Alice Purser in Chapter 9 for further info and reassurance.

The same principles apply as with letter writing in Chapter 2. Keep it brief and to the point, include all of your contact details, along with whatever marketing materials you have and clearly state when, where and what the production is. It's also an idea to communicate with your fellow actors to see who they intend to write to etc. and/or who their agents may be bringing. If a casting director has been invited by an actor it doesn't mean that they will only be watching that actor does it?! Follow it up, tell them that you know they were in etc. I have worked on a couple of productions where there were a few 'youngsters' who started a list in the Green Room so that the whole company were aware who had been in to see the production, who had been invited and who we might be expecting on any given day. We are all in the same boat; if we paddle together we will get further, faster.

Letters are important and most directors and casting people I've spoken to agree. Yes, it is an expense for you and yes, it is a time-consuming job for them (their assistants) to sift through the piles, but it can and does have the desired effect and saves them searching for you.

A friend from drama school who was incredibly capable but didn't get an agent following graduation (god only knows why) struggled with sporadic bouts of small-scale work and eventually began doing a series of other jobs outside of acting. Though this was the case, she always kept her eye on what was happening in the business and kept plugging away relentlessly. One day she wrote to a casting director who replied and called her in for an audition for a small part in a rather successful West End production. She read for that part and was then asked to audition for another, bigger part, which she got. She had the pleasure of working in *War Horse* for two years – all because she kept the faith and kept marketing herself.

Moral to the story? All write to the casting director of *War Horse*… No don't. Well do if you're right for it but… Oh god, I'm going to end this paragraph.

CONNECTIONS

As I mentioned earlier, you will quickly discover that the world of acting is a web, where everyone is connected to someone else; in a room of actors at least two or three people will have mutual friends or will have worked with the same people, possibly repeatedly. Word of mouth has, since forever, been a powerful means of promotion and as we've already discussed, professional reputation is the perfect sales tool. The most you should aim for is being known as good, pleasant, interesting and interested whilst being confident about what you do and who you are; this shouldn't be a premeditated image that you create and portray, it should be what you are! Ultimately, just be aware of how you come across, because directors drink with casting directors, actors socialize with producers, and most of the aforementioned sleep with each other; everybody, everybody loves to share information. And fluids apparently. So, put simply, be yourself (as long as you're not a dick; if you are a dick, please stop it. No one likes a dick)… I'm going to resist the temptation to go any further with that.

On theatre jobs (especially) you will make some very special bonds and friends, which is indeed a wonderful part of our job. The lengths of time spent together and the intensity of what you go through as an ensemble can cement some of the most rewarding relationships that you may go on to cherish for years to come. You are likely to 'get on with' the majority of people you work with; actors by nature are sociable, open and fun which promises for good times ahead on any job you're fortunate enough to get. Whether colleagues and associates turn out to be real 'buddies' or not, simply conversing with all and sundry can be beneficial and it can be useful to be able to refer to other actors and their performances, therefore steadily identifying the 'webs' of actors you come across. Some may see this as some disgusting, forced version of proving one's acceptance into a clique, which is fine, I suppose it depends on the vein in which it is done. I see it as knowing your shit (that's your not you're – Oh how punctuation matters). Quietly researching for yourself who is who, and how people are connected is a clever and astute thing to do in my opinion and only those full of hot air would view it as anything different.

Now go and make some awesome theatre!!!

6. WORKING ON SCREEN

Hurrah! (and hard work)

RANDOM: You what? You're gonna be ont'ele box? WICKED…

… Standard comment from, what shall we call him? … Stanley. From Stanley, who works in…Mechanics, why not. Obviously in this instance Stanley is Northern – note the cliché ont' type comedy – (I use the word comedy loosely). It's ok, I'm from the Midlands and am therefore allowed to take the piss out of pretty much everyone, up, down or sideways (we have to cover up our lack of identity somehow).

So, back to the point, which was about 'Stanley's' reaction to the news that you have a television job. The following type of chat may now occur, either throughout the conversation you have with 'Stanley', or with anyone else who happens to be eavesdropping within the vicinity; this type of conversation will be a regular source of annoyance/amusement for the duration of your time as an actor.

STANLEY: What famous people's numbers have you got in your phone?

ACTOR: Er…I haven't got, I mean…we didn't… It's not really erm…

Followed by an unimpressed grunt from STANLEY.

STANLEY: When are you on?

ACTOR: Huh, I haven't even had my costume fitting yet. So…

A blank stare.

…A while yet.

STANLEY: Have you met thingy jig, what's his name, the one off…
(Clicking his fingers expectantly.) you know, that programme with the doctors, all of the doctors?…

ACTOR: …*Doctors*?

STANLEY: Yeah, and he was in a car chase with that bird off *Loose Women*?

ACTOR: I don't know I'm afraid, I'm not sure you who you mean.

STANLEY: Call yourself an Actor mate! …
Eh, don't forget me when you're famous will ya?!

ACTOR: *(Under breath.)* Already have. 'Mate'.

I jest. In truth, it's lovely that our industry creates such intrigue and excitement amongst the masses. After all it's their belief, support, and enjoyment for what we do that provide an industry pool in which we all happily swim. However, the usual innocent shows of interest, manifested in sentences such as 'How do you learn your lines', seem to graduate into Actor's Question Time once you either announce, let slip (or have it announced for you), that indeed you shall be appearing upon the big sheet of glass in excitable 'Stanley's' living room within the next 3-9 months – possibly for all of 45 seconds...

Being an actor you will already be familiar with the sometimes irrational reaction to our work from Civvies (I like to call non-industry folk Civvies, in an attempt to counterbalance their 'lovey' title for us; pathetic yet satisfying). You will naturally learn to dodge idiotic questions, humor ridiculous comments and, quite rightly, learn how to put everything in layman's terms. You speak a different language you see, a language you aren't even aware you speak – how clever is that?! For example, after my first theatre job:

MUM: How was the show?

ME: *(Casually.)* Fred didn't make his cue USL, the rake still felt wrong, the speed-run before the half helped the pace but Carol is still masking me, which almost made me dry during the business in 2.1.

...I thought the signal had gone on my phone, but no, I was speaking 'actor' and she hadn't a clue what I was talking about. It's a club we're in, quite an exclusive club as it happens, and one that we often forget to be proud that we're a part of. However, it's perhaps useful to remember that the public provides us with this club; not only their money but also their presence is vital to the survival of our profession. So, it's always a fairly good idea to appreciate the general public wherever possible (humouring their intrigue and only making fun of them secretly with other club members)... Cheeky.

Working in/on television catapults one into a different realm of 'interesting' in the eyes of onlookers. Admitting that you are a theatre actor seems to go something like this:

STANLEY: You're an Actor are you?

Sheepish nod.

     What you been in? Would I have seen you in owt?

ACTOR: I work in the theatre mainly.

STANLEY: What, Shakespeare and that?

ACTOR: Yes, he's…he's one of the many, MANY playwrights we work with, yes.

STANLEY: Don't you wanna do films then?

ACTOR wants to impale themselves onto the nearest sharp object.

ACTOR: Film would be great, yeah…but, theatre's also rather wonderful.

STANLEY: Never been to the theatre.

ACTOR: Right.

Many (Joe public) have either never been to the theatre so daren't engage in conversation about it, or they assume that you can't be that good an actor because you aren't on the BAFTA guest list. Theatre can be seen as some sort of consolation prize, and by being a 'thespian' (which as far as I can gather is a label not a job description, like gaffer or bricky??) you are expected to be one of 'those' – weird extroverts who can't start a sentence without 'DARLING'… Let's be clear, there is some truth in this, clichés aren't simply imagined; their foundations are formed from easily identifiable themes and the predominant and regular ones amongst them are then highlighted (and exaggerated). Some of us are more guilty of providing these themes than others admittedly (usually the ones who are trying to prove themselves as serious actors in every other way possible than actually being good at acting) but as a breed we do carry our work with us, we are our work and the general public has a knack of sensing it! (Especially if one wears a big swooshing scarf, grips a 2 litre bottle of Evian and carries a copy of Sir Peter Brook's *The Empty Space* EVERYWHERE…) Darlingitis is a highly infectious plague where symptoms can go undetected right up until the disease becomes terminal – we know, fine, but for gods sake it was an epidemic that peaked in the '70s and takes hold of far fewer of the acting population now, so get over it Civvies!

These wild notions don't end with theatre, they span across the board, and television is no exception. If you work (certainly as a regular) on television then yes, people hurriedly put themselves forward to have their pictures taken with you, but these same eager 'fans', when looking at that picture on their phones later that night in the pub, will instigate a half-hour long conversation about how you've sold out artistically and must be shagging directors. The 'respect' nosedives, you become a walking cliché, and, apparently, everyone else's business.

Public perception of our industry and its players is nothing if not entertaining, and it is within the safeguards of our own 'club' that we can share the amusement of their judgments. That's not to say that this club of ours is a judgment-free zone, FAR from it, there are clubs within cliques, within clubs! The lovely George put it brilliantly:

**'There is a strange pecking order among actors.
Theatre actors look down on film actors, who look down
on TV actors. Thank god for reality shows, or we wouldn't
have anybody to look down on...'
George Clooney**

Dealing with the public and their perceptions of our trade isn't always necessarily about being 'famous', in fact, it hardly ever is; as we know playing small parts on television every now and again doesn't equal fame. Regardless of our professional 'profile', we have what seems to still be (certainly in the eyes of the general public) the controversial label of 'actor', which means that we are required to learn to deal with the fact that the majority of people we meet and speak to will for some reason take more of an interest, and possibly have more of an opinion about our job than any other vocation or current affair throughout the history of mankind. Don't get me wrong, it can be wonderful being able to chat about work with everyone and anyone, and that they will, for reasons that may be favourable (e.g. they're genuinely interested) or not so favourable (e.g. ask you to sign a beer mat in case they can one day sell it on eBay), listen and be genuinely supportive. But god this can be tiring – especially the next time you see star-struck Stanley and you aren't going to be 'ont'ele box', instead you're serving him in KFC...

Despite my rambling, this chapter isn't about public perceptions and misconceptions of our work, even though I do consider this to be 'part of the deal that I was never warned about', hence why I thought it was worth a mention. (I may have thought it an adequate opportunity to be a tad entertaining too? I'll leave that one hanging)...

Right, let's stop giving a shit what people think about our job and focus on actually doing it. Many of you reading this may have television experience, your drama school may have prepared you well, or you may have already been out into the world and tasted the honey. I use the word honey because television/film work involves hard graft to make it, is sought after by swarms of busy workers and is ultimately... SWEET! See what I did there?... (Crap analogies weren't exactly an objective for the book, but who am I to block an organically recurring theme...) Whilst you may be experienced, or feel ready to take on the world of screen, I know many of you will not. It is more than likely that you have trained at a theatre school, which means you may have had limited time in front of a camera, resulting in many of you being baffled and alarmed by the myths and hand-me-down stories about it. This section is for everyone, whether it is a confirmative companion or an educational and thought-provoking tool. The skill is in the doing...

Create opportunities to play, play some more and then play a bit more. It is through the playing that truth and confidence will emerge.

Point one about this chapter is that I am not going to be telling you 'how to act on camera', how the hell would I know?! I've only been doing it for a short time myself. In fact I'm not going to be 'telling' you anything – as I mentioned earlier, I disagree with books that claim to 'teach' subjects that are fundamentally practical. Perhaps these types of books can be a guide in addition to the practical experimentation of methods but can never solely teach, and in my opinion can be in danger of theorising something far too beautiful to be contained within the covers of a book. Rant one done and two major points reiterated; that what I say is an offering not an instruction, and that where camera acting is concerned it is the doing that must be done in order to develop.

I want to help you conquer any existing anxieties regarding camera work, whether they are about auditions or actually working as a screen actor. In my eyes these anxieties fall into two simple categories, the doing and the knowing:

1) The doing – A lack of practical experience.

2) The knowing – A lack of technical knowledge.

Sadly most graduates will feel a sense of both as they walk into their first screen audition. Many manage to get by and many others blossom, but so many crumble. I believe that two major elements that contribute to great screen presence are equal measures of confidence and calm; a focus that is second to none. Only when they are in place can actors be free enough to submerge themselves into a whole other realm of existence, the realm of our characters. With a basic foundation of technical understanding and an awareness of surroundings (the knowing), as well as with an ease that comes from repetition and familiarity (the doing), that focus is achievable, and will provide the subtle truth that the camera so desperately requires from us.

I am assuming if you have purchased or are browsing through this book that you can act? Possibly a dangerous assumption to make, but we're seven chapters in, so I'm going to go with it! The skills you have as an actor are the same whatever medium/genre you're faced with; it's delivering them with conviction, confidence and accuracy under pressure that counts. I hope that this chapter goes some way to helping you realize how.

So… Screen.

SCREEN AUDITIONS, THE DIFFERENCE

It's not different, it's acting. In the same way you would automatically adjust depending on whether you were playing at the Gate or the Garrick. You have a core set of skills, and through practice and play your instincts will quickly acclimatize, according to whatever medium you are working in.

Why is one camera scarier than 500 people? It isn't. First you must acknowledge any anxieties, before you are able to break them down and combat them! So there's a camera? Don't make it into a bigger deal than it is or your nerves will screw you. The camera will see everything you're feeling, that's the beauty of it, so if nerves and terror are not your character's emotions, make sure that they're not in the shot! I built up an anxiety for screen without even knowing it. The auditions I went for were ok, but in no way did I feel the same as I did when leaving auditions for plays, and I now know that was because I felt differently on the way in. Feeling that way was unnerving; I lacked control and knew I was in a psychological rut, which irritated me greatly and was preventing my skill from being seen. I spent a lot of time trying to figure out why there was such a difference in my psychological approach, and you will need to do the same in order to progress. You may not think you're fazed in the slightest, but these things might be lurking in your subconscious, ruining your chances...

- Playback – (ugh).
- I'm trained in theatre, what if I do 'too much' and am too theatrical?
- I have no background information on the character, how am I meant to create a believable three-dimensional human being?
- I feel unattractive.
- Producers scare the shit out of me.
- The 'character' looks and sounds exactly like me. Is this acting?
- I'm fine with the acting, it's the chatty, interview bit!

So, *Playback*...

In an audition situation this is almost never going to happen; firstly because there isn't time, secondly because I'm not sure there are many directors that would be cruel enough to force that upon someone they've just met, and lastly because the chances that the casting director, producer or assistant can operate the camera well enough to skip forwards and backwards as well as pressing stop and record are minimal! Producers, I am of course joking. Producers are great – (Say that sentence again with the same inflection as the 'I'm Ron Burgandy?' line from *Anchorman*)... You haven't seen *Anchorman*?

Seriously, you can read this later, go and watch *Anchorman* if you've never seen it, it makes the world a better place.

Welcome back – watched it? It's beyond hilarious right?

Many, many actors despise seeing themselves on screen. I think Julie Walters has avoided seeing most, if not all, of her own work. This is understandable; we linger in a sequence of beautiful, imaginative moments when we act, believing that we are what we say we are, existing only in the world we've created – watching playback is like seeing the tooth fairy walk into Ladbrokes – the illusion is broken, the magic diminished and the ideal tarnished.

Though I'm no huge fan of watching rushes, I do make myself watch the finished product as I believe that healthy assessment of one's work is the key to improvement. (Plus it's rather nice to see yourself and your colleagues as an ensemble, complemented by everyone else's vision and hard work.) I don't play it on repeat or agonize for hours over each choice, intonation and facial movement, but I do listen carefully to the reactions around me (something we do in the theatre whether we admit it or not). Also, I make a mental note of anything that I felt just didn't work and why; therefore the next time I walk on set I have a private little agenda of things to try, things to avoid and things to enjoy. A lot of these lessons will come through your director, your main informant. Remember though, that a director's objective is to create the overall vision of the piece, and though guiding and helping you is a way he or she will achieve this, being on set is not like being in a classroom; it is not their responsibility to 'teach' you. Time is always of the essence and self-education is a major part of the development process; finding the lessons within everything for yourself and working out how to apply them next time you have the opportunity to do so. As an actor you should constantly evolve; I see playback as a way to aid that evolution, rather than it being some sort of obstructive torment for vanity. Learn from it, take what is useful and then discard what is not. Go on, at least try! And then, if you find that you simply cannot feel comfortable with it, it is a personal choice that you are perfectly within your rights to make. (But be aware that this means you could miss out on some seriously cool screenings/premieres/free bars!)

I am trained in the theatre, what if I'm too theatrical?

DIRECTOR: … You're doing too much!

… Take it down!

… Nope, do less!

… Stop showing me.

ACTOR: Shit.

These are some of the most common variations of a tired old note, regularly given from screen directors to actors. I think the main reason for this is that we, by nature and by nurture, are intended and groomed for the stage rather than the screen. We go to *stage* school, and we excel in the works of Chekhov, Ibsen and Wilde. We are encouraged to embrace theatricality, its timelessness and its flamboyancy. So much time is spent celebrating this style that others are worryingly neglected and the gap between them widens. Most budding actors get up 'on stage', or 'in a space' everyday of their lives, probably for around five years (including college/sixth form and drama school) so taking the hundreds of times an actor has performed live into consideration, it is clear to see that it's a well-trodden path, and therefore a home from home. With that in mind, it is not surprising that, for many, it feels like the more comfortable medium.

In contrast, the camera can feel like an alien invader, a judgmental magnifying glass ready to intimidate and demean; all because it is less familiar and more permanent. We exist for a single moment in the theatre; we exist forever on screen and that is, quite understandably, a little scary.

COMFORT IS KEY!
Experience and knowledge of a new medium will provide comfort, and comfort holds hands with confidence. Soon enough assurance will ooze from you on set, just as it does when walking onto the stage from the wings.

The vital things to remember before, and during an audition for television or film, are to think it and feel it as opposed to doing it and showing it. This is an obvious note for any performance, and a silly one to throw out without further explanation, but it's so important, especially on screen; something that can take practice and perseverance.

Cameras are in everyone's possession these days, I can't do anything without a video or photo of it being uploaded somewhere (well, almost anything – I HOPE) – this is a perk of our age, so put it to some use! Get actor mates together and film some sketches or monologues, anything that gets you playing is good news; you can find useable, up-to-date scripts online, or simply make 'em up – it doesn't matter what the text is. Take it in turns both acting and observing (and I mean observing others act, as well as watching yourself on playback – both are very useful)! Failing that, if you don't have a mobile phone (weirdo) or you don't have any friends (poor weirdo) then get on to the film schools and put yourself forward for their student films. This is a fabulous way to get used to hearing camera lingo and to get that vital practice time in front of the lens.

When you do get in front of the camera, play with techniques and experiment with shades of emotions; play until you forget the camera is there. If and when you get the chance to observe the results of your efforts, be very clear of your objectives; you are not doing it to assess how old you're starting to look or how big your nose is in comparison to the rest of your face; there is no place here for vanity. Instead, assess your levels of intensity, levels of emotion, levels of movement. You are a paint chart; notice your shades and tones and then remember how they felt.

Acting for camera classes can be very useful to you, but for a trained actor it may be an unnecessary or unmanageable expense. Acting is acting, whether on screen or not; at this point you don't need to be 'taught', you need to practice. In doing so, the techniques used by actors who switch between mediums effortlessly, should emerge for you too. And if you attempt to make a friend of the camera instead of an enemy, who knows, you might even enjoy it! The only way to make friends is to spend time together, getting used to one another, learning to understand them and allowing them to get the best from you.

I have no background information on the character, how am I meant to create a believable three-dimensional human being?

This used to seriously stress me out. I'd get a script through for audition with the following information attached:

> Mandy. Female. Early twenties. Stubborn. Had an affair with John and dislikes cats.

Brilliant – see you on set…

I felt that I had no use for this vague, generic (and often random) excuse for information, like it was simply a casting director's artless tick box.

However, look again – any information is useful, they're clues! It's what you do with the clues that counts, whether you take the initiative to invent and have the balls to challenge. If you do attempt to 'invent' a background for your character though be careful not to go off on a tangent or else:

> Mandy. Female. Early twenties. Stubborn. Had an affair with
> John and dislikes cats.

May turn into:

> Now Mandy but used to be Matthew. Early twenties.
> Stubborn because her father abused her. John was her savior,
> until she realized she was allergic to his cat. She kills the cat.

Suddenly we've made her an abused, trans-sexual murderer. Which is possibly not what the film requires?

VERY IMPORTANT POINT: Don't make characters what you want them to be or what you fancy playing – look at the evidence and serve the text.

In addition to the character breakdown that you may or may not receive, glean what you can from the text and use your judgment of how it is relevant to your character's individual story. There will be a clear arc (for any good film, episode or series), which you can use to inform your 'choices'. In fact, don't make choices, but do generate ideas – (great actors offer ideas continuously but know that the finished 'thing', whether it be a play or a film, is a team effort; any big 'choices' should be made through organic playtime and/or discussion with your director).

You will notice quite a difference between screenplays and play scripts, and it may take a bit of time to acquaint yourself with this different way of storytelling; not to mention the different layout. It is likely that you will be more accustomed to long stretches of uninterrupted text and won't have the foggiest what to make of this:

INT. C/UP SANDRA. DISSOLVE TO MIKE POV

And you don't have to; this above instructs the crew that it is an Internal (indoor) scene and that initially there is a Close-Up on Sandra which should then Dissolve or Fade into a separate camera angle, which is of Mike's Point Of View. Though this kind of information may or may not be present on a shooting script, it's good for you to have a basic understanding of this stuff, without stressing yourself out about it; master what is expected of you first! This being the dialogue and the delivery of it.

Though the inclusion of such technical language may not directly affect you hugely as a new artist, the story told through them is vital. The scripts you are dealing with will tell a story very differently depending on whether it's a theatre, television or film script that you are working from. Not only the formats and layouts are different, but getting used to the different choices preferred by different genres can take time and practice to get a handle on. As a performer, you are the translator of that story and I think it is imperative that we understand why we are telling the story the way we're telling it.

Most actors are very used to the playtext way of storytelling; its format is familiar and the structures and devices it employs are embedded into us. Despite the fact that television and film will probably have been a presence in our lives far more than theatre will have been, actually seeing the blueprint for the entertainment we so casually take for granted in our lounges suddenly seems rather confusing.

What are a few things that a screenplay might have that a play may not?

- Shorter scenes.
- More description about what we see than what the actors should 'do'.
- More characters.
- More locations.
- More elaborate storytelling.
- Montages.

What are a few things that a playtext might have that a screenplay may not?

- Long scenes.
- Stage directions.
- More description about the characters and how they feel.
- Labelled acts.
- Monologues and lengthier chunks of text.

These are not 'rules' but are the basic basics, and important things to note and observe. It may not occur to many actors graduating from a theatrical training to ask the question 'What is the difference between the scripts?' until a screenplay is thrust into your hand and the audition for your first film is the following day. Knowing not only how to read both types of scripts but also how to use the differences between them to inform and enhance your performance is so very important. And so very impressive.

So, with this in mind I have taken a scene from a project I'm currently working on and have created two versions of it, one a screenplay and one a playtext, in an attempt to show you one plot told through two mediums. Use the examples to note the formats; to get a feel for the differing approaches and their results, and then experiment with the contrasting ways you might play them.

Peg
An extract from the stage play

By Natalie Burt

The scene takes place in the auditorium of a theatre on Broadway, so on a bare stage that represents this. The year is 1924, it is summer and though the temperature has soared during the day, the late afternoon delivers a cooling breeze as the sun lowers.

The stage is empty and without set, merely a platform devoid of decoration; however it is littered with scripts which are the remnants of an acting class that has recently ended.

BLANCHE, a tall, dark actress in her late forties picks up the scattered scripts, enjoying the peace and quiet of the deserted space in which she is so comfortable. She is slender and harsh-looking and though her shape has dissolved and her face shows the exhaustion of a full life, it is still evident that she was probably once a beauty. She groans every now and again when she bends, vocalising her own dismay at the aging process. She hears the side door swing and as she looks around she sees PEG enter through the auditorium.

PEG is 18 years old, sweet-looking with an inoffensive facial configuration and a soft yet assertive air. She approaches the stage where BLANCHE continues with her task, unaffected by PEG's presence. PEG takes in the space, as if revisiting an old friend. BLANCHE speaks with a thick New York accent.

BLANCHE: We're done for today; you wanna be an actor try getting here at the start of the class instead of the end of it.

PEG: Oh I wasn't here for the class, Mam.

BLANCHE: What are you, the cleaner?

PEG: No mam. I saw your Ranevskaya at the Imperial.

BLANCHE: I see – you're a fan. *(She sighs lightly.)* Well, I've touched every one of these scripts; you help me pick 'em up, I'll sign one for you.

PEG: Er, ok.

They pick up the scripts in silence.

So do you like teaching actors how to act?

BLANCHE: I don't teach 'em how to act; I teach 'em how to realise they already can. *(Beat.)* Either that or I tell 'em they stink.

PEG: *(Smiling at this.)* My father used to say that acting was either in your blood at birth or it wasn't and if it wasn't there was no way of injecting it in.

BLANCHE: Huh – Pops is an actor is he?

PEG: *(She nods.)* He used to bring me along to the weekday matinees here at this very theatre; we never queued outside because my father tutored one of the usherettes and she used to let us in that side door, where I just came in – as payment. He'd give her some acting advice behind that curtain there for five or so minutes and in return she'd get us in for free. I used to sit and wait staring at the empty stage; thrilled by its sense of anticipation and duty; I'd imagine it was a person, waiting to fulfil the most important moment of his or her life; a person who held all the secrets of the magic that was about to take place upon it. *(Pause as she breathes in.)* And the smell in here, a strange yet comforting mix of toffees and sweat; I used to think to myself that hard work smelt so sweet; huh, the perfume of the thespians. *(She smiles to herself.)* I'd sit quite happily here on one of these seats, swinging my legs 'cause they didn't touch the ground back then, wondering what Rosalind or Portia or Kate Hardcastle were going to look like and sound like today, what they were going to tell me and teach me; then I'd fantasize about how Romeo or Captain Jack were going to make me fall hopelessly in love with them. I'd pretend the actors knew I was waiting for them as they put on their make-up; then I'd imagine that when they looked out into the crowds of adoring spectators in the curtain call that what they were in fact doing was searching the sea of strangers for me. *(Slight pause.)* It's a lot to think in five minutes huh? Sometimes they were there longer behind the curtain, and if they were, the usherette would sneak us two wafers and sit us nearer the front. She was always real happy to see my father. He was a great actor.

BLANCHE: *(A knowing tone.)* Was, but not anymore?

PEG: Well, no Mam.

BLANCHE: Yeah, many don't stick at it; it's understandable.

PEG: Understandable?

BLANCHE: Sure, understandable that over time the struggle with money, the lack of work, the battle with one's self-esteem can just become too much. The rejection, it kills actors you know.

PEG: So do bread vans.

BLANCHE stops still and scoffs. PEG continues to pick up the scripts.

BLANCHE: What?

PEG: Vans. That deliver bread. My father was hit by one and killed – his self-esteem was doing fine until then.

BLANCHE bursts into laughter. This has really tickled her. She shakes her head and gets out a cigarette. PEG, straight-faced and unaffected by this reaction, continues to pick up scripts.

BLANCHE: Sorry, that's far from funny, it's just…the way you… *(Beat.)* You have a peculiar mind don't you?

PEG: *(She shrugs.)* I live inside of it Mam, so I'm probably the only person in the world who can't answer that with any kind of objectivity.

BLANCHE smokes and studies the young girl.

BLANCHE: And what's it like living in your mind young lady?

PEG: Oh you know, sometimes a party, sometimes a wake.

BLANCHE: Oh yeah, and which is it today?

PEG: That all depends on you Mam.

BLANCHE: *(Smiles a knowing smile.)* Does it now?

There is a pause as PEG stops and looks attentively at one of the scripts.

PEG: I can do this better than anyone in your class.

BLANCHE: So you're not a 'fan'.

PEG: Oh I am yeah, sure. But – I want way more from you than a scribble on a scrap of paper. Who you are is immaterial to me; it's what you know that I'm after.

BLANCHE: *(Dismissively.)* So join my class.

BLANCHE sucks on her cigarette and starts to pack her things into a bag.

PEG: No.

BLANCHE stops. Gradually musical instruments can be heard warming up in the wings during the next.

I want you and me – your knowledge, my potential with no distractions.

BLANCHE puts down her bag. The musical instruments get louder and BLANCHE has to throw her voice over them to be heard.

BLANCHE: And just what the hell makes you think that you're different to the twenty thousand other dough-eyed hopefuls in this town?

PEG: *(Handing her the scripts.)* I'm not them.

The band strike up a song (unseen in the wings). PEG grins at its poignancy.

Blackout.

Peg
An extract from the screenplay

By Natalie Burt

1. <u>INT. THE AUDITORIUM OF A THEATRE ON BROADWAY.
    1924. LATE AFTERNOON.</u>

BLANCHE, a tall actress in her late 40s picks up scripts that are scattered on
the stage. She's been teaching a class in the space. She speaks with a thick
New York accent.

PEG, a mousey-haired girl, 18 years old, creeps in through a side door.

> **BLANCHE**
> We're done for today; you wanna be an actor try getting here
> at the start of the class instead of the end of it.

> **PEG**
> Oh I wasn't here for the class, Mam.

> **BLANCHE**
> What are you, the cleaner?

> **PEG**
> No mam. I saw your Ranevskaya at the Imperial.

> **BLANCHE**
> I see – you're a fan. Well, I've touched every one of these
> scripts; you help me pick 'em up, I'll sign one for you.

> **PEG**
> Er, Ok.

They pick up the scripts in silence.

> So do you like teaching actors how to act?

> **BLANCHE**
> I don't teach 'em how to act; I teach 'em how to realise they
> already can. Either that or I tell 'em they stink.

> PEG
> (Smiling at this.)

My father used to say that acting was either in your blood at birth or it wasn't and if it wasn't there was no way of injecting it in.

> BLANCHE
> Huh – Pops is an actor is he?

> CUT TO FLASHBACK:

2   INT. THE CORRIDOR & AUDITORIUM OF THE SAME THEATRE.
      1912. EARLY AFTERNOON.

A young PEG is being pulled along by her father, a dashing but not classically good looking man. A pretty usherette rushes them down a corridor that leads to the side door of the auditorium. It is obvious that she is sneaking them in; there is an urgency but mostly, for the adults anyway, a sexy sense of danger.

> FATHER
> Now sit here Peg, this acting tutorial won't take long today.

The USHERETTE makes a mockingly disappointed groan and then giggles as he slaps her bottom and playfully manhandles her behind a curtain. PEG sits on the edge of a row in the auditorium. After a second he reappears.

> FATHER (CONT'D)
> And don't touch anything.

He goes to disappear again.

> Hey Peg, told you I'd get us in to see it – Sold out my eye.

He winks and PEG beams at her father, her hero. PEG looks out to the vast theatre space in wonder.

> CUT BACK TO:

3   INT. THE AUDITORIUM OF A THEATRE ON BROADWAY.
      1924. LATE AFTERNOON.

> PEG
> Er, yes Mam, he was. He was a great actor.

> BLANCHE
> Was, but not anymore?

PEG

Well, no Mam.

BLANCHE

Yeah, many don't stick at it; it's understandable.

PEG

Understandable?

BLANCHE

Sure, understandable that over time the struggle with money,
the lack of work, the battle with one's self-esteem can just,
become too much. The rejection, it kills actors you know.

PEG

So do bread vans.

BLANCHE stops still and scoffs. PEG continues to pick up the scripts.

BLANCHE

What?

PEG

Vans. That deliver bread. My father was hit by one and killed
– His self-esteem was doing fine until then.

BLANCHE bursts into laughter. She shakes her head and gets out a cigarette.
PEG, unaffected by this reaction, continues to pick up scripts.

BLANCHE

Sorry, that's far from funny, it's just… the way you… You have
a peculiar mind don't you?

PEG
(She shrugs.)

I live inside of it Mam, so I'm probably the only person in the
world who can't answer that with any kind of objectivity.

BLANCHE smokes and studies the young girl.

BLANCHE

And what's it like living in your mind young lady?

> PEG

Oh you know, sometimes a party, sometimes a wake.

> BLANCHE

Oh yeah, and which is it today?

> PEG

That all depends on you Mam.

> BLANCHE

Does it now?

Pause. PEG stops and looks attentively at one of the scripts.

> PEG

I can do this better than anyone in your class.

> BLANCHE

So you're not a 'fan'.

> PEG

Oh I am yeah, sure. But – I want way more from you than a scribble on a scrap of paper. Who you are is immaterial to me; it's what you know that I'm after.

> BLANCHE
> (Dismissively.)

So join my class.

BLANCHE sucks on her cigarette and starts to pack her things into a bag.

> PEG

No.

BLANCHE stops. MUSICAL INSTRUMENTS can be heard in the wings as musicians beginning to warm up approach the stage.

> PEG (CONT.)

I want you and me; your knowledge, my potential with no distractions.

BLANCHE puts down her bag. Band members start entering from the wings, flooding the stage with people and sounds.

BLANCHE

And just what the hell makes you think that you're different to the twenty thousand other dough-eyed hopefuls in this town?

PEG

I'm not them.

She hands her the scripts. We linger on BLANCHE's bemused but intrigued face. The band strike up a song and PEG grins at her.

❧

One of the most important things for an actor to observe when looking at a screenplay is that it is predominantly a visual vehicle. What we might say in a two-page monologue in a play, we might be asked to convey in a look and a grin on film. It's not more work for the actor and it certainly isn't less, it's different; knowing those differences will set you apart from those who either haven't bothered to ask the question or who haven't even realized that they need to.

Further script examples are easy to locate and it's a really good exercise to read the script of your favourite film so that you can actually see how they made what you know and love from the script you now have in your hand.

A lot of the time, the scenes (or 'sides') you will receive for a television role will be rather self-explanatory, as each scene (though it's still part of a story) exists for its own isolated reason, it is delivering a specific message to the audience. You must know what those reasons and messages are. Always ask to see a full episode, but if this is not possible then at least consider what the point of the scene you have is (both for the audience and for your character). If you have questions, note them down and wait for an appropriate time to bring them up. But for god sake don't ask questions just for the sheer hell of it!

DIRECTOR: Any questions?

Actor thinks: Is this a trick? If I haven't got a question will they think I'm an idiot or that I don't want the part enough??!!

ACTOR: Er... Are you looking forward to directing it?

Epic fail.

If they put this question to you, you may be tempted to ask something, anything; partly just so that you can stay in the room a little longer, but mainly because you imagine that it is some sort of elaborate test of your intellect and artistry. It's not! Only ask a question if you truly have one about the character or the production.

I feel unattractive.

So do most of us, worry about this on your own time. I know this sounds harsh, but when you're working it should be a break from vanity not a holiday with it; you are being somebody else – enjoy it! As far as others' perceptions of you go, just look after yourself and be hygienic; everything else is subjective (/ridiculous/not worthy of your concern).

Obviously use your common sense and don't have a large Big Mac before an audition as this may hinder your energy levels, and make you feel like crud. (But do eat something as not doing so will too!)

Producers scare the shit out of me.

They hold all the cards; they can be scary, especially if you make them out to be so. They're in a powerful position but shouldn't be seen as a threat, you are screwing yourself over before you've begun if you let that happen. They want you to be good, just like the casting director does. (Of course one cannot predict how that 'want' will present itself, or if indeed it will at all, but rest assured that if they've got money tied up in a project and four hours to find a vital piece of said project, they will be cheering you on more than most!) Remember, you have a right to be there and a skill they admire (and probably wish they had themselves… It's fine; no producers will read this… will they?… Well, if they do the next section should screw me over nicely…)

I think I got one job because I caught the producer out. Here's what happened:

PRODUCER: Good Natalie, that was nice. This time can you be a bit more 'taken aback' by Freddie, remember it is the first time you meet him so let us see that, let us enjoy the fresh intrigue there is between them.

I pause in thought. The DIRECTOR looks up.

ME: *(Quietly but assertively.)* It's, it's not the first time they've met, actually… They met two scenes prior to this one.

PRODUCER: Did they?

I smile sweetly.

DIRECTOR: That's why your job is to sign the sodding cheques!

Laughter. Slight embarrassment.

PRODUCER: I should read the fucking script at some point, it sounds rather good. In that case, let's do another take for luck but what you did there was spot on.

More laughter.

I got the part. A hairy moment, but I'm so glad I had the balls to call him on it. (He'll kill me for putting this story in if anyone works out which project it was for!! Or he may deny it, and people listen to producers over unemployed actresses all the time!)

The 'character' looks and sounds exactly like me. Is this acting?
HUGH GRANT. Discuss.

I'm fine with the acting, it's the chatty, interview bit!
Apparently in auditions in the US the actor enters the room, possibly exchanges a polite 'Good Morning', and then goes straight into the read; any discussion, questions or comments are then left until afterwards in order to preserve and respect the character the actor has presumably 'awoken' within themselves minutes and hours before the meeting. I so wish we could take a bit of a leaf out of their book here! Some actors can switch from themselves into characters, to moods and imaginary situations like a TV channel, which is a very useful skill, especially when dealing with long waits on set (abruptly brought to a close by the 1st AD bellowing 'Ready, and rolling!') However, most actors (and there are some who take this to the point of ridiculous, of whom we shall discuss/slag off later) find a minor run-up and some preparation time useful to centre and to focus themselves. At the risk of sounding rather precious, it can be a ritualistic metamorphosis; one that is too often disregarded, disrespected and ruined by the audition process. It is an issue relevant to some and not others and it depends largely on the individual actor and their personal approach. It also depends on the nature of the piece being performed; more sensitive pieces perhaps require more of an emotional through-line from waiting room to camera. Most directors I've encountered are sensitive to this, as they want to witness the truest and most accurate performance you're capable of. But when all's said and done, they don't know your preferred ways of working and are usually too pushed for time to enquire/give a shit, so if you need a few seconds before 'action', take them – it shows that you are aware of what needs to be accomplished and how you're going to get yourself there.

My audition belongs to me, it is mine and not theirs and I will endeavour to take control of it in any way that I see fit. This does not mean that I am overbearing, controlling or overtly uncooperative, it simply means that I try and engineer what I need to happen in order for me to perform to the best of my abilities. (Please though, please never be wanky for the sake of being wanky; it impresses and fools no one and your charlatanism will be sussed out as soon as you begin to deliver an empty performance. We know it's a special skill; trying to reinforce the fact for the sake of onlookers only devalues it and us.)

Auditions are a playground, so dare to risk, make it count and take control. By 'take control' I'm not suggesting that you say 'Can we just get on with it', or that you attempt to conduct the whole interview 'in character' (both of these crazy approaches will probably ensure that you remain unemployed for the foreseeable future). Stay focused and take your time; when they are ready for you to perform, make sure that you take a second to check back in with the preparation you've done, it'll be there.

A lot of actors are highly uncomfortable being 'themselves'! I don't think you can necessarily teach 'Interview Techniques', but you can certainly improve by following a simple formula:

Preparation + Focus = Confidence

We've talked about focus, and preparation for 'the day of the audition' was discussed in Chapter 4. Preparation of the actual text has a simple checklist you'll already be aware of:

- Be familiar with, or have learnt the lines.
- Read the WHOLE script (if possible).
- Understand the scene's/scenes' place in the character's journey.
- Have created a character that you feel is most suitable considering the evidence the material has given you.
- Understand or be inquisitive about your character's relationships with other characters.
- Have a list of questions or quandaries about your character and/or the plot.

As well as the material prep there is also a lot of other useful research that can be done in order to better prepare yourself for the meeting (that's if you have time – it's currently 4pm, I have an audition tomorrow and I haven't received the script yet; so, not much research gonna happen there! Luckily the role is a tired, stressed and continuously hungry author in her mid-late twenties who has backache and a tendency to find herself funnier than she is…should be fairly simple to portray).

Research:
- *Who is the director, producer and casting director and what have they done?*

This will give you a good knowledge of the projects they tend to take on, the actors they've worked with repeatedly and how long they've been in the game.

- *Watch any work that they've created (if there's time).*
  This may offer you a good understanding of the acting styles they lean towards and provide background knowledge for you should they reference past projects.

- *Research the writer.*
  This is a must with theatre but also very important in film and television. It may flag up any regularly used patterns and styles regarding plot and character.

So, basically, get to know the backgrounds of the people you're meeting with and find out everything you can (this doesn't mean that you have to get every inch of that research into the 4-minute conversation, but if nothing else, knowing that you are well informed, will boost your confidence). An obvious, but seemingly common, mistake is actors not realising they've met someone before. Please don't do this, it looks shit and sloppy and sloppy shit is not desirable. If you have a rubbish memory (how do you learn lines??) make a note when you meet someone and check the list when you have a meeting. A friend of a friend of mine didn't have a list, or a brain by all counts:

CASTING DIRECTOR: So, Tom (blatantly not called Tom), what have you been up to recently?

TOM: Not a lot unfortunately, it's been really quiet. I did this god-awful ident thing a few months ago, a travel agency ident with all these tacky tag lines, awful. But not much since then.

Pause.

CASTING DIRECTOR: What, the one with the parrot and the catchphrase?

TOM: Yeah that's it. Don't judge me, work's work eh?!

TOM laughs. Another pause.

CASTING DIRECTOR: That was our company's ident.

Gulp.

TOM: Ah.

CASTING
DIRECTOR: That'll be all for today.

TOM leaves.

True story. What a dick. Be very careful who and what you slag off, it really is a SMALL WORLD!! I'm quite pleased it happened because a) it is a very funny story (and boy do we need those) and b) it is the perfect way to warn other actors of a very simple but costly mistake!

So, if you've done the prep and you're calm and focused, all there is left to do is deliver what you've prepared.

For screen I'd definitely recommend (as I've mentioned) to have learnt or be very familiar with the lines. On a practical level the camera needs to see your face, and most importantly it needs to have a relationship with your eyes; they are the windows to the soul and can leak emotion in a beautifully subtle way; this cannot be appreciated by a theatre audience in quite the same way, and is an important storytelling tool that should be taken advantage of on camera. Learning lines also shows that you are committed, and on a basic level – able. (I know that sounds daft, all actors can learn lines, right? But when the audition is for a continuing drama whose turnover is rapid and schedule is tight, it's good to confirm that you are an actor who is capable of learning many scripts, out of sequence and with little or no time!)

If you have an audition for a 'soap', (or 'continuing drama'), they won't release the script to you before the day and will only allow you to collect it an hour or so before your meeting. Get there early and collect it, then find a quiet corner or toilet cubicle (yes, I have done this) and become as familiar with the text as you can. The scenes will be fairly brief so this is manageable; but don't agonise over it or you will achieve nothing and be a jibbering wreck by the time you enter the room. A good tip is to select a few poignant moments to learn well so that you can lift those moments right off of the page and deliver them with conviction and confidence.

Earlier when I mentioned taking control of your audition, these are some of the things I meant:

- Enquire how big or small the frame is, i.e. how close in on you they are, as this dictates how much movement you have. (Don't ask for the sake of it, it's not clever; only ask if this is useful for you or you think it may be relevant.)

- Ask to go again if there was something you weren't happy with (but gauge this – if they're really complimentary and happy, just run with it for now and nail it on set!)
- Even if you are miserable with being out of work, remember to be passionate and enthusiastic about work, or else what's the point?

Finally, don't crumble, stumble, or over-compensate when the oh so common yet debilitating question comes up:

DIRECTOR: So, what have you been doing recently?

Although your paranoia and misery might be at an all-time high if you've been out of work, I promise you that this question is NOT a trick, or in any way a spiteful 'You're not doing very well' dig. They can see your CV, if the last job listed was in December and it's now June, they can see that. These answers may not be ideal:

ACTOR 1:   My imbecile of an agent hasn't been getting me any auditions.

ACTOR 2:   I've had loads of auditions I just haven't gotten any of them. Weird huh?

ACTOR 3:   I've been doing an amateur puppet show in a car park in Cleethorpes but didn't list it on my CV.

ACTOR 4:   Er... *(Red face, big gulps, tears well up, voice disappears.)*

These four actors may have just blown the first sniff they've had of a job in six months, all because they let their own self-doubt and deprecation mute the fascinating person within them. Every actor has 'out of work' times, every director knows this and knows that every actor wants to work and hates being out of it; all is common knowledge and to be expected of freelancers, so don't apologise for it. Instead, make sure that you are using the out-of-work time wisely. I write when I'm unemployed, as you can see! It gives me a creative outlet, I feel worthwhile when I do it, like I'm achieving, I have control over it, and it gives me something to discuss when that dreaded question comes up. (In fact, I'm rather disappointed these days if they don't ask!) I'm not saying that every actor should write, of course not, but inertia isn't attractive or constructive, and you must find ways to stimulate yourself in between work. Surely these sound better?

ACTOR 1:   I haven't had any acting work lately but I took a short course in philosophy and it was fascinating.

ACTOR 2:   I haven't had any acting work lately but I've always
           been interested in photography, so I've been building
           a portfolio of work that I've named 'Seek and ye shall
           find' (quite a good idea actually... I've lost the lead to
           charge my camera, so that's scuppered that idea).

ACTOR 3:   I haven't had any acting work lately but used the
           opportunity to travel a bit.

You get the drift; these are far more endearing answers to hear, and far more healthy choices to make (obviously the idea being that you do these, not just use them as 'lie' answers). You will hear me say this time and time again, the 'out of work' times are as important, as informative and as influential to you as an actor and a human being as the 'in work' times. If you observe and obey that mantra, when you do get an audition you can be:

Focused, prepared, calm, interesting and good.

STEP BY STEP, CASTING TO AIRDATE

BEFORE FILMING

You've nailed the audition, you've been offered the part and you've accepted (small celebration dance). Then what?! Well, depending on the schedule you may feel a bit like a sitting duck; there are so many people in the team who will need to be notified of your acceptance, each of them then having a job to do in regards to you and your involvement in the project. (On the flipside of course, you could get the job and start filming three days later, causing a rather wonderfully manic 72 hours before 'action'!)

You will receive two phone calls. Firstly, one from the 2nd Assistant Director (see description coming up) – who will welcome you to the production and make it abundantly clear that they are your 'go to' person. Any questions or worries and they're your point of contact (much the same as your Company Manager is in the theatre). They will take charge of you and organise any travel or accommodation you require. They will also post or email an up-to-date draft of the script to you with any changes, along with a call sheet (once one is available).

This varies slightly on each job of course, as the turnaround and scheduling is different for each production company on each project. (But this is pretty much the standard, and what you should expect.)

The next phone call is likely to be from the costume department who will ask for measurements, or will arrange for you to come for a fitting – again, this varies and the 2nd AD may act as the go-between and arrange all that for you.

The next step could either be a fitting, a reading, or it could be arriving at the location (whether that be at a hotel they've arranged for you or straight to set. Nice huh?!)

It's important that you feel comfortable, informed and prepared for your shoot days, and the team is there to help you, so always ask questions and never feel silly for admitting you're new to this side of the industry; we all gotta start somewhere!

Once you have the script, do as much preparation on it as you can, as rehearsal time will be limited, and possibly non-existent! This will be a very new and slightly unnerving way of working for a lot of you, but by using the same principles you did for your audition (preparation and focus) you will arrive feeling confident, ready to play, listening to your instincts, and eager to have the time of your life!

A CALLSHEET TEMPLATE

Once you receive this baffling document you may wonder what the blue fuck to do with it. Never fear! Though a lot of it will become clear (and will be self-explanatory), I very much appreciated a friend explaining the call sheet to me before I was handed one on set. As his guidance worked so nicely for me, I decided it would be useful to do the same for you.

Firstly, the call sheet, is actually more for the crew than the actors, and though it is important (I think) that you know how to read one, you will have a team of people ushering you from pillar to post, putting you where you need to be, informing you of everything and checking you are ok every five or six seconds.

Each crew member, cast member, supporting artist, driver and caterer will work from the same schedule.

In the grid highlighted in orange is information directly connected to you: the Actor.

The actor's movements
(Similar grid beneath for the non-speaking roles in the production)

No: Number – this is your character number. It is used to place you in a scene on the schedule without having to put your name every time. You won't be referred to as this number (well, you shouldn't be!) The crew will know your name, both of them (character and professional).

Artist: This is your professional name.

Character: This is your character name.

So you will notice that mine is:

16 –   Natalie Burt   –   Pandora

To the right of this are the times you are scheduled to be arriving into certain departments. This lets the 2nd/3rd ADs know where you need to be, and also lets the departments know when to expect you.

P/up: This is the time that you will be picked up by a driver from either your home, hotel or arranged location. You will be informed of this time the night before (probably when you receive the callsheet).

Costume: This is roughly what time you will arrive at your trailer or dressing room. You will be taken there, probably by the 2nd AD, or you may be met by the designer who will chat through the costume and ask you to get into it. A good production team will have anticipated that you may need help dressing, or will offer. Always take help with corsets or fiddly/delicate garments, firstly because you shouldn't have to struggle and secondly because a lot of costumes are hired and damage to them can cost time and money.

M/up: This is the time you will be expected to arrive into Make-up. Depending on the requirements of your character, a certain amount of time will have been allocated. (Usually the make-up artists will say 'It's not bloody long enough!' You'll get the hang of this overworked department rather quickly.)

Meal: When a meal has been scheduled during the working day for you i.e. a break for you to grab lunch, or dinner (if it's a night shoot).

A UNIT

Director:	**DATE**	2nd Assistant Director:
Executive Producer:		3rd Assistant Director:
Executive Producer:	**BLANDINGS**	Location Manager:
Producer:		Assistant Location Manager
Line Producer:	**CALL SHEET NO: 18**	
Production Co-oridinator:	**Production Company**	
Production Assistant:	**Production Office Address**	
CAST/CREW TRANSPORT ON LAST PAGE OF CALLSHEET		

UNIT CALL:	0800	Breakfast: 0700 - 0800	Sunrise: 0553

WEATHER:	Partly cloudy and sunny all day with showers around 1100 & 1500 - max temp 10c, Realfeel 7 C

NOTES:	• PLEASE NOTE CALL TIME IS 0800

LOCATIONS	UNIT BASE
Loc 1 - Drawing Room, location address	UB - ADDRESS
Loc 2 - Main Hall, location address	
Loc 3 - Conservatory, location address	

SC	SET/SYNOPSIS		D/N	CAST & S/As	PGS
2/3C	Loc 1	INT - BLANDINGS - DRAWING ROOM (BLUE PAGES) Pandora has procured a dog for Connie	D5	Clarence (1), Connie (2), Beach (3), Freddie (4), Pandora (16)	1 4/8
2/30pt1		INT - BLANDINGS - DRAWING ROOM (BLUE PAGES) The ceiling collapses on Baxter	D6	Clarence (1), Connie (2), Beach (3), Freddie (4), Baxter (5), Pandora (16), Veronica Schoonmaker (26, Jimmy Schoonmaker (27	1 4/8
MOVE TO HALL					
1/13A Loc 2		INT/EXT -BLANDINGS - HALL (NEW SCENE) Beach and Connie drill the troops	D2	Connie (2), Beach (3), Freddie (4) A, B, C	1 4/8
MOVE TO THE CONSERVATORY					
6/13 Loc 3		EXT - BLANDINGS - LAWN (SPLIT SCENE) Clarence's wheelchair trip is interrupted	D12	Clarence (1), Connie (2), Beach (3), Daphne (14)	1 6/8

No	Artist	Character	P/Up	Costume	M/Up	Meal	Travel	M/up Artist	On Set
1		Clarence	0650	0700	0720	After Reh			0800
2		Connie	0655	0810	0700	After Reh			0800
3		Beach	O/T	0720	0700	0740			0800
4		Freddie	0650	0720	After Reh	0740			0800
16	Natalie Burt	Pandora	0740	0800	0700	After Reh			0800
5		Baxter		0950	1010				1030
26		Veronica Schoonmaker	0825	0855	0915				1030
27		Jimmy Schoonmaker	0840	0910	0940				1030
14		Daphne	1500	1530	1550				1700

ID	Num	Supporting Artists Role	Call	Costume	M/up	Hair	Meal	Travel	On set
A	3 x	Footmen	1200	1200	TBC	TBC	TBC	TBC	1430
B	2 X	Maid	1200	TBC	1200	TBC	TBC	TBC	1430
C	1 X	Older Butler	1200	TBC	1200	TBC	TBC	TBC	1430
									Total 6

ADDITIONAL INFORMATION/INSTRUCTION/REQUIREMENTS	
SET VISITS	
ADDITIONAL CREW/EQUIPMENT	As per - coordinator - 2nd Camera and Steadicam - operator
CAMERA	As per
GRIPS	As per
COSTUME	As per
DESIGN/ART DEPT/SET DRESSING	As per
ELECTRICAL	As per

The callsheet as you will receive it:

A UNIT

Director: Executive Producer: Executive Producer: Producer: Line Producer: Production Co-oridinator: Production Assistant: **CAST/CREW TRANSPORT** **ON LAST PAGE OF CALLSHEET**	**DATE** **BLANDINGS** CALL SHEET NO: **18** Production Company Production Office Address	2nd Assistant Director: 3rd Assistant Director: Location Manager: Assistant Location Manager

UNIT CALL:	0800	Breakfast: 0700 - 0800		Sunrise: 0553

WEATHER:	Partly cloudy and sunny all day with showers around 1100 & 1500 - max temp 10c, Realfeel 7 C

NOTES:	• PLEASE NOTE CALL TIME IS 0800

LOCATIONS	UNIT BASE
Loc 1 - Drawing Room, location address Loc 2 - Main Hall, location address Loc 3 - Conservatory, location address	UB - ADDRESS

SC		SET/SYNOPSIS	D/N	CAST & S/As	PGS	
2/3C	Loc 1	INT - BLANDINGS - DRAWING ROOM (BLUE PAGES) Pandora has procured a dog for Connie	D5	Clarence (1), Connie (2), Beach (3), Freddie (4), Pandora (16)	1	4/8
2/30pt1		INT - BLANDINGS - DRAWING ROOM (BLUE PAGES) The ceiling collapses on Baxter	D6	Clarence (1), Connie (2), Beach (3), Freddie (4), Baxter (5), Pandora (16), Veronica Schoonmaker (26, Jimmy Schoonmaker (27	1	4/8
		MOVE TO HALL				
1/13A	Loc 2	INT/EXT -BLANDINGS - HALL (NEW SCENE) Beach and Connie drill the troops	D2	Connie (2), Beach (3), Freddie (4) A, B, C	1	4/8
		MOVE TO THE CONSERVATORY				
6/13 Loc 3		EXT - BLANDINGS - LAWN (SPLIT SCENE) Clarence's wheelchair trip is interrupted	D12	Clarence (1), Connie (2), Beach (3), Daphne (14)	1	6/8

No	Artist	Character	P/Up	Costume	M/Up	Meal	Travel	M/up Artist	On Set
1		Clarence	0650	0700	0720	After Reh			0800
2		Connie	0655	0810	0700	After Reh			0800
3		Beach	O/T	0720	0700	0740			0800
4		Freddie	0650	0720	After Reh	0740			0800
16	Natalie Burt	Pandora	0740	0800	0700	After Reh			0800
5		Baxter		0950	1010				1030
26		Veronica Schoonmaker	0825	0855	0915				1030
27		Jimmy Schoonmaker	0840	0910	0940				1030
14		Daphne	1500	1530	1550				1700

ID	Num	Supporting Artists Role	Call	Costume	M/up	Hair	Meal	Travel	On set
A	3 x	Footmen	1200	1200	TBC	TBC	TBC	TBC	1430
B	2 X	Maid	1200	TBC	1200	TBC	TBC	TBC	1430
C	1 X	Older Butler	1200	TBC	1200	TBC	TBC	TBC	1430
									Total 6

ADDITIONAL INFORMATION/INSTRUCTION/REQUIREMENTS	
SET VISITS	
ADDITIONAL CREW/EQUIPMENT	As per - coordinator - 2nd Camera and Steadicam - operator
CAMERA	As per
GRIPS	As per
COSTUME	As per
DESIGN/ART DEPT/SET DRESSING	As per
ELECTRICAL	As per

Travel: If the preparation departments (dressing rooms and make-up) are in a different place to the location to the set then this will be the time that a driver will arrive to transfer you.

M/Up Artist: The name of your allocated Make-Up Artist who will 'travel' to set with you.

On set: The time that the rest of the crew on set will expect the actors to arrive to shoot the scheduled scene.

The times in the orange grid are simply a guide for you; it is the individual crew member's responsibility to stick to them and the 2nd/3rd AD's job to orchestrate it all. It is not for you to worry about, so don't; if you're running late, you're running late and someone else will be getting the flack for that, not you – just keep focused on the job in hand. (Flustered actors are not good for the final edit.)

So, now we move onto the green grid:

This is the schedule for the scenes that are to be shot that day, and includes all of the relevant information to do with that.

SC: The scene number on the script.

Loc: What Location (listed in the red grid) the scene is at.

Set/Synopsis: A brief description of what happens in the scene and details about the environment of the scene.

INT/EXT: Whether the scene is to be filmed inside or outside.

Cast & S/As: What characters and supporting actors are in that scene.

Pages: Pages of the script to be filmed.

The rows in between scenes containing information like: 'Move to Hall' are indicators for the crew that they will need to move the unit (all the equipment) to another location or room.

In the red grids you will find the following FYI type notes:

Useful info and reference points

LOCATIONS: Are the different places in which the filming will be taking place that day. They are also given a number for quick reference.

UNIT BASE: Is where the make-up department, trailers/dressing rooms, catering van, and production offices are based.

NOTES: Exactly that, any further information, specific to that day that the crew will need to be made aware of.

WEATHER: The predicted forecast for the day (this may affect locations and exterior shots. It also may effect equipment).

The information in the blue grids is:

All 'other' relevant information.

A UNIT: There may be more than one unit (and therefore more than one crew) filming simultaneously. If this is so, then other schedules titled B unit and C unit will operate in conjunction with the existing one. A crew member is assigned to a specific unit but an actor might shoot scenes with all of the different units at different times.

DATE: The date for that schedule.

TITLE: The title of the production.

CALLSHEET: The shooting day. The first day of filming is one. This indicates how long the shoot has been running and is a quick reference for pick ups. (You'll notice that in the blue grid it says 18. If all is not completed on Day 18's schedule then 'P/UPS from Day 18' would appear in the green grid on the day that those shots were to be completed.)

Production Company & Office address: The name of the company making the programme or film.

UNIT CALL: What time the crew is expected on set.

BREAKS: Breakfast and Lunch times for the Crew.

SUNRISE/SUNSET: Exactly that, so that the crew know how many hours of daylight they have.

NAMES: Listed to the right and left of the blue grid are the Production team, Producers, Assistants, Managers etc.

At the bottom in the yellow grid are notes for the crew; staff changes, equipment information etc.

WHO'S WHO

An important part of being a screen actor is realising what a vital, but very small part of the team you are. There is the cast, and then there is the crew. The crew and 'production team' are the many, many others who make the production happen; who run, manage and supervise the set, the schedule and every other element that goes into creating the finished product. I think it is essential that actors understand what all the other cogs in the machine do. I'm not saying you must learn to wire a plug or change a gel in order to be able to empathise with the crew around you (I'm sure the majority of them have next to no interest in reciting Steven Berkoff monologues) but a basic understanding of the work going on around you is both polite and useful. Being able to place people quickly, know their area of expertise and understand their responsibilities so that you can comply, makes for a speedy and efficient experience for all.

There will be jobs that I've not mentioned here, just look at how long the credits take to roll after a film and you'll understand why! However, I have listed everyone that you are likely to come into contact with on set, people you will communicate with on a professional basis and people whose work directly or indirectly affects your own. The descriptions are brief and basic; designed to arm you with a concise understanding rather than a degree on the subject.

Departments and jobs and how they might be relevant to you

The 'Crew' is divided into different departments, each of which specialises in a certain aspect of production.

DIRECTION
Director

The Director is responsible for the creative realisation of the project; selecting images, sounds, music and performance that will achieve the vision he or she has. They are also responsible for hiring members of the cast and crew – Obviously!

You'll have met them in the audition. You may have rehearsals with them, or in some cases (especially in a lot of television filming) the next time you see them will be on set before you start to film. They are there to work with you and direct you and you must use them as much as needed regardless of how little time or patience they might have on that given day! Be sensitive to their task but also attentive to your own. You may end up communicating more with the 1st AD, which is absolutely fine.

1st Assistant Director (1st AD)

The primary role of the 1st AD is to help the Director in the making of the film in the time allowed, whilst observing the budget allocated. They must ensure that the production sticks to the schedule and must be sensitive to the director's artistic ambitions, but they must do so in a practical way that obeys time and budget restrictions.

Amongst many other things, the 1st is responsible for producing the shooting schedule and callsheet and for liaising with all of the heads of departments on the production. On set you will probably hear their voice far more than the director's. They will be attentive to you and you must use them accordingly, whilst being aware that they are also that 'go to' person for everyone else on set!

2nd Assistant Director (2nd AD)

The 2nd AD is an assistant to the 1st AD, helping to achieve the targets of the day but primarily their role is to look after the artists; orchestrating transport for them and delivering them to the correct department at the required times. They work very long hours (as do most, if not all of the crew) and are your main source of assistance. They will be your first port of call when you arrive on set and will keep you well informed of all scheduling that affects you. They liaise between the set, the base and the production office and will ensure that you are safe, happy and where you should be, at the time you should be there! They may be on set with you at times but a lot of their work will be away from it, running from set to office, to location, to set. They will usually distribute diems too.

3rd Assistant Director (3rd AD)

The 3rd (as you might have guessed), assists the 1st and 2nd ADs but is the main assistant to the 1st as the 2nd will be occupied with the artists. Their job is to help with whatever the 1st needs them to do, taking on delegated tasks as and when needed. This can involve assisting different departments and turning their hand to a number of duties. Their place is on set with the 1st and they will take over looking after you (the artist) once the 2nd leaves you on set. Any problems or issues regarding pretty much anything can be directed at the 3rd – they will arrange someone to help you if they can't.

Runner

They are the most junior member of the production team and will get involved in all aspects of the production from making tea, picking up props to moving vehicles.

Be kind to them; be kind to everyone, but especially to them, as they will be trying to impress (just as you are). Help make their lives a little easier wherever and whenever possible. (Plus bear in mind that runners get promoted over time and may just be directors one day…)

CAMERA

Director of Photography or Cinematographer

DOPs are key heads of department and have a major creative role in the filming process. The DOP, Director and Production Designer work very closely to give the film its visual signature.

DOPs must discover the photographic heart of a screenplay, creating the desired look using lighting, framing and camera movement. This is achieved with the cooperation of the crew and the collaboration of the other heads of departments.

The DOP is a very important presence on set and though your interaction may be minimal or non-existent (as their focus is on the technical and the visual), you will be in direct contact with them. It is a fascinating job in my opinion, and a highly skilled one that deserves your respect and acknowledgement.

1st Assistant Camera Operator, Focus puller

The 1st ACO gives hands-on support to the DOP and Camera Operatives whilst being responsible for keeping the camera in focus as it's shooting.

2nd Assistant Camera Operator, Clapper & Loader

They have more specific responsibilities involving camera maintenance and are required to keep meticulous records including daily camera reports and time code details for takes.

They are also in charge of the clapperboard at the beginning of a take, (otherwise called 'slating'). The clapperboard ensures that the sound recording can be perfectly synchronised with the film image in post production.

In addition to those responsibilities the 2nd ACO also takes care of loading and unloading the camera magazine (a removable section of the camera that houses each roll of film). Now most filming is in HD the loading and unloading of a memory card or chip is the norm.

Assistant Camera Operator

They support senior members of the Camera Department and take on responsibilities from them, as and when they are delegated. They are generally in charge of setting up the cameras and having ready the required lens etc. for that day.

SOUND

Sound Designer

The Sound Designer or Supervising Sound Editor is in charge of the sound in post-production (once filming is complete and editing has begun).

Production Sound Mixer

They are responsible for ensuring that dialogue recorded during filming is suitably clear, of an acceptable quality and ultimately usable. The Sound Mixer and Boom Operator plan where to place the microphones to obtain the best sound quality.

Boom Operator

Operates the boom! The boom is the fluffy-looking mic on a pole that is dangled above the actors (out of shot, ideally), to obtain the clearest sound quality from the dialogue. Either the boom or sound assistants will fix your microphone to you and collect it at the end of the scene/day.

ELECTRICAL

Chief Electrician or Chief Spark

The Chief Electrician is in charge of all electrics on set and head of the electrical department – jointly responsible for the design and execution of the lighting plan for a production with the Gaffer.

Best Boy to the Chief Spark

1st Assistant to the Chief Electrician.

Electrician/Spark

There to support and work with the Chief Spark and Best Boy. They set up, control and are responsible for all electrical equipment on set.

LIGHTING AND CREW

The Gaffer or Chief Lighting Technician

A key head of department and head of Lighting on set who works closely with the DOP to prepare the set and to achieve the correct lighting and blocking for the vision they'll have created together.

Best Boy to Gaffer

Chief Assistant to the Chief Lighting Technician.

Technicians

Are trained lighting and rigging specialists. The main responsibilities of a technician are to work closely with the electrical department to put in the lighting set ups for a shot. They assist, support and work with the Gaffer and the Best Boy.

Key Grip
Is responsible for assembling and operating heavy camera accessories such as the Dolly (FYI a Dolly is any apparatus upon which a camera can be mounted, enabling the smooth movement of a shot), Crane or Tripods. A Dolly Grip is in charge of operating the camera dolly specifically. Other Grips also work to assist and support the Key Grip.

DESIGN
Production Designer
Is one of the heads of departments – the Art Department. They work closely with the Director and DOP to achieve the 'look' of the production. The Production designer concentrates on the physical, visual appearance of the shoot, including location, set, furniture, costume, make-up etc.

Art Director
Is second in charge to the Production Designer. They basically put into practice everything that the Production Designer asks for. They are highly skilled and work closely with the other members of the art department.

Set Decorator
Works closely with the Production Designer and Art Director to achieve the correct look for the set.

Set Dresser
Dresses the set with the chosen furnishings, carpets, curtains etc. Every detail will have been planned by the production designer and is then created by the Set Dresser.

Props Master
Responsible for finding and managing all the props that appear in the production.
You will have direct contact with this person and can ask them anything about any objects you use in the scenes.

Costume Designer
Responsible for all the clothing and costumes worn in the production by the actors and supporting artists. They are also in charge of designing, planning and organizing the construction of the garments, down to the fabrics, colours and sizes. They work closely with the Director to understand

and interpret the 'characters' and liaise continuously with the production designer and make-up and hair department to achieve the chosen look.

This may be the first person you come into contact with, either at a fitting or moments after you arrive on set.

Assistant Costume Designer

Assists the costume designer, frequently appearing on set with needle and thread! They will make sure that you aren't creased or marked and will generally be on hand if you have any costume queries or mishaps.

Hair & Make-Up Designer

In charge of the Make-Up artists, overseeing their work and liaising with the Costume Designer and Production Designer regarding each character's look.

Make-Up Artist & Hair Stylist

Apply make-up to, or manage the hairstyle of, anyone appearing on screen; closely following the plans set out by the design team and taking special care to observe meticulous continuity.

You will be 'allocated' a Make-Up Artist who will create your initial look, accompany you onto the set and attend to you throughout the shoot.

FYI You find out all of the set gossip in the Make-Up van/department.

PRODUCTION

Executive Producer

Supervises the producer on behalf of the studio, the financiers and/or the distributors. They ensure that the project is completed on time, within budget and to the technical and artistic standards agreed at the beginning of pre-production.

Typically Execs are not involved in the technical aspects of filming but may have played a crucial financial or creative role in ensuring that the project goes into production. They are now, more often than not, involved in the casting process and have creative say too.

You may have dinner with them on bigger projects, or they might swing by the set to meet you (check up on you). Otherwise your roles are worlds apart. Know who they are though!

Producer

The producer oversees the whole production; they are often responsible for the initial concept and occasionally for raising essential finance. They have creative control during pre- and post-production and will work closely with the Director and DOP to ensure that the project is on course both financially and creatively.

They are usually involved in the entire or later stages of the casting process so you will probably meet them in audition. When you go to an audition and are 'put on tape', that footage will be more than likely then sent to the producer.

They may be there on set regularly but aren't always a constant presence, it depends on the project. And the producer!

Production Manager/Line Producer/Associate Producer

Their focus is the business, finance and employment end of things. The likelihood is that you won't come into contact, but one of their assistants may contact you or your agent for various reasons. They provide the producer with weekly updates during the shoot regarding the budget and progress of the project from a financial point of view.

Production Coordinator

They co-ordinate the production! Apart from dealing with everyone and everything else in the entire world, they will also organise any travel and accommodation needs for you, keeping you informed of call times/days, and always delivering a schedule to you on time. They are directly linked to the Line Producer.

Production Accountant

Pays you! And manages the overall accounts and budgeting for the production.

Script Supervisor / 'Continuity'

Supervises the continuity of storyline, of action and of dialogue and records and assesses all information regarding the screenplay. They match action and dialogue during the shoot and take reference pictures of set, costumes etc. for matching purposes.

They will be monitoring the script closely and will whisper in your ear if you are making any dialogue mistakes that may later affect continuity. They will also remind you of certain actions or gestures you did in previous takes if you are required to repeat them. Always a good plan to know your script supervisor's name; they are a crucial part of your presence on set and the accuracy of your performance.

Drivers

My favourite members of the crew; the first face you see in the morning and the last when work is done. They are usually down to earth and awfully pleasant; keeping you company, keeping you safe and warm and most importantly, keeping you well informed! (Whatever the make-up department forgot to mention gossip-wise the drivers will deliver!)

FYI They talk about actors so make sure they only have nice things to say about you on their next job!

… And we all know what the Casting Director does!

Quite an extensive list isn't it? And depending on the size of the production (and the budget) there may be four or more people for many of those roles, and/or several Units operating simultaneously.

I didn't know any of that when I did my first telly job, and the difference I feel walking on set knowing it is huge. The more confident I've become, the more I've wanted to make it easier for all young actors to do the same. Possessing all of this information beforehand, it becoming ingrained in your subconscious, frees up the conscious mind to tackle the responsibilities that your own job demands of you! Again, any knowledge that makes an actor feel more at home and at ease on set is worth its weight in gold; it makes us a little more confident and a little freer. Oh, and respected by the crew – which is always a nice feeling!

One important last point on this subject is learn people's names! It can be quite an extensive task, but my god does it matter. Obviously if you are a day player (someone just filming for the day) this is nigh on impossible, so give it a go but don't stress about it! ('Oi' does work.) Make a mental note when someone introduces themselves – Not only is it polite to remember, but it's also so much easier, when you need to ask a question or have a problem, if you've made friends with someone who will probably know the answer. (And if you've learnt the list above you'll know the relevant person to ask too)… Besides from anything else, it makes the whole experience (and most importantly, the wrap party) much more fun!

Some quick tips:

- You will have a trailer. Be cool about it and secretly squeal when you are alone. But remember the walls of these things are paper thin!

- When the car arrives to collect you, know that where you sit is telling. I always make a point of sitting up front with the driver, especially if it's a first day. It doesn't mean that you are a pompous git if you do sit in the back, and if you have scenes to look over then by all means politely explain this to your driver and get on with them. But be aware that just slouching in the back without so much as a 'good morning, what's your name' will get you a reputation for being an arrogant, unfriendly cock. Just a thought.

- You will wait around a lot on set, it's a certainty. Take a book if you have the sort of mind that can switch from fiction to fiction easily (I struggle with this – whilst preparing to create one world I can't submerge myself into another). A newspaper or magazine work best I find. However you pass the time whether it be reading, listening to your iPod, getting off with fellow artists – remember that you are always on call; at any given moment there could be a knock at the trailer door and the golden words 'We're ready to travel you to set' could be uttered. Don't be caught out or caught off guard; sleepy, flustered or bored shitless actors don't look great on screen. Be alert and ready for the job you're about to kick the shit out of.

- If the crew offer you a 'keep warm' (a big filming coat) take it. Take hand warmers and hot water bottle too if they offer. You may be cosy in your trailer but waiting on a pier in a dressing gown for thirty minutes while they rig another light could get a tad chilly. Shivering, goose pimply, pissed off actors don't look good on screen either!

- Start acting when they shout 'Rolling'. By acting I do not mean start the scene (i.e. the dialogue) but enter the world and consciousness of your character. Usually that will give you a few seconds of 'being them' before 'Action' is shouted. Rolling is a preparation stage, a warning call, an on your marks – all the other departments use it, so should you.

- When 'final checks' are called that means that the Costume, Hair & Make up, Set dressers etc. will launch into action. This instruction will result in you being surrounded by swarms of design type people who will be making sure every hair is in place, that there are no shiny noses, that the ruffle on your coat that you keep moving is back to the position it should be in at the top of the scene for continuity and that you are happy and ready to roll. They are doing their job to make sure you look perfect when you do yours, so behave and let them poke and prod.

- MOST IMPORTANT TIP: You may, at times, be referred to as 'the talent'. This is production's alternative for artist. I hate it. But, what you gonna do?! My tip is to acknowledge being 'the talent', enjoy being 'the talent' but never act like you're 'the talent' and certainly never like you're the only 'talent'. Basically do your job but don't be a twat.

UTILISING THE EXPERIENCE

Here we are again, utilising. So filming is pretty wonderful and you must embrace and enjoy every second of the experience; never forgetting in the midst of wonderment that it is in fact a job. You will benefit from it as a practical lesson in screen acting, and then use the post-production period to market your forthcoming exposure.

You must ensure that people know you've done it. (Obviously I'm not referring to a quick text to Uncle Bill or a Facebook status to brag – vile).

Your agent (if you have one) should be working closely with you to get the news out, however you are able to do this yourself too:

- Your credits on Spotlight must be updated with project title, director, character etc. – information can also be written in the notes section as mentioned earlier (especially once you have an airdate).
- You can also update IMDb, Casting Call Pro and any other 'exposure' sights you are signed up to.
- Your agent should have the information clearly on their website (if they display actors' CVs).
- You can write to casting directors and directors, especially ones you know and ones who cast similar projects.

Once you have an airdate it may be worth letting them know again, whilst updating all of the above as well.

Once you have footage you can create or update your showreel and send it out!

What you've just filmed might be the most astounding performance ever delivered but it means jack if no one sees it, or knows it's you. You must take responsibility for this, communicating regularly with your agent to make sure you aren't doubling up (if they're going to contact someone leave them to it). Don't allow complacency; it's all too easy to be seduced into thinking you're the 'cock of the walk' after having filmed something – you're not! Remember you are only as good as your last job and the airdate of something you're in is an especially vital time to remain focused, driven and thorough, whilst always shaking hands with modesty – no one likes an arrogant arse.

THE FAME GAME

'If a man loves the labour of his trade, apart from any questions of success or fame, the gods have called him'.
Robert Louis Stevenson

Fame – it's a bag of bollocks. A fairly complex bag admittedly, filled with superficiality, unfairness, ridiculousness, idolism, idealism, huge amounts of talent and bigger amounts of mediocrity; it explodes and implodes, sometimes without rhyme or reason. It is a club so many long to be a member of, a club of extreme extremes, a club that ignites and extinguishes without warning, and certainly without mercy. You may encounter it, and if you do you will see that it comes in many shapes. You may be in the presence of it, or you may experience it yourself. It may be cruel, it may be kind but you can guarantee it will be turbulent and peculiar either way. I think one of the most important factors of the fame game is never to turn your back on the fact that it is a man-made entity, an overwhelming fabrication and a farce, which is better to laugh at than be infected by.

WORKING AMONGST IT

As an 'unknown' (a title suggesting that one is not famous), the experience of colliding with fame is like opening that Christmas present you've been eyeing up since October; sometimes it's everything you thought it would be, and sometimes it's rubbish, and you wish you'd asked for money. On the one hand you may find yourself suddenly thrust on to a set working with, laughing with and learning from an actor who has mystified you from infancy. On the other hand, those same 'idols' can become rather abruptly humanized and nosedive straight off the pedestal you put them on. Fame affects everyone in different ways, and hopefully the majority of 'celebrities' (now a filthy title that means little in terms of talent or achievement) will be down to earth, pleasant and accommodating. However, some may not!

Fame is power and that power can be used for good or for evil (as in all good stories!) How fame has 'affected' a person will determine how they use it, or how they let it use them. If it has manifested itself into evil you may encounter difficult, selfish, demanding, spoilt, arrogant, ignorant people; but if they have taken to the fame game well, and it is being kind to them or they are content with their indifference to it, you may encounter a stupendous confidence that radiates and breeds calm, fun and reassurance. And if you're really lucky, they may be aware of their presence and use it to help, teach and inspire all those around them.

I don't think most famous actors fit neatly into a camp of 'good or evil', though some unintentionally give the impression of the latter. Whilst I don't think this should be 'excused' exactly, I do think one can choose to allow, to a certain degree. The pressure, exhaustion, constant and relentless scrutiny of their personal and professional movements, plus the immense superficiality all around them is almost inevitably going to be a breeding ground for loneliness, bad tempers, cynicism and diva-like tendencies. (We've all heard the stories and know the usual suspects.)

I've had a few encounters with this insane world now and am pleased to report that so far most encounters have been wonderful, either because a taste of opulence is always fun for a girl from a modest background, or because I've wound up acting with seemingly normal people who, both single-handedly and collectively, had a part in my decision to go into the profession. Having said that, I've also met a few utter arseholes! Interestingly it seems to be the people who (though they'd never admit it) aren't comfortable with or proud of how they achieved their status, nor are confident with their ability to sustain it, who are more often than not the biggest arseholes… Food for thought? Make the behaviour you encounter act as a blueprint for your own conduct.

THE THREAT/TEMPTATION/HOPE OF BECOMING PART OF IT

(Whichever thought process applies to you.)

My gut instinct is to say that if you're in this for fame, get out and don't be daft. Earning respect in one's field and yearning for the admiration of one's peers is understandable; everyone is seeking approval deep down, whether it be from society in general, a workplace or boss, even a loved one – it's all about approval and acceptance. But fame is a wild and sometimes vicious version of this, which seduces and corrodes simultaneously. Your drive should be about the craft, the journey, the lessons and the art – yes, I know, wanky wanky wank wank – but it's true. Unfortunately, we do currently live in a society that applauds quick fixes and celebrates minimal input and maximum output. Let the rewards you reap be justified because of the genuine talent and passion that earned them. It is up to the true artists among us to prove the Budgens to Broadway-type theories wrong, and to fly the flag of integrity long after this new wave of idiocy has faded.

Rant over. I felt it needed to be said! I've been really good at not mentioning art sucking, freak show reality sh… Over, rant over.

… Well, just one more thing:

'We must be careful that this fad is calmed or better still, stopped sooner rather than later; if we don't we may wake up one morning to find the Thames littered with lifeless young hopefuls and Sally Gunnell playing Medea at The National.'
Natalie Burt. Pissed and riled.

Ok, now the rant's over.

Be determined, be driven, be ambitious, be relentless, be focused but point all of that towards creating, making and doing not gaining, having and basking. Most importantly try and make sense of it for yourself. Any actor, (though there is more chance statistically of being bitten by a shark or hit by lightning) runs the risk of dipping a toe, falling into, or drowning in the sea of fame – every actor. Ask yourself what it's all really about and rationalise it for yourself. If you do it will make understanding the famous people you work with easier, and may therefore be a more rewarding experience; it may also equip you with the right state of mind to withstand the match should you ever find yourself in the game.

'Talent is god given. Be humble. Fame is man-given. Be grateful. Conceit is self-given. Be careful.'
John Woode

7. WORK IN VOICEOVERS AND COMMERCIALS

£. Fact.

Let's all be artistic, sure, we love the art; but also let's know when to forget the art and make some bloody money too! Both voiceovers and commercials (or adverts) are a fine way of earning a mint for doing next to nothing. Welcome to the wonderful world of advertising! And what's more, you have the skills that said advertisers need in order to make money – boom.

Let's start with voiceovers – they're a good idea. Not a straightforward one, granted, but a good one nevertheless.

One of the things I hear actors moan about most frequently is making money when they're not acting (and a lot of the time the money they're not making when they are acting!) and to be honest, whether said moan is a flippant whimper, a mumbled groan or quite an embarrassing snot-infused tantrum, they are, I feel, totally justified; it's a bitch. Jesting aside (not for long) it is a real problem, and one that has unfortunately dealt the fatal blow to many a promising career. Though I will be discussing budgeting properly in the next chapter and will be dealing with temp work in Chapter 9, the inevitability of being out of work and the certainty that your funds will suffer as a result are such relevant issues to an actor, I feel it necessary to mention these two little darling subjects now. We need to make money; but sadly, as actors this can be quite difficult and no matter how hard we try and whichever way round we look at the situation, we cannot escape the bare bones of our plight:

- Lack of flexible jobs that we are able to drop at a moment's notice.
- Lack of work in the country on the whole.
- Lack of jobs that can offer us enough work.
- Lack of jobs that pay enough for us to live on.
- Lack of jobs that don't cause us to hyperventilate at the thought of doing them.

Massive sigh, swig of gin (or tipple of choice) – stay with me.

Some actors (and parents of actors) are of the opinion that drama schools should teach other 'useful' skills alongside the craft of acting, such as typing, bookkeeping etc.; skills that will enable us to be employed when unemployed; skills that may also enable us to undertake slightly more challenging (lucrative) roles than the ones we seem doomed to accept, such as dishing out champagne to posh people or spraying perfume at 6 million randoms per day (yes, I have done both of these thrilling jobs). Whilst many think that it would be beneficial to have these 'extra'/'just in case' skills taught to actors during their training, in anticipation and preparation for the hard times ahead, some think of it as being defeatist; that it would take precious time away from learning the craft and practice of acting. I'm not sure what your opinion is on that? I can see both sides. I do not consider it necessarily 'negative' or 'defeatist' to pre-empt and prepare for turbulence; bouts of unemployment are an inevitability for most, no matter how temporary or infrequent those bouts end up being. However, I would have been bloody livid if drama school had said:

'Your voice class and Meyerhold workshop are cancelled this afternoon and being replaced by two BORING lectures titled "Typing for Idiots Stage 1" and "Filling out a CRB application in 3 Easy steps"'.

Joy. Who's Joy?… Regardless of who Joy is, I would have flipped, as I'm sure most of you would; I don't know about you but I went to drama school to do drama! And perhaps the more time taken away from nurturing the craft within us, the more they would be increasing the inevitability of unemployment? Maybe it isn't necessarily a drama school's responsibility to coach for hardship, and maybe the people who are realistic and pragmatic enough to think about back-up plans at such an exciting stage weren't born for a life of imagination and magic? All of that aside, I do still wonder whether more could be done to assist and encourage students not only to take responsibility in facing the hurdles ahead, but also to consider how they may jump them? If one is expecting a storm, one puts on a rain mac and decides how to sit it out, does one not? One has suddenly become rather posh in the rain. One is sorry. Enough. My point was anticipating a problem and forming possible strategies for survival before the problem arises – Obviously! (It's never a great joke if you have to explain it; same goes for analogies.) Basically, simply hoping for the best is a cack idea.

So, perhaps drama schools shouldn't be responsible for additional lessons in typing or mixing cement, fine; but what they could do is make damn sure you know how to thoroughly utilise the skills that they have armed you with. This could mean many things. The skills you acquire on a drama degree are relevant and useful in so many professions; simply by having the ability to be articulate and the confidence to be personable you are leagues ahead of most. Teaching, customer services, promotions etc. etc. are all areas that you will be welcomed into as an actor, because you are (supposedly) a people person. I despise the general public and yes, I have 'excellent customer service skills' on my temping CV. What did I say about telling the truth on your CV… I should have specified that I meant be totally honest on your acting CV and totally full of whatever horseshit will get you work on the other! Aside from the obvious attributes you may possess (most of which are really more to do with your personality than your profession), there is something else, something you are already a master of, and something that can be very profitable without diverting or distracting you from your career. Yep, your voice. As a trained actor you've spent hours and hours and HO-URS perfecting a skill, which unfortunately tends to be fairly dormant when you are out of work. Exercising your voice is important and by doing voiceovers not only do you accomplish that, and make money but it's also all in a way that does not encroach upon your career – Boo-yakka-shar. (Not sure that reads as well as it sounds.) This is a good thing, a very good thing; but more often than not, a good thing is not only difficult to obtain but also widely sought after; both of which are true in this case. But we're actors, right? We can cope with the odds being stacked against us?…

'He who dares Rodney, he who dares…'
Derek Trotter

It's sought after, obviously because all actors want flexible, non-committal work that provides maximum output for a minimal amount of input (big bucks for three hours' work) and it's no wonder it's difficult to obtain because the market is now massively overcrowded with people who have cottoned on to the fact! But, in true Natalie Burt style, I say that it is better to have tried and failed than never to have tried. Though I hate to fail so I very carefully pick the things I attempt… Did I just undo my own point? Whatever.

Let's get practical and strategic about this – how does one 'try' to get into voiceovers? As with most things (certainly with this industry) there is no 'one way', and there are certainly no secrets to spill that will lead you to a long and lucrative voiceover career (if I had those, I would damn well use them myself). However, I can aim to highlight a few ideas and dish out a few tips to assist you in your quest. There are things you can try which will hopefully lead to happy accidents occurring, but to me the main ingredient to eventual success is that P word again (no, not Prostitution)… Persistence.

Saying that, my entry to this lovely sideline was pretty much down to luck. An actor I had worked with twice recommended me for a VO job. So actually, it was luck but I had done the groundwork which provided that 'luck' – always making sure that I do my best to impress people in the hope that I will be remembered in a favourable light. And I was – score! Luck born from good work. Anyway, this actor's girlfriend was a producer – useful (a partner choice I intend to put into practice myself at some juncture). She needed a female voiceover artist without a 'voiceovery' tone for a job she was working on with a big mobile phone company (cue Natalie who had no experience in the voiceover industry whatsoever and used her cheeky regional tones to sound familiar and conversational). As a result of that gig going well I did more work with that particular client and more work with other clients belonging to her production company, which led me to my agent and the development of my repertoire and voicereel. I don't make millions, FAR from it and I am still very much on the bottom rung of the ladder, but my foot is in the door and that's perhaps half the battle?

So am I attempting to write a section on something that is essentially down to luck? Sort of, I mean you're lucky if the VO agent you approach happens, on that morning, to be in a gambling mood, but if you don't write the letter or send the email in the first place it won't matter what mood they're in, they won't be signing you! If you invest too much trust in Lady Luck then this whole book is a waste of time I guess (I've waited till Chapter 7 to test you on this one, in the hope that there's no way you'll still be standing in the shop which means you must have purchased the book – gotcha. What, you've got a receipt? Ah don't…) Luck, if it seems to be in your favour, is great, but if it's not it's all too easy to relinquish control and give up without taking responsibility for the fact that you are choosing to do so. I believe we can and should make our own luck as well as and in addition to the hand that either fate and/or other people deals us. Each opportunity feeds an achievement and each ounce of effort creates an opportunity; it's all interlinked which makes the source of any 'luck' mostly unidentifiable. If you want something you should do everything within your power to get it and the first step towards doing that is knowing how. So (short of accidentally impressing actors with producer girlfriends) what the hell are you meant to do to get your foot in this VO door? Good question. There is no one answer, but in a nutshell, these things…

PRODUCING A VOICEREEL & GETTING AN AGENT

…. Are a good place to start. Quite a major chicken and the egg situation here though! How do I get an agent without a voicereel, and how do I get samples of voice work or know what to include on a voicereel without an agent? Getting an agent is an utter cowbag, so we'll deal with that in a minute. As for voicereels, you don't necessarily need to include real voice work you've been paid for if you don't have any yet; mock-up samples should do the job of marketing your unique voice well enough at this stage, if they're done professionally. It's far easier to mock up a voice sample for a reel than it is to 'create' footage for a showreel! (And far more acceptable.)

VOICEREELS

Knowing your product

ASSESSING YOUR VOICE – If you are interested in doing voiceovers then start to listen to the ones around you. Assess the kinds of voices being used and what specific products they're being used for etc. Record your own voice and start to compare it to the ones you hear on the radio and on the television (in order to identify your personal tone and recognise styles, not in an attempt to mimic). Play around with different types of voiceovers and see what seems to suit/work. As well as 'sales' samples and adverts, give narration a go; anything David Attenborough-style will be a good exercise, and Channel 4 documentaries and television channel announcers are useful too. There's a vast and complex market out there; the more you experiment, the more versatile you will become (enabling you to get more work). Plus, the more informed you are about the market on the whole, the better your chances of breaking into it are.

VOCAL QUALITIES – Note the different vocal qualities that are used for different products and try to identify what yours are so that you (and your agent – current or future) can target areas of the industry that you may be best suited to. For example a very soft, warm and mature-sounding female might be used for baby products, whilst a northern, young and energetic male might be good for an alcohol or pie of some sort. Sweeping generalizations and massive stereotypes, yeah? Yeah, get used to it, and then use it! Remember that this is not about pigeon-holing you as an actor; it's about selling a product and using your tools to make that sale; so go with it and don't give a shit. This is one area where creative integrity doesn't exist, just do the job and make the dollar.

ACCENTS – As actors we are supposed to be able to do these, we apparently have a 'good ear' for them and regularly use them in our quest to portray other people. However, in this area of business there are so many actors/ artists to choose from that the current trend is simply to get exactly what they need instead of asking someone to pretend to be what they need, i.e. if they would like a soft Scottish voice for a salmon advert, why would they use a Liverpudlian pretending to be a Scott? The product people (technical term) have such a huge and varied pool from which to choose nowadays, that they can source exactly what is required without asking performers to be anything other than natural. The Liverpudlian might get the job over the Scott if it was an acting gig and he was the better actor for the part (one might hope) but with this, it's reading and using your voice – there are only a couple of shades of how good you can be at it. (There are quite a few shades of how bad though!) With this in mind it is important to identify your USPs (unique selling points, as mentioned earlier). If you have a regional accent, use it! Accents come in and out of fashion like stripes and denim on a catwalk, and though it is unlikely that a particular accent is ever especially 'out of fashion', trends do certainly seem to waft in and out of what is. For that reason, it is important that you know when yours is in so that you can take full advantage! You may need your accent abilities for some projects, I'm not saying you definitely won't, but most of the time it will be your 'natural voice' that they're interested in, where minimal tweaking of vocal qualities in accordance with the product you are selling/introducing/endorsing, will be required. I speak with a loose RP accent with southern vowels but can quickly revert back to a Midlands drawl (usually when drunk or angry), if needed. I am therefore quite lucky that I sort of have two native accents; and because of this I will always give them the option at the beginning of a session (I will obviously only do this if the accent hasn't already been stipulated by that point).

USING ALL OF THAT TO CREATE YOUR REEL – So, once you've done some research on what's around/what's being used within the market, and after you've assessed your own instrument and identified where your strengths may lie, then you can start to plan a reel that will show off and sell those USPs to agents and/or clients. You'll know, having done the research, what kind of voice you have and therefore what kind of ads you should perhaps target. For instance, if you have a lowish voice that is described as velvety or husky you may want to make sure that you have a chocolate or perfume ad on there – this kind of voice is linked to pleasure and sensuality and fits these products perfectly. If you have quite a strong and direct quality to your voice you may want to include something instructional or authoritative like a government tax ad or a drink awareness campaign? You get the gist, and once you've played around a bit you will have loads of ideas for what should go onto your reel in order to give the broadest example of your vocal capabilities. Obviously we can change accent and vocal qualities, we're actors, so do make sure that you include enough variety on your reel to show off versatility. But I would, certainly for now, focus on playing to your obvious strengths.

AGENTS

WHO TO TARGET – Have a look through *Contacts* and start to research a few agencies. On their websites you will be able to see their existing client list and you should also be able to listen to their clients reels and samples. On most websites you can refine your search, making it possible for you to choose 'female', 'northern', 'bubbly' etc. In doing this you will be able to see who they have on their books, who has what vocal attributes, and whether they might already have a client 'like' you. (Even if they have it may still be worth a shot, but it's good to be aware of anyway and to maybe even flag up to them that you are – whilst vehemently expressing how you think you can be 'interestingly different'.)

Recommendations are always useful, so do ask around and note down any agents that sound promising. If you hear a voice on the television that you recognize, it is easy to find out who an actor's voice over agent is usually by Googling them. The more you do this the more you will begin to form an idea of the main players, the medium agencies and the smaller companies operating within the industry; along with the differing levels of clients and varied types of projects they're involved with.

RATES – They will vary, but this is fairly standard:

Agent takes 12.5-15% of the fee paid on each job + VAT.

If an Agent suggests anything wildly different I would certainly query it and have someone at Equity or a fellow colleague look over your contract before signing with an agent. Some VO agents don't even ask you to sign a contract. This can sometimes work in your favour but I'm not sure where you stand legally on receiving payment if there's no contract so it's probably best to check with Equity if you're unsure.

NB. A voice over agent has NO RIGHTS over your acting work, or earnings that you receive from acting. You must make sure that this is clear if you sign any type of contract or agreement. Equally, your acting agent is separate from your voice work and won't profit from the voiceovers that you do (though it may be polite to let them know that you are signing with a voiceover agency; it's always good to keep them informed and some acting agencies have voice over departments too, which is ideal – two birds, one stone!) If you do have separate agents always make sure you inform your acting agent when you've been booked for a voiceover job; they need to know your availability and it is your responsibility to communicate with them about it.

CONTACTING THEM – Write to agents, and always enclose a CV, photograph and letter describing your experience and acting background. If you have a voicereel you can include this too. Alternatively you can email them and attach all of the above which is more cost-effective and less time-consuming, but may provide more opportunity for it to be slung into their computer's trash can without having been read? The method of contact is up to you, but do look on agency websites as they usually give some guidelines regarding their preferences when it comes to submissions. If they do, obey this wherever possible – if they've bothered to state what they want, you might as well get off on the right foot and follow their instructions!

Writing to voiceover agents will require patience and persistence. The competition is fierce and the door will not only be regularly slammed in our faces, but padlocked and bolted behind us too. There are a zillion other actors in the race, plus the non-actors whose main job is being a voiceover artist, not to mention the scores of celebs who 'voice' things for masses of dough. Forget all of them, sod all of them; keep practising, keep observing and learning about the market, and no matter how many times they slam that bastard door, stand your ground and keep knocking.

BEGINNERS TIPS

Warm up – Obvious right? Well, when you haven't got a voice department barking at you every seventh second it is all too easy to become lazy and complacent about such things. The microphone is like a magnifying glass for the voice; therefore you must warm up and be vocally healthy whenever you are required to use it professionally. By healthy I mean that you do not go out raving the night before, screaming above thumping music until the wee small hours; neither do you have a quiet night out but take part in a smokeathon. I have no doubt you'll be sensible, especially when you see how much money is at stake if you're not! Having said that, if 'gruff', 'husky', 'no middle or higher register' and 'slurred' are on the breakdown then go and have a ball the night before…

Always take a pencil – Seems terribly obvious, because it is, but still worth a mention. You may want to annotate your script, and the direction you receive can and will change from take to take, so maybe take a rubber along too! If at all possible it is rather useful to have seen the script before your session begins. Always ask your agent if you can see the material beforehand in order to prep it. This may or may not be possible but usually studios and production companies won't have a problem with it as it means less takes and less time (which means less money)! Of course if the script isn't written and/or ready, you will have to prep quickly and whilst being watched and that's fine too – you'll find your style.

Smile in your voice – This sounds a little daft, and I too thought 'get a life' when I was advised to do it, but my god it works. Physically smiling as you speak does something wonderful to your voice; it lightens it, lifts it, ensures that you sound engaged with the subject you're speaking about and makes it easy for the listener to believe you (which is obviously important with sales, but is vital across the board). Plus, the more times you do a take you will perhaps (quite unintentionally, and only marginally) lose interest or become frustrated; this will be heard in your voice and can be prevented by using this simple technique. (You'll look like some insane Butlins rep, but you should sound great!)

Translating direction – The 'directors' you will encounter in this area of the business are more likely to have the actual job title of production assistant or marketing assistant etc. They are not 'directors' (as we understand the term) and we should not expect them to be nor need them to be. These jobs will not be artistically complex. The people in charge (either production people, marketing teams or product developers) will have a vision for what they want and it is your function to realise that for them. The scripts you will receive will be fairly self-explanatory (zero subtext!) and should be approached as such. I always ask a lot about the product/company/campaign as soon as I meet the contact just before I step into the booth. I listen carefully to what they say, how they talk about the product, whilst taking careful note of the vibe they give out; this is them selling the idea or concept to me, which I can then utilize when I sell it back to them during the session. When giving direction they won't speak in a language that you are used to, they will say things like 'Yeah, I liked it, but that bit felt... I dunno... not quite, right...' You must be highly observant about what it is that you deliver on any given take, jotting down notes if this helps; that way you can suggest what it is you've presented and give contrasting alternatives for the next take. Notes from them may include very specific technical issues such as downward inflections, pauses in between points, emphasis choices and word pronunciations; they might also attempt to analyse a feeling or certain emotion you were focusing on by expressing how it made them feel. Learn to be clinical rather than artistic here. We are not searching the depths of our souls; we're selling and obeying – so take the pressure off yourself and resist the temptation to be an arty farty tit.

Taking control – I've sort of already touched on this in the previous paragraph but to expand slightly, you must be interested in their product from the off as not only will your interest generate conversation about the product (providing you with information and clues) but also your intrigue will enthuse the team around you in regards to their product, and ultimately in you as a professional – win, win! Ask questions and get involved in their world for the short period of the time that you are in it; it will benefit everyone, especially you.

When I say take control, I don't mean start dictating and bossing around, of course not (you are not in charge, you are hired to execute what is required of you) but you do have a job to do and you are the professional they've hired to do it, therefore there is nothing wrong with being assertive in the way that you work. This means that if you require water and haven't brought or been offered any, ask for some, if you are unsure of any pronunciations, check with them, if something doesn't read right, have a conversation about it. Being in control and assertive makes you seem professional and gives off the impression that you give a shit whether the end result from the session is a success or not.

Become acquainted with your style and way of working – Be aware of how you like to work best and I guarantee that they will accommodate and do whatever is required (within reason) to get the job done quickly and effectively – these are busy business people who have deadlines and bosses to contend with remember. Having said that, don't be rushed if they are a bit manic or pressed for time! Make sure you are happy with what you are producing and query anything that you are unsure about – It's your voice attached to it at the end of the day.

I have formed my own ways of working the more experiences I've had. I always ask to read through the text quietly on my own before the levels are tested, which gives me an opportunity to make some notes and to become familiar with the text, its direction and its journey before I am 'put on the spot' so to speak. I also insist on having a hard copy of the script instead of reading from a screen so that I can make notes. When I make mistakes I don't break the take; instead I take a second of silence (to possibly swear) and then start again from either the start of the paragraph, section or sentence without making a song or dance about it. The technician soon grasps that this is how I do things and they also understand that this way they have more options when editing.

And so, there you have it. It is a hard game to get into, a game that requires the player to be persistent and able to ignore the word 'no'. But really how does this differ from the acting game? We should have a separate degree in laughing at dead ends, right? I take the disappointment and rejection from acting in my stride, as much as I can, but opening yourself up to take it from yet another source is not an altogether easy thing to do and one that should be done with care. With this in mind you must try to cleverly time when you make lunges, ensuring that your heart and mind are in a resilient enough place to stay strong when the inevitable 'nos' do start rolling in. Remember that this is a kind of lottery where tens of thousands of people have tickets and never win. But also remember that only the ones who invest in the ticket in the first place stand any chance of winning; you have to be in it to win it.

Once you're in, enjoy how it differs from the acting world, making sure you're never complacent about it. I enjoy the isolation of being in a booth and the freedom that not being looked at gives me. I also find it interesting and challenging using only my voice to persuade and sell; a lesson that has further informed the way I am able to use my voice in performance. And apart from anything, you are in effect attending a sort of vocal gym every time you do a voiceover, which is of course beneficial in regards to your actual career. Of course we all wake up an hour early every morning to spout six sonnets, do three tongue twisters, two heavenly waters and some sirens

OBVIOUSLY…but, you know, on the days when you forget, a voiceover's just as good…and it pays the bills!!!! Thumbs up and many thanks.

'Sorry? There's another way to make some serious dollar, whilst using my skills as a performer, that won't interfere with my career as an actor?'

'Yep.'

'How lovely. Is there a downside?'

'Well, you'll probably feel like an absolute tit doing it.'

'Ah. Ok… Sod it, if it's good pay I can feel like a tit.'

'Great, let's talk about it.'

COMMERCIALS/ADVERTS

Times have certainly changed. Back in the day adverts were sneered at by the artistic world, and an actor was seen to be 'lowering themselves' by appearing in one. Nowadays, every actor's unashamedly (and rightly so) an opportunist. We slave away for shit pay, we endure weeks and months of unemployment and poverty forces us to consume way more cuppa soup than is recommended. Is it any wonder that actors seek ways to bump up their earnings?

Another difference between adverts gone by and the trend today is that adverts are simply…well, cooler now. I think Budweis-eeeeeeeeeeeeeeer was definitely a turning point for the 'cool' ad, do you remember that?! Everyone above 20 remembers that, surely! Nowadays the likes of Virgin and Ikea, and obviously perfume and car ads fly the flag of 'cool' in the ad world. Ads are funnier too – comedy has become the most powerful way to sell (next to sex, but I think that's kind of lost its shine these days) and marketers using the right people to achieve this helps enormously – Stephen Merchant and Barclays (only someone that funny could make us smile at an advert for a bloody bank in this economic climate), Paul Whitehouse and Aviva (I have absolutely no interest in the product but I watch the ad in its entirety just to catch a glimpse of someone who should be on our screens more), Dawn French with various chocolate ads, and the wonderful Jennifer Saunders somehow making us chuckle about a chocolate-flavoured spreadable cheese. Even Specsavers and WKD ads are better than a lot of the comedy that's commissioned. Ads now, seem to be either cool, funny or taking the piss out of themselves for being extremely irritating – My niece recently wandered into the lounge and said to her mum (Midlands accent):

'I hate that Barry Scott'.

Who knew that the Cillit Bang advert is so annoying that it could piss off a three-year-old. If they don't get rid of the Go Compare dude and the Safestyle UK wanker soon she'll end up in therapy.

But how is all this relevant to us? It's relevant not because celebrities are being used to endorse products (this has happened since television began so we should get over it), but because the ads are better i.e. cooler and funnier, acting in an advert is no longer some embarrassing money-making venture that hopefully people forget about quickly, no, instead they're actual showcasing opportunities; a chance for exposure and to demonstrate acting and sometimes comic ability – great! Naturally, if you do a 'Bloated? Constipated?' type ad or anything involving tampons, Durex or STDs then you will obviously and quite rightly be ridiculed for it until the end of time. However, before the end of time you will be able to skip past your piss-taking mates (who are crying over a payday loan website) on the way to buy diamonds and cars.

MINDSET

I cannot tell you how to get a job in a commercial. Mainly because I never have!

My explanation of why I've never done an advert may therefore serve well as some 'What Not To Do' guide?! It is a skill outside of our skillset and there is a knack to auditioning for them that some people master and others don't. On top of that, there is a shitload of luck and peculiar subjectivity thrown into the mix as well. I believe that adverts and advert castings are mainly about mindset and attitude. I certainly was, and probably still am, a creative snob. If the script interests and excites me then I will open my heart and mind to it unconditionally and without hesitation. However, if the script bores, embarrasses, annoys or ridicules me then I cannot, or possibly *will* not play ball. It is not surprising then that I have not been given a commercial; Shakespeare it ain't. To be fair, I haven't been up for many commercials over the years and I got close a couple of times. I was 'pencilled' for an MFI ad once. 'Pencilled' is a delightful phrase you'll hear, which means they've pretty much booked you but you have no idea whether that booking will go ahead. IDEAL! Not. As you may be able to gather, I had a three ad deal, probably to the value of about £12,000 wafted in front of my face and then given to someone else. Nobody said this money-making venture was fair! I'll tell you the story of that audition in the next section. It was…interesting.

I am probably much more able to laugh at the situation now than I was when I was younger and desperate for recognition as a 'real actress' – whatever the fuck that is, Kerry Katona is apparently one of those now according to a newspaper report I read recently. I might adopt her attitude and decide tomorrow that I'd like to be an astronaut. Sorry, that had jack shit to do with this but it needed saying.

I play lower status quite easily on stage but I struggle with it somewhat off stage, which is not terribly great for commercial castings! You are one of many people possibly capable of appearing in a commercial; those people will consist of actors, models and dancers – ERGO THIS IS NOT ABOUT WINNING OSCARS. It's the same idea as the voiceovers, it's about hearing what they want, putting your artistic instincts aside and delivering what they've asked for effectively and immediately – whilst having (or making a damn good job of making it look like you're having) 'fun'. Being enthusiastic, open, willing, patient and uninhibited are the key factors you need when taking part in a commercial casting. Skepticism, a dark sense of humour, and an intolerance of jobsworths and darlings ain't gonna get results – hence why I've probably never managed it! Many, many actors thrive on pleasing and can easily leave their dignity at the door. (These are the people with mortgages and motor vehicles!) You must be able to take the whole experience with a pinch of salt, ignore that there are people making judgments (and that there is a camera recording the ordeal, providing evidence of what a twat you were made to look for all eternity). I'm partly joking of course; the money you get for a commercial will more than compensate for any loss of respect or dignity in a casting suite, and don't forget that the money earned will obviously aid your acting career and take the pressure off of you during the quiet times; it comes down to the sacrifices we, as individuals, are willing and able to make. Though I jest about my nausea regarding commercial castings, when I was faced with one I always did my damnedest to hide my discomfort and dealt with the task at hand, as we all must. Don't take it personally and certainly don't take it professionally! It does not mean that you cannot act if you do not get commercials, it does not mean that you can act if you do; it doesn't mean that you're too fat or thin or tall or ginger; it means you didn't fit the product, the mood, the style, the costume! There are a billion reasons someone else gets a commercial instead of you and attempting to guess which reason it was is tiresome and pointless. This is a 'throw enough shit at a wall and some will stick' kind of a deal; try to be as flippant with getting them and going for them as they are with giving them to you. Commercials are a bonus, not a necessity.

AUDITIONS

So we've talked about mindset. To be honest, that is a section in which I had more to talk about than this one. We've already discussed earlier in the book about not necessarily being able to predict what will happen during an audition and that preparation is the key to coping with that. However, huh, that ain't the story here. With commercial castings there is usually no preparation to do or any hint of what might be expected of you; reacting in the moment, improvising well and going with the insanity you are faced with is all you can do. I intend to be in the hiccupping/giggly stages of intoxication if I ever get another commercial casting – I think I'd be much more successful! This is what I meant by it being a skill, a knack; tapping into what it is that they want (despite the nonsensical notes they've given) and attacking what you do with conviction and confidence. This is quite literally all you can do. Don't get bogged down with detail, or hung up on realism, just try to get a sense of the product and attempt to fit it!

Obviously if you are told before an audition what the product is then you may want to do a little research to try and find out what tone they usually go for; but don't be surprised if that has little to no relevance when you walk into the room as most marketing campaigns happen because of a 'change of direction' or a 'rebrand'. So do what you can, but unless you're asked to prepare I certainly wouldn't cancel any plans to sit on YouTube sifting through ads all night if I were you!

Basic points to remember:

- Always be prompt.
- Always know who you're meeting and what for.
- Dress accordingly (if you have been given a clue).
- Have your agent's number, your height, weight, dress size, shoe size, bra size, hat size to hand if possible so that you can fill out the form they will inevitably give you easily and quickly.
- Understand what doing your 'profile' is. (Looking to camera, pause, then looking to your right, pause, then looking to your left, pause, then back to the camera.)
- Don't be thrown by any bitchiness/weirdness/awkwardness in the waiting room – you're all in the same boat. I tend to make conversation whether the other people want to or not; what are they doing 'getting into character?' I think not.
- Turn off your phone.
- Smile more than usual.
- If you're drunk have a mint so they can't smell it.

If there any other secrets to commercial stardom, I am not aware of them. Now for storytime:

The MFI ad. MY. GOD. For this particular audition we were recalled in pairs. Yep, that's recalled for an ADVERT. Fine. I was 22 and it didn't occur to me to care much at the time, I was just excited that somebody liked me (Freud would have a field day with that one). During the recall we were given this note:

'So, young couple, new relationship, horny. When we shout "action" we want you to get it on. Just go for it.'

I sheepishly grinned at the complete stranger who was about to learn what I taste like and the room fell silent in preparation for the commencement of the scene. Just before action, as a million and one things flew through my mind, I opened my mouth and as my voice did that embarrassing wobbly thing I said:

'Tell me why again?' Silence. 'It's fine, it's absolutely fine, I've no problem…"getting it on"…erm, I just wondered *why*.'

The director answered, as if justification and motivation were obscenely pointless:

'Because they're shopping in MFI and then they fancy a fuck.'

After a second I nodded, feigning complete satisfaction with his answer.

'Ah. Great, thought so. Right, here goes. I'm ready when you are, buckle up.'

Action was called and I leaped onto the poor, rather genteel actor opposite me, and proceeded to dry hump him until the director shouted 'Cut!'

The director was happy, the cameraman was somewhere between pleased and satisfied (if you get my drift), the poor actor panted in shock and I was more than a little horrified. Needless to say, I was *pencilled* for that gig but never did the job; which a more sensitive person than myself might assume to mean that my dry humping was good, but not good enough. Shame.

There is a really brilliant sketch by Cardinal Burns on YouTube called 'Fiery Hawk', but it's also known as 'The Audition'. It so beautifully encapsulates the eagerness of actors and the ridiculousness of the casting situation that after you've watched it you won't know whether to laugh or kill yourself. The former is advised.

PLUSES AND PITFALLS

We've kind of covered the pitfalls here but the one I haven't mentioned is becoming a commercial casting regular. Am I going to suggest that repeatedly being given the opportunity to make lots of cash is bad? No, in fact you probably need to be seen for about twenty to get one. However, if you regularly do commercials there are two dangers. One is that you will become recognisable as an advert face; though the exposure is good, it is the last area that you want to be known for (in my opinion). And though this will provide many lovely cheques, it may also limit what else you are seen for. It's worth also bearing in mind that a string of adverts can't continue for long as marketing people won't want the faces of other brands to be theirs. One of the pluses that can come from this of course, which seems to be quite a trend right now, is repeat casting with a single brand. Look at how long the Adam & June campaign ran for BT using those same two actors, look how well the Malteser girls and the Boots girls have done out of the ongoing storyline they were given. It's nice to see normal everyday actors being used to endorse products because the actor's characterization and the team's storylines have worked well together. So this is an exception to the 'don't do too many ads' suggestion!

The second danger to doing loads of ads is that your agent will possibly, like a footballer's wife, become accustomed to the regular deposits of cash and see you more as a profit provider than a skilled professional. Some actors I know are only put up for commercials – this is not what we want. Whilst these can be dangers, they are certainly not major deterrents; being aware of them is all that is required and using the same level of self-awareness and objectivity as you're using for your career on the whole is what is recommended.

A FINAL NOTE

Apart from being about minimum input and maximum output (which, as a side line, is what we're all after to accompany the exhaustiveness of trying to be an actor), the actual 'doing' of voiceovers and commercials can be a fun experience. For a commercial you may be whisked away to some exotic location, shoved in a 5* hotel and paid well for the privilege. You may also meet some really interesting crew; camera people and ADs who are honing their skills and simultaneously trying to make ends meet just as you are. And though voiceovers are more likely to be in Soho rather than Shanghai, you will be paid well and the overall experience is likely to be brief but pleasing.

Give yourself a break and take the pressure off yourself; leave pompousness for the RSC and being a diva for when you get to Hollywood. Now is the time to make money where you can, to laugh at every opportunity and above all to remember why on earth it is that we put ourselves through this shit!

8. FINANCE

Ugh, bloody hell, I hear ya.

YOUR FINANCES

How can it be that there is no real preparation during training for the financial challenges and hardship that an actor stands to face during their career?

Sure, snide comments and bitter anecdotes regarding poverty are in abundance; tales of woe billow out of us all (usually as a result of copious amounts of vodka) accomplishing nothing but some sort of chorus of injustice for the jobbing actor, like there's camaraderie to be found in our collective ignorance and acceptance? I think a big part of why many actors feel this sense of injustice has far more to do with not feeling ready or able to deal with the hardship, rather than the basic fact that it's happening; if there's one thing we cannot escape as students it's being told of the possibility of unemployment and poverty (statistics and clichés are not in short supply) but why then, if it's so inevitable, so expected, aren't we equipped with the knowledge and skills to cope with it? In my view feeling jaded and let down by an institution that grooms and polishes its products, only to send over three quarters of them out like lambs to the slaughter, is a fair complaint. Sadly, what then happens is that the cycle of bitterness continues through the generations and becomes the accepted trend – 'Actors are poor a lot of the time and artistic types know nothing about finance and are indifferent to business'… Surely there's a more constructive and pragmatic way to deal with such inevitability? Surely in this day, age and economic climate we can give ourselves a little more credit than being luvvies who get high on art? In my opinion, it's time to break this cycle; victims we are not.

I dread to think how many promising careers have crumbled under the pressure of earning money and managing debt; how many promising careers have dissolved as a result of the actor not being equipped with the knowledge and foresight to combat financial turbulence. This subject, if ignored or overlooked, ends careers; it's as simple, as dramatic and as tragic as that. Today's young actor should be encouraged to be an entrepreneur as well as an artist; managing financial affairs, creating profitable opportunities and making choices that will help to sustain a fruitful business, all of which should coincide and work in harmony with their artistry.

Obviously every single one of you will have had very different experiences with money throughout your lives so far, so instead of attempting to make this relevant to all I have focused on the scenarios that will need most attention, or those which I consider are most likely to be yours at this present time. If you're anything like I was you may be graduating (or starting your professional life) not only penniless but with a hefty suitcase full of debt in your hand. I was fortunate that I was awarded a scholarship for drama school (I couldn't have gone otherwise) but still, the overdraft, credit card and student loan were enough to make starting out as a professional actor bloody hard; so hard that I am still paying for it now, quite literally. So we'll talk about debt. Many of you may not have debt issues, but assistance with managing everyday finances and some clarity on the finer details of being self-employed may be useful; so we'll also talk about budgeting and accountancy too. As an actor (whether debt is an issue for you or not), managing and living on a turbulent income is no easy task. No one expects you to be naturally 'in the know', or vastly interested in being so for that matter! But, if you can manage to stay awake for the next few pages (I'll try to keep it brief), I think you'll be pleased that you did.

The unpredictability of your financial situation can affect your entire life; where you go, who you meet, what you eat, what you wear, what you experience; and ultimately the control, ability and freedom to choose all, any or none of those things. We work in a profession of extremes; sometimes you will feel as if you've won the lottery and other times Supernoodles will become your Mon-Fri delicacy. Those lottery numbers may take a lifetime to come up, and possibly never will (to an extent that *buys* the boat instead of teasingly rocking it). Most of us play this lottery by default rather than by design, as it is part and parcel of the job we love, and whilst as a breed we admirably pursue our passion in the face of this uncertainty, we must do ourselves a favour by focusing on how to survive in the meantime. This immense unpredictability means that we can never get particularly 'used' to one way of living, meaning that we must try to be careful and considered with what we spend without becoming a slave to what we 'shouldn't' and 'cannot' have and do. Being adaptable, smart and realistic are the ways to achieve this.

Not only is learning how to live and function within ever-changing parameters important, so is striking a good balance between controlling your finances and being careful not to let those finances dictate (too strongly) the creative path you build for yourself. Especially in the early days I believe that you should be (and hope that you are) making decisions mainly based upon your artistic ambitions and not much else – because now is the time, before commitments and responsibilities come into play, for you to be selfish and insular about your artistic goals. By laying these foundations hopefully it will lead to greater artistic achievement and eventually perhaps, some form of financial reward too. Different things drive different people; some live solely for their art and are content with the poverty and limitations that may come with it, some find a balance of art and monetary reward, taking different jobs for different reasons, and others become understandably seduced by (sometimes trapped in) the more lucrative end of things. There is no judgment here as to which one(s) you choose, or find yourself in; realistically, life ain't a fairytale and money makes the world go around. You must work out what it is that you want, how you think you might get it, how you're going to fund doing so, and what you're willing to endure along the way in order to dictate (as much as possible) the pattern of your own fate. Sticking to any sort of 'plan' in our industry is fairly impossible but look to any warfare throughout history – launching an attack without an initial strategy is basically suicide. Did I just make a likeness between the acting profession and war? Yep, on purpose.

I think it's a fair and simple observation that a jobbing actor who is in and out of work and whose wages vary from job to job, can't/shouldn't overspend grotesquely during the infrequent phases of affluence.

One must allow for treats of course but never forget that a bleak time could be just around the corner (cheery). If you have the luxury of being able to save or keep money aside from a lucrative job, or inheritance or whatever, then do it, as this can be an invaluable back up for you when you don't get a job, or when someone fails to pay you on time, or if your laptop/car/leg breaks. The crippling panic when you have NO money is not a good state of mind when you are auditioning and trying to impress people, believe me, and so always try to plan ahead a little. If at all possible.

A float is obviously one of the best ways of planning ahead but I used the word 'luxury' earlier because I know that most of you, (especially those of you who have just been through years of student life), will not have one at your disposal. Most of you will be living month-to-month or even week-to-week and as freelancing means gaps in earnings, most pay from a job will be quickly used to settle debts that you incurred during the quiet time leading up to the job. I know, it's a vicious cycle and this may unfortunately be your reality for a while, but remember that with each low-pay/no-pay job or each audition you do well in, you are investing in your artistic future and laying those foundations so that at some point or another chunks of money will come along, regularly enough to either momentarily or (fingers crossed) permanently break the cycle. However, in the present tense, in the early days, there is no way of knowing how long the cycle may last for you; it is therefore so important that when you do make money you are clever with it.

Thinking ahead and preparing for the array of eventualities you face is imperative, but having said that so is rewarding your damn self every once in a while! (Splash out on a ridiculously expensive new pair of shoes, but perhaps resist the second pair and put that chunk into a savings account instead – boring, but effective). If you are in the cycle then the likelihood is that you will need to use whatever is in the float soon after having saved it, but nevertheless it will have served its purpose in preventing you from being up shit creek and should provide you with the incentive to repeat the exercise when you are next able. By looking after our finances we are prolonging our artistic shelf life – passion for art cannot pay the bills, and not being able to pay the bills soon starts to kill the passion.

What's that you're screaming at me?...

> 'How the hell am I meant to manage my money if I don't fucking have any?'

Ah, yes, well this is quite a pickle. Don't for a moment think that I am not aware that this is a problem, or that I have not yelled that very sentence out myself on many a rent day. It's tough and no matter what you do hard times are a-coming! Being on a limited budget for unpredictable amounts of time, with differing amounts coming in and out and no guarantee of receiving payments when they are expected is a bitch, we can all agree on that; it is tiring, demeaning, soul-destroying and a lot of the time nigh on impossible to prevent, but there are ways to make it easier and I intend to highlight them as best I can within this section. It's about prevention instead of damage control, making it a little easier before it gets too hard.

In offering this advice I am not suggesting that you are crap with or clueless about money, far from it. In a way, above all, I intend for this chapter to reassure you that you are not alone. Most actors suffer in this area (continuously and intermittently) and if you find yourself in a bad situation, whether getting there has been beyond your control or because of bad judgment, know that self-flagellation is not constructive; it can make you ill and if you're ill you're no use to anyone. By reading this chapter and taking responsibility for your affairs you are taking a very important step towards being serious about the quality and longevity of your career. So, you've earned yourself a wee break before we move on to this cowbag... (Go and make a cup of tea/stiff whiskey...)

MANAGING DEBT

STUDENT LOANS – The amounts borrowed vary (as do the ways in which they are spent!) Whatever your circumstances this is a loan you are entitled to if you wish to study at a place of further education, and the payback system is the same for all who are self-employed as you are/will be – (we'll cover registering as such later). A student loan is 'income contingent', so how much you repay depends on what you earn, not how much you borrowed.

Self-employed loan repayments are assessed on your profit (after expenses) as opposed to overall income, as with those who are employed. Once you register self-employed you will be required to pay back this loan when your income (your profit, after expenses) exceeds £15,795 per year – if you started your course before 1st September 2012 – or £21,000 per year – if you started it after 1st September 2012. When your income does exceed that amount you will be required to make payments that reflect your earnings at that time – at the minute repayments are 9% of anything you earn over the figure mentioned above. If your income drops below this amount repayments will stop. Needless to say, most actors don't need to worry too much about paying it back for a while after graduation unless you get a whacker of a job straight out of drama school!

Some good news – I heard that apparently if you die or if you leave the country for a silly amount of years (like, your whole life), then you become exempt from paying back the loan… SCORE! It'll only cost you your life or never seeing your family again… As an alternative to those sterling solutions, it might be best for now to keep the balance reminder letters in a little pile somewhere out of sight and only acknowledge repaying it when you have to/ are able to. Interest is charged on a student loan (don't even get me started) so, if you earn a mint it may be worth chipping away at the old loan asap.

More info on student loans here:

http://www.direct.gov.uk/prod_consum_dg/groups/
dg_digitalassets/@dg/@en/@educ/documents/digitalasset/
dg_200475.pdf

http://www.studentloanrepayment.co.uk

https://www.gov.uk/student-finance

OVERDRAFTS – The most cost-effective form of financial 'help' (apart from rich relatives and sugar daddies that is). These can vary from £200 – £5,000 depending on your credit rating and the bank's policies and services. As a student you will get a certain amount of time in the overdraft that is interest free and then the longer you are in that overdraft, the more charges may be applied. The idea is to use the facility when you are a student (to replace income) or in periods of hardship when you have graduated with a view to then pay your way out of it when you are able, either gradually or in a lump sum. Of course this is far easier to do if you graduate from a uni course, go into a well-paid full-time job and can set aside money from your set income each month in order to do this; not so easy if your situation is completely unpredictable like ours. The overdraft can become the float I mentioned earlier and you will probably end up 'living in it', its function being a sort of safety net. (However most students leaving further education will have already had to max this facility so an overdraft can feel more like a trap than a net!)

Being stuck in an overdraft isn't a nice feeling, but in my opinion it is the lesser of quite a few evils. Only concern yourself with it when you find your professional and financial feet or when you come into a significant enough amount of money to make a dent in it. If this happens and you are able to pay it (or a chunk of it) off, you can then request that the overdraft facility be reduced, resulting (hopefully) in you eventually being in and staying in credit. However, even if you are in credit and aren't in your overdraft, I would (if you can be disciplined with 'available funds') keep the facility for a while, just to act as an emergency float in times of need. If your overdraft is your only debt you could make payments into it from another account, and reduce it gradually without giving up the safety net. Depends on how debt-conscious you are!

CREDIT CARDS – These are the actual spawn of Satan! Admittedly they are 'useful' and can get us out of some serious scrapes, but they can also seduce us into thinking that we have more money than we actually do (later biting us on the ass with interest and charges). If you can get a credit card with an interest-free period of time attached then great, but be aware that you must make full payment within the specified time in order to avoid obnoxious charges. ALWAYS check what the % APR is (interest rate you'll be charged) before applying for a card, and shop around for the lowest percentage over the longest amount of time. If you haven't managed to pay back the amount during the months of free credit you were given then you will be slammed with an APR which could make your monthly payments much higher or mean that you are no longer reducing the balance but simply paying off the interest.

Gloomy as hell right?! Of course the ideal answer is not to have a credit card if you can help it! (Or at least not until you are in a more stable situation.) But sadly, ideal goes out of the window when you're brassic! So, if you must have a credit card, do try and keep it for emergencies only, make regular payments or pay it off in full as soon as you are able (before racking up a balance that you cannot manage). Also be careful not to miss credit card payments, as this will affect your credit rating.

PAWNING/SELLING ITEMS – This seems a rather old fashioned, extreme course of action in a day and age where credit is available to all and sundry, but it's still an option. Exhaust every other possibility before you sell or pawn something of sentimental value, you will torment yourself if not, and living with regret is a horrible feeling.

If you are looking to sell household goods, electrical goods etc. then eBay and Gumtree are adequate enough places to do so, but for god sake don't invite complete strangers to your address without having someone at home with you and always demand payment up front. Please, please beware that anyone on Gumtree requesting that you transfer or pay funds to them via Western Union is likely to be a thieving lowlife. There are many scams and shitheads out there, so keep your wits about you. It's cynical not to trust, I know, but it's necessary I'm afraid – look at Little Red Riding Hood, she got it wrong didn't she…

If you are selling jewellery then shop around before doing so. Jewelers, (especially predatory ones in London) will try and pay as little as they possibly can in order to make the highest profit possible (obviously) so if you aren't going to have your items valued, then at least test the fence with a few jewelers to see if what they all offer is similar before settling on a price – if you don't you might be missing out on quite a significant amount of dosh!

NEXT DAY/PAYDAY LOANS – Be careful. I think that's the only way to start this section. There are many companies out there whose business it is to make money out of the venerable. So, if you are in trouble, i.e. an unexpected bill has come in or you haven't received payment for something and your rent is due and you've exhausted every other possibility then shop around for a payday type loan to tide you over. But be aware that you will be paying back about 50% of what was lent **on top** of the initial amount you borrowed. It is quick and easy and often online (so you don't have to go through the humiliation of explaining yourself to a judgmental telephonist), but if there is any other way to borrow I'd do it; the charges are too high and we usually don't know when our next 'payday' is anyway so paying it back can be problematic.

PREVENTING FURTHER DEBT

Don't be afraid to admit to companies and banks that you are having trouble paying money back. It will be far worse if you keep quiet, ignore the phone and don't open the post – plus if you do that you simply look irresponsible and untrustworthy to lenders, and you may incur charges and affect your credit rating. As devastating and humiliating as it can be to admit to a complete stranger who doesn't give a toss about you that you are struggling, you have to muster the strength as it is the only way out; the debt problem will only grow if it is not addressed. There may be payment plans, payment holidays or debt management strategies in place to help you tackle the issue. If you don't ask, you won't get.

When organising and agreeing to new credit/loans etc., remember that lenders make money out of people's inability to meet the payments they've agreed to, so if it seems easy to get credit it is probably because it will eventually be a win-win situation for them and not you! Think ahead when agreeing to any kind of monthly payments. Will you be able to make them in six months? The likelihood is that you won't know, so always err on the side of caution if you can, and only agree to realistically manageable amounts (if the monthly payment is some sort of subscription then make sure that you can cancel it whenever you may need to).

Be careful not to pile up debt, justifying it with a 'when I make it' attitude, because you will be slightly buggered if you don't 'make it'! (Whatever the hell 'make it' means!) You must attempt to live within your means, and I know that this can be very difficult when your 'means' are ever-changing and sometimes fairly non-existent. The only way to keep a handle on everything is to keep a close eye on your finances, to readapt your budget to fit your circumstances as they change, always attempting to pre-empt when those changes may occur and insuring yourself against the unpredictability as best you can.

BUDGETING

Is a bitch and a ball ache but a necessity if we are to prosper in a financially challenging industry. I think one of the best ways to do this is to have two bank accounts, one for income and one for payments (or outgoings). If you have the accounts with the same bank you will be able to transfer money quickly and easily online should you need to and you can keep a close eye on both at the same time. The advantage of doing this is that you will calculate an exact figure that your predictable outgoings come to (by predictable outgoings I mean your rent, mobile phone bill, utility bills etc.) You will also know what dates they are all due on and can organise direct debits to be staggered throughout the month or taken altogether, depending on your preference. Each month you could transfer the required lump sum from your income account to cover all of the outgoings coming out of your other account, leaving the income account clearly showing what you have left to 'play' with or save for the rest of the month or however long. Not only will this hopefully prevent you from running out of money to eat and travel, it will also give you a good understanding of how much you have to earn in order to cover all bases. The common problem here of course, will be that you don't have enough income arriving into your account to ensure that this plan is as bloody ideal as it sounds! I know. Freelance work is tiresomely turbulent and the economic climate certainly isn't helping the temping situation we intermittently find ourselves in. I won't talk too much about temp work as we'll cover that in Chapter 9 but however you are comfortable living, whether lavishly or sparingly, if you budget you will immediately know the least amount that you have to make every month and the most that you are able to splash. This is the situation we're in, and we have to face it, evaluate it and deal with it as best as we can. Trust me, there is nothing more pointless and counterproductive than running away from or ignoring financial hardship; it will not simply go away, it will catch up with you and running from it is actually more stressful than facing it.

'Need', as I've mentioned, will become an overused word for you if you are living hand to mouth; do I need that new jacket? Do I need to go to the hairdressers? Do I need to eat? You will soon become a professional prioritiser! (That's not a word...) Sometimes we should be sensible and calculated and sometimes we all *need* to throw caution to the wind and have a nonsensical blow out! Do your sums, assess your own situation and judge when you can be/should be which. No one wants to have to penny pinch – and when we have no choice but to scrimp the guilt that accompanies buying or paying for anything contaminates almost everything we do, which is desperately difficult to live with.

Instead of berating yourself, every time a bill comes in that you're going to struggle to pay, why not remind yourself that you are in a tiny minority of people who are attempting to realise their ambition; you have abandoned the norm and the easy route and must take pride in that everyday. A healthy attitude will make you strong enough to face the financial problems you'll encounter, and make it far more likely that you will shine professionally when you're required to – thus, hopefully ending the financial plight, for a while at least! For most, acting work is a respite rather than a solution – but for god sake enjoy that respite and use it to recuperate; it's the only way to make it through the next drought.

Despite all of this doom and gloom make sure that you do have fun when you can; you must allow yourself this, however tight the budget belt is. There are many ways to have cheap fun and as I've said, the great thing about having mates in the same industry is that most of you will be in the same boat! (See Chapter 12 for where to find cheap ale.)

As well as your domestic finances you have your financial obligation to the government and to the country; this comes in the wonderful form of TAX! Almost every young actor I've spoken to seems clueless and petrified about the subject (if they're awake long enough to finish their sentence). We have two main problems: firstly, this country caters better for people who are PAYE rather than self-employed, and secondly that a self-employed person's tax details are so unique to them that advice and education regarding the subject are difficult to provide without being unhelpfully generic.

With this in mind, I have borrowed the mind of a lovely young accountant at MGM Accountancy to answer the core questions surrounding the area of tax as a self-employed actor.

A CONVERSATION
WITH ACCOUNTANT MARK LIVERMORE

(MGM Accountants)

MGM are not my accountants but I came across them at the *Surviving Actors Conference* and after chatting to one of their team I soon felt that they were exactly the kind of company I needed help from to write this section of the book. As well as dealing with a whole host of clients from other walks of life they do pride themselves on being sensitive to and knowledgeable of the entertainment industry; they use such conferences as the one I met them at to make themselves known to actors who are struggling with the financial aspects of their career.

I asked Mark if he would be willing to answer a few questions for me so that I can give an accurate account of tax and finance information (rather than a slightly blagged version using the bits of knowledge that I've gathered over the seven years that I've been unemployed…I mean, self-employed).

GENERAL QUESTIONS

Q. What is PAYE?

PAYE stands for Pay As You Earn and relates to an employed job where the employer operates a payroll scheme and as such is required to deduct tax before paying you your wages.

Q. Can I be both PAYE and Self-Employed?

You can and often will be. Many of our clients, actors and writers who work in the entertainment industry, have a 'second job' in addition to the work they do as performers. This means that though they sometimes work PAYE they still need to be registered self-employed.

Q. How soon after graduating do I need to register as Self-Employed?

Ideally, immediately. Formally, once you start looking for self-employed work you are self-employed and as such you should register with HMRC. The thing to remember is that even if you are not getting paid work straight away you are still spending money on travel, headshots, showreels etc. and these costs are all claimable so register and start keeping your receipts so that when you do get the paid work you can claim back as many expenses as possible.

Q. If I am registered Self-Employed but work a temp PAYE job will I be taxed twice?
No, you should never be taxed twice on the same source of income. Employment and self-employment are two different tax schedules (D & E). When you come to complete your self-assessment tax return they go in different areas and as such are subject to slightly different treatment. The only rub is that on occasion you can be over taxed through your employment if HMRC issues the wrong tax code to your employer. This is usually resolved during the tax year but if for some reason it isn't it will come out in the wash when you complete and submit your tax return.

Q. How do I know what tax code I am in, if asked?
If you are employed (working in a bar or an office for example) and are paid under a PAYE system whereby your employer deducts National Insurance and tax from your wages directly (at source) then HMRC will have told the employer what your tax code is and it should appear on your payslips.

Q. When will I start owing tax from?
If you graduate in June or July and register for self-employment immediately then your first tax year end is the following 5th April. This period June/July to the following April is due to be submitted to HMRC in the form of a self-assessment tax return by the following 31st January, along with any tax due.

Q. Do I have to register as Self-Employed?
If you are looking for self-employed work and ultimately acting as if you are self-employed then yes. It is not a choice and a failure to do so in a timely fashion can result in fines and penalties. In the past if you did not register within 3 months of becoming self-employed there was a mandatory £100 fine; this has now been relaxed, although the threat of fines and penalties remains the same.

If your first job happens to be employed (PAYE) work then obviously you don't have to register immediately, however you may still be incurring expenses that would be claimable were you registered self-employed so unless you don't intend to work as self-employed at all (which is of course unlikely) I would recommend that you register.

Q. How do I register Self-Employed?
There are 3 main ways you can do it:

Forms – Download and complete the form CWF1.
http://www.hmrc.gov.uk/forms/cwf1.pdf

Phone – The Newly Self-Employed helpline: 0845 915 4515

Online – The quickest and most convenient way to register. https://online.hmrc.gov.uk/registration/newbusiness/introduction

The information you will need to provide in order to register:

- Name
- Address
- National Insurance number
- Date of birth
- Contact telephone number
- Contact email address
- Date your self-employment commenced
- Nature of your business
- Business address
- Business telephone number

It's worth making sure you have all this to hand, especially if you are registering online as you cannot save the details and return at a later date once you start to complete the online form!

Q. If I am Self-Employed how do I pay National Insurance?

There are two forms of National Insurance for the self-employed, Class 2 and Class 4.

Class 2 is often referred to as your 'stamps' and is currently £2.70 per week billed by HMRC every six months and can be taken by direct debit (monthly) or paid by transfer/cheque. You will automatically become registered to pay Class 2 once you register as self-employed. If however you are going to earn less than £5,725 then you can claim an exemption to Class 2 NIC by filling in and submitting form CF10 (http://www.hmrc.gov.uk/forms/cf10.pdf). One thing to bear in mind however is that Class 2 NI counts towards state benefits such as maternity pay and the basic state pension so it may be worth paying even if you are under the exemption level.

Class 4 is calculated on your profit at a rate of 9% on profits between £7,755 and £41,450 and 2 per cent on any profit over that amount. This is obligatory and there are no exemptions unless you are under 16 years of age, over pensionable age or not resident in the UK. Class 4 contributions are worked out when you complete and submit your self-assessment tax return, and you pay them as one lump when you pay your tax bill.

Your National Insurance number (in a format similar to DQ123456A) will be on the card that you receive when you turn 16. Alternatively, it appears on letters from social security, documents sent to you from the HMRC and on payslips, P45s and P60s. You will need this number when registering yourself as self-employed. If you do not have one you can call Jobcentre Plus on 0845 6000 643.

Q. What is a UTR number, how do I get one and what will I need one for?

A UTR number stands for 'Unique Tax Reference number' and will automatically be generated for you when you register as self-employed. It will be quoted on previously issued self-assessment correspondence. It's made up of ten digits, for example... UTR: 12345 67890

Q. I won't owe tax if I have earned beneath a certain amount, is that right? What is the amount?

The personal allowance is currently £9,440, so you can earn up to this amount of profit when self-employed without paying tax. If you also have another employed job (or several) then this personal allowance is not doubled, but split between all your sources of income.

Q. Can I accept cash in hand work?

Yes you can, although it should be stated that HMRC dislike cash in general! Many jobs do still retain an element of cash payment even if it is only for the PDs (per diems). As long as you still keep accurate records of the cash then you are on safe ground.

Q. Can I pay my tax in installments or do I have to pay a lump sum every January?

As a self-employed individual, once you start completing tax returns you pay your tax in three installments anyway. The first installment is a 50% payment on account for the year you are in (based on the previous year's tax), payable by 31st January. The second installment is the second 50% payment on account for the year you have just finished (based on the previous year's tax), payable by 31st July. The third installment is the difference between the actual tax liability and the tax paid, and this is due by 31st January following.

If you still cannot afford to pay your tax then as long as you talk to HMRC they are generally fairly lenient with setting up a payment plan over 3/6 months. Don't just pay a bit of the tax due and leave the rest without speaking to them, they will fine you for not paying in full unless you agree a payment plan with them!

Q. If I try and save my tax as I earn, what percentage of my wages should I realistically be putting away?

The basic rate of tax in the UK is currently calculated on your profit at a rate of 20% on profits between £9,441 and £41,450; a rate of 40% on profits between £41,451 and £150,000; and a rate of 45% above £150,001. Most newly self-employed people are firmly in a profit range that puts you in the basic rate of tax, however you will also be charged the 9% Class 4 NI as mentioned earlier so the actual rate is 29%.

When you base your tax savings on your income we recommend putting aside 20% (when you are in the basic rate band). This is because once we deduct as many expenses as we can the rate of tax and NI based on your income tends to be around and often below the 20% mark.

So try to save at least 20% of your earnings throughout the year and you won't be stung with a tax bill you cannot pay!

If however you know you have a job that is paying you well above the basic rate band (so earning over £40,000 per year) then you should move this percentage up to 25 – 30% to make sure you don't get caught short.

Q. Will I get taxed on royalties etc. as well as my acting 'fees'?

All income derived from your self-employment is subject to UK income tax. Some forms of income are taxed at different rates, but all sources of income (except for the rarest of exceptions – such as gambling!) are subject to income tax.

See you all at the casino. Sorry, couldn't resist. Next question…

Q. Do savings or pensions affect how much tax I will owe?

Savings are taxed slightly differently to earned income and there are some exceptions. If you earn below the personal allowance then it is possible that your savings will not be subject to tax, or that they will be subject to a lower 10% rate. Also certain types of savings such as ISAs are not subject to income tax. Generally however, once you are earning enough to pay tax then your savings (excluding those exempt) are subject to income tax at the same rate as your earned income.

Pensions can also affect tax. If you are paying into a pension then the amount which you pay in can in turn increase the basic rate income tax band and as such reduce your tax bill (from the 40% band back to the 20%). So if you pay £1,000 per year into a personal pension scheme then you can extend the basic rate band by £1,000 and pay 20% less tax; thereby saving you £200.

Do remember though, as HMRC are giving you a tax break on monies paid into a pension, once you start receiving a pension HMRC treat this as taxable income and as such you will be taxed!

SELF-ASSESSMENT

Self-Assessment was based on a system operated in the US, which puts the onus on the individual taxpayer to:

1. Notify HM Revenue and Customs within specified time limits of having a liability to either Income Tax or Capital Gains Tax.

2. Request the correct Income Tax forms for completion.

3. Submit the forms by the due date.

4. Pay any tax due at the correct time.

5. Keep adequate records for HM Revenue and Customs to verify the figures shown on a Tax Return form (should these be requested).

Q. What are the dates of the 'financial year'?
The UK financial year runs 6th April to 5th April. This means unless you happen to register on 6 April, your first year will in fact only be a part year!

Q. What is the deadline to have submitted a self-assessed tax return?
If you want to submit a paper return the deadline is 31st October, however if you move with the times and submit online then you have until the following 31st January. Income Tax Returns must be submitted by this date at the very latest, if they are not then there is an automatic penalty of £100.

Q. What is the deadline to have paid my tax by?
Any balancing payment is due by 31st January (following a return filed 5th April the previous year).
1st payment on account (of 50% of the previous year's tax) is due by 31st January.
2nd payment on account (of 50% of the previous year's tax) is due by 31st July.

Q. What information will I need to complete a self-assessment tax return?
You need to keep accurate records of all income and allowable business expenses.

We give lots of our clients basic bookkeeping spreadsheets, which help to track your income and keep your expenses by 'type'. They also provide a guide to saving tax based on your income.

> *Proving Income:*
> *Keeping invoices, payslips and a record of any money you have been paid is important. You can either keep track as you go, inserting them into a file on your computer, or can refer to your bank statements annually and work out the year's earnings that way.*

The list of claimable expenses is long and varied and often depends on specific details and even geographic location! It is difficult to give a concise list, however the following is a fair example of the types of expense that are usually in some way claimable and those which are not.

Expenses that are usually claimable even if it is only a percentage:

- Establishment Expenses/Upkeep Of Studio
- Agent's Commision
- Clothes and Accessories
- Stage / Appearance-related Hairdressing and Manicure
- Laundry and Dry Cleaning
- Telephone
- Visits To Theatre, Cinema, etc.
- Travelling and Subsistence
- Baggage, Porterage, Tips to Stage Doorman, etc.
- Subscriptions
- Assistance
- Photographs & Showreel
- Accountancy
- Cds, Dvds and Music
- Car Expenses
- Stage Make-Up/Cosmetics
- Magazines, Newspapers, etc.

Expenses that are usually not claimable:

- Cosmetic Dentistry/Contact Lenses
- Cosmetic Surgery
- Home Improvements

- Gardening supplies
- Holidays
- Any purely personal expenses that are not related to your career

I have a drawer with envelopes in for each claimable category listed above. As the receipts come in, they go into their relevant envelope. Doing this every couple of weeks means that gradually I can build up and keep track of my receipts ready to submit to my accountant (or complete a self-assessment tax return myself).

As a general guide, keep every receipt and any invoices you raise, also keep your bank statements as these can be invaluable in claiming expenses for things which you have lost the receipt.

Q. Do I need to enter information regarding both Self-employed and PAYE jobs?
In order to complete your tax return you need all P60s or P45s from employed PAYE jobs; all self-employment income and expense details; all savings and bank interest certificates/details; all trust fund details; all rental income and expense properties you own; your student loan details; and any capital gains and/or inheritance tax issues.

If you have all of the above information you will have covered most bases. However some of that will not be relevant to you.

Wow. We made it!
(Please bear in mind that what is correct today could well alter in a forthcoming budget, HMRC has us constantly changing and updating the rates and requirements, so always check!)
Cheers Mark.

TO SUBMIT ONESELF OR TO BE A LAZY GIT – THAT IS THE QUESTION!

If I had to advise either way, I would say to get an accountant (especially if you can spread the accountancy fees over the year or into a few more manageable installments). Many of my actor friends complete their own tax returns quite capably; I only recommend not doing so because it works well for me! The reason I have an accountant is simply because I think I have enough stress to deal with in my career and I take great comfort in the fact that it is all taken care of for me by someone who knows what they're doing. I've had no guidance with self-assessment. If you have parents or siblings who are self-employed they may make it easy for you to learn how to complete a tax return with relatively little stress (then you can go and blow the two hundred quid you've saved on an accountant on something ridiculous). Even without 'help', you can go online and read the guidelines available to you. Personally, I have neither the time nor the inclination to know about self-assessment and openly admit that I am too lazy to enquire further about it! Having an accountant is one of the FEW luxuries I allow myself, and though finding the fees is not always fun or easy (especially in sodding January) I feel that it is totally worth it. If work is bitty and sporadic it makes things far more complicated when doing your own tax return, and so at least if my accountant handles it I know there won't be any accidental mistakes or problems. I'm sure a lot of you may be a lot less idle than myself, but if not, you can sift through the myriad of accountancy firms in *Contacts* or research other options online. The accountant I am with came through a personal recommendation (which is an ideal way for it to happen as there's a lot of trust involved when you allow someone to deal with your finances).

MGM ACCOUNTANTS AS AN EXAMPLE

Q. What are the advantages to hiring an accountant?

We basically act like your mum and nag you until you meet the deadlines and file everything! Accountants will try and make sure everything is done on time and as accurately as possible. We are also more up to date with the current legislation than anyone else and therefore know what changes and when better than your mate down the pub…

Q. What is your fee?

Most accountants will complete a self-assessment tax return for a set fee and this will often vary depending on the state of the records you give to the accountant and if there are more levels of complexity. Some of the things that add complexity and therefore fees are dividends from shares held, rental property accounts, capital gains and a few other bits besides.

MGM will tend to charge £200 plus VAT for a set of self-employed accounts and a self-assessment tax return, although this will depend on what is mentioned above, and also on whether you turn up very close to the deadline with a suitcase full of every piece of paper/receipt you have ever been given!

As a general note, the better organized you are the lower the fees.

Q. What does your fee include?

The fees include a set of self-employed accounts and the completion and submission of a self-assessment tax return. We don't tend to charge for phone calls, meetings, e-mails etc. as we would rather have lots of communication so that we get to know our clients better and so we can therefore give better advice.

Q. Is your fee payable in full or can I spread the cost?

We have lots of clients who pay in full once the work is complete, but we also have lots who like to pay monthly over 3/6/12 months. We are happy however you pay, although we prefer British Pounds over say...magic beans.

Q. As my earnings go up will your fee also increase?

There is no direct correlation between fees and income. What we often find though is that the busier our clients are the less time they spend looking after their own books and the more work we are asked to complete, therefore our fees do go up.

Also there are often more fees as once a client earns more they may suit a different structure (such as a Limited Company) or require different treatment (VAT registration) and as such there is often more work for us to do and therefore higher fees.

Q. Can I contact you for advice throughout the year or only when you are doing my tax return?

You are welcome to contact us as often as the need arises. We encourage clients to pop in to our offices for a chat and a cup of tea so we keep up to date on their lives and careers in order for us to offer the best advice. We try and be as welcoming as possible and try and keep our office environment as far from a typical accountant's as possible so that our clients don't feel intimidated or put off coming to see us.

We are based in Covent Garden and since most people involved in the acting trade either front or back of camera are in the area fairly frequently, it is easy to keep in touch.

Q. If I earn a lump sum of money will you be able to advise me how best to prepare for taxation or would I need a financial advisor?

We will always be happy to advise you how to make sure you save enough for tax and do our best to ensure that you are not caught out by any unexpected tax liabilities. Going further than that we work with some lovely financial advisors who are like-minded and offer a relaxed, more informal service to creative people.

Q. Likewise can you offer advice on debt and other financial matters or is that not your area?

We will generally be happy to offer an opinion, however most accountancy practices are not FAS registered and therefore will not be able to give structured financial advice. We do however deal with financial advisors who work in similar ways to ourselves and we would be happy to pass you over for some advice from people we trust.

Q. Top tips for financing as an actor?

- Register as Self-Employed on time and keep every receipt.
- Be prepared for a hard slog.
- Save as much as you can during the good times.
- Be patient.
- Keep good organized records and if you know you are rubbish with paperwork pay someone to do it for you, just be honest with yourself.
- If you don't know something ask someone who does as HMRC don't accept ignorance as an excuse for missing deadlines etc.

Useful websites for financial advice and information:

http://www.hmrc.gov.uk/sa/understand-online.htm#1

http://www.hmrc.gov.uk/sa/complete-tax-return.htm

Self Assessment helpline: 0845 900 0444

http://www.moneysavingexpert.com/

Now go and have a drink and don't talk about money for at least 48-72 hours!

9. NOT WORKING

Certainly not sodding 'resting'

'RESTING'

Ok. Deep breath…

RANT ALERT!! … Anyone who describes what an actor does when not acting as 'resting' is either clueless, desperately searching for something to say and clutching at clichés to avoid exposing their cluelessness, or just a blatant out-and-out arsehole who is ignorant of the agony that unemployment causes. None of them are malicious, however all are as irritating, and almost as painful as thrush. Being out of work is pretty tough for anyone who wishes to feel purposeful and valued, but for the actor it is a two-pronged dilemma; not only do we contend with the anxiety and disconcertedness caused by not knowing how else to make ends meet, but simultaneously we endure the emotional torment that comes with being prevented from doing the thing that we love and are good at. It's like having your bank balance frozen and your heart ripped out in one fell swoop and it happens fairly regularly, and there is no way of knowing when it will end, or indeed when it will begin again. (This was never going to be a happy clappy sit-round-the-campfire kind of a chapter, sorry.) I used the word prevented just now because as we know, our professional schedules lie mainly in the laps of others, for them to tweak, mess with, and forget about as suits them. Dealing with the lack of tweaking, coping with the unsettlement of their messing, whilst juggling the quest to prevent them from forgetting is a 24-hour job and one that can certainly never be described as 'resting' without some cruel sense of fucking irony. I'm sure that the term may have been conceived to 'ease' or disguise the *shame* of being out of work; but in this day and age I find the implications of it insulting, and the suggestion that I am somehow not aware of, or at ease with my status as a freelancer, banal. To me it has become one of the most inaccurate assumptions there are about actors and a term that is inflicted upon us rather than used by us.

And release… Bit of a bugbear of mine that, in case you hadn't guessed.

These periods in an actor's life, though inevitable (and to a degree) acceptable to us, seem incomprehensible and weirdly fascinating to others, which can unfortunately result in many a conversation where inaccurate assumptions and unfair flippancy are bred and aired, regardless of who is listening. Just because we aren't and shouldn't be ashamed of it, doesn't mean the pain of living it is any less, and the baseless perceptions of others can cause misplaced embarrassment and awkwardness that add to an actor's distress. I think one of the best ways, and maybe one of the only ways to combat the blues that come from both being in the situation and being judged on the situation, is to make peace with it ourselves as a temporary inconvenience that will soon be rectified. I want to try as hard as I can to dispel the ridiculous stigma that being 'out of work' has, at a time when it seems to be more of a problem than ever before.

All of the best actors become busy immediately and never stop working? Correct? If only it were as clear-cut as that. It takes many years for most actors to be truly recognised, if ever! Also, there are a dozen different perceptions of what that actually is too – what the hell does it mean to be recognised in your opinion? Even if someone is 'recognised', take it as red that they will have taken many, many knocks in the form of rejection and crippling disappointment, before and during the climb up the ladder of recognition. Once more, even those who 'get there' may not 'stay there'; to me success is not something that you own, it's something you must sustain.

To be an actor, in or out of work, you will need a degree in bouncing back and enough endurance to withstand what may be a one step forward, three steps back cycle for an unpredictable, possibly even an indefinite amount of time. Thrilling prospect huh? Basically, I need you to buckle up because you're in for a bumpy ride! Whatever shape or form your turbulence comes in, we're going to assess it all in this chapter, gently moving through how to cope with it, combat it and be victorious against it. No victories were ever won without going into battle. I consider this to be probably the most important section of the book, not only because the subject matter is sure to affect us all at one time or another, but also because I feel that this is yet another inevitability that is hushed up and ignored by training establishments and industry professionals. In my mind, it's a subject that needs to be faced, accepted and dealt with…rather like an STI…

There are some things in this chapter that you may not want to hear but I promise you that this chapter, above all of the other chapters, is the one that will save you; save you from yourself and from a trying industry that will repeatedly goad you into crumbling under the pressure. If you are good and you love your job then you deserve some help with defending your mind, heart and career against the harshness that comes with it.

It is not my intention to focus on the doom and gloom of being an actor, this is not a section titled 'woe is me', quite the contrary. I simply feel that admitting the pitfalls instead of sweeping them under the carpet will put anyone hoping to survive as an actor in a much better position to thrive. There must be at least one place (other than in the pub or in therapy) that we can vent, analyse and learn. This chapter is about doing just that. I do not wish to dwell on the struggle; I aim to deal with the fight.

So let's have it.

A. Being 'out of work' can come in many forms and with varied surrounding circumstances. To attempt to reach and understand all of you, here are some statements that may sound familiar/be relevant to you…

Things haven't gone your way (a phrase we all have to get used to) and you find yourself spending the majority of your time in temp/alternative work.

This is an incredibly difficult phase to be in. Difficult firstly from the point of view that you are having to spend every day doing jobs that you don't give a flying crap about, probably surrounded by people who make you feel ten times worse about the situation than you already do; secondly, because the redirection of your energies into temping makes it feel like your actual career is slipping away from you. I've been there, and it sucks. Remember that acting is a skill that you have, that you possess, but it is also something that should be practiced; without the time, energy or opportunity to do so you can soon forget how capable you are – cue doubt and other evil thoughts such as 'Will I ever act again', 'Even if I did, would I be able to do it'. Sounds dramatic I know, but this can be a dark phase and there ain't no point flowering it up. That's the bad news, and the harsh truth that you will no doubt recognise if you're there right now or have been recently. The good news, which we must always search for, is:

- **Regular income** – It means that you are able to pay for things/have things/ do things.

- **Being occupied** – Inertia kills actors; drains them and dims their sparkle.

- **Feel your worth** – Never underestimate how important it is to feel like you're good at something. If the opportunity is there to be good at something else, take it as long as you keep your eye on the prize, you are not cheating on acting!

- **Hope** – As long as this exists you can use the strength that 'working to survive' is giving you to drive your main aim, taking comfort in the fact that you are still very much in the game. No one blows the whistle on that game but you.

Take in all of these positives and use them to your advantage, they will keep your mind strong and your ambition solid. However, I do just want to offer a small word of warning to you if you are currently in this phase: When working, and perhaps temporarily residing in another world, it is all too easy to slip gently, so subtly that not even you detect the change, from having a 'temp' job, to 'a semi-permanent' job, to a 'full-time' commitment to another career. One can be seduced by security and wooed by routine; by all means please do succumb to the natural progression of a good prospect, *as long as you are fully aware of and in agreement with the fact that it is happening.* Don't wake up one day and wonder why you're not an actor or how that happened – you owe yourself more honesty than that. Refer to Chapter 10 if this is an issue for you right now.

B. You have a stream of steady acting work but need to temp in between.

Lovely, you are laying the foundations of your career, planting seeds and making good impressions on influential people whilst practising your craft – aces. You are building your CV and therefore creating the springboard from which you will (at the right time) be elevated. The downside to this scenario is that you may not really be making much of a 'living' from it (from neither acting nor temping). You will more than likely be financially worse off than everyone in category A and therefore more trapped, limited, frustrated and stressed. On the flip side your career does have wings and you are getting to do your job (if somewhat intermittently); a little fact that must remain in the forefront of your mind when your bankcard is declined or when you have to wear your winter coat for the fifth year on the trot.

Another element of scenario B, which is an utter bitch, is that temp jobs won't necessarily rely on you and therefore may not continue to re-employ you/use you over category A (who are around more and leave them in the lurch less) – therefore after the completion of every acting job you are forced to play the 'find a job to pay the rent' game; the jollity begins all over again (unless you get a nice telly job and that can 'see you through' – see Chapter 8 for managing money). This can be stressful, time-consuming, soul-destroying and financially difficult to orchestrate.

Both of these scenarios are tough for very different reasons and whilst the inhabitants of one category will look on into the other enviously, rest assured that those looking back will be doing the same. It's about making the best out of whichever scenario you find yourself in and remaining positive and focused on how to change things for the better, whilst acknowledging that this may take time.

Those in Category B remember:

- The acting work you're doing, whether it's one scene on *Doctors*, a little part in a regional theatre production, or a profit share tour, all matter; from the lessons you learn in the playing of it, to the people you meet during the doing of it. Seeds are being planted and you are a progression in motion.

- Any job has the possibility to lead to a next one. There's that word HOPE again.

- You must swallow your pride and take the shit jobs when you have to in order to fund yourself until the next opportunity comes; keeping yourself fed, clothed, presentable, in good shape and relatively happy is a must.

The opportunity will come and you must be ready for it when it does, but patience is a massive part of this game.

C. You work a lot.

Great, enjoy! But don't take on too many direct debits or get too cocky! Pay off some debts (if you have any), or open an ISA and save some dough if you can. Don't commit to expensive accommodation either, there are absolutely no guarantees and without trying to piss on your chips, you will, at some point, for a period of time be back in category B. The way you handle the good times will see you through the not so good times (as discussed in Chapter 8).

Never take 'success' (in whatever form that comes) for granted, or imagine that it will always be there at your convenience; you can never know when a phase will end, and most of the time there may not be any plausible reason for it having done so. Acting success is like the ocean – completely unpredictable; totally wild one minute and disconcertingly flat the next.

Each category comes with pros and cons that affect the everyday living situation of any actor. All of the above can be difficult to stomach in different ways, presenting their own sets of problems and frustrations. (Obviously we all hope that we're fortunate enough to be in category C, but the majority of us will be dotting between A and B, certainly to start with.) Whichever you are in now or find yourself in over the next few years try and always focus on the positives I've outlined, accepting that this is your path and that not everyone's can or should be the same. It is highly likely that you'll be sliding between the categories for most, if not all, of your career and must learn to deal with the peaks and pitfalls of each.

So being out of work is a lottery then? Not exactly. As I've mentioned so many times, lady luck is present but she ain't running the show, she ain't in control, you are. You control how many plays you read, what shows you see, what press nights you appear at; you decide what company you keep, what you eat, how much you drink, whether you exercise, whether you go to the cinema, whether you find other interests and whether you challenge and inspire yourself on a daily basis; whether you hone your skills and perfect your craft. You are in control of so much; in fact you control everything that goes into making yours the best case for victory. This control thing is like the sadness in the sinking sand scene in *The NeverEnding Story*; the second that hope is lost and control is relinquished, you will be sucked under, never to be seen again…

'ARTEX!!!!!!!!!!'

(Possibly wasted on anyone who wasn't a child of the 80s…it's a scene with some mud and a rather depressed horse…if you didn't see it first time round, I wouldn't bother now, it'll just look weird.)

Moving on… I am fully aware that saying all of this is a damn site easier than doing it. Know that it's not empty advice; I've been so close to rock bottom that my face was grazed and therefore I can whole-heartedly emphasise the importance of prevention instead of cure. If I'm honest, this is exactly the reason I am writing this book. If I can warn and I can prepare, if I can support and I can assist even one of you talented people then I am one happy Author. It ain't a solo sport, we're a community, a breed, an ensemble; let's find camaraderie amidst the misery! We, as a collective group must stick together, loving it and learning from it together.

Keep the word 'hope' at the forefront of your mind every morning.

In no way do I assume that everyone who reads this book has it in them to go all the way, whether what stops them is talent, commitment or inclination. But, if you've come this far then you're in with a fighting chance; it's orchestrating your opportunities, surpassing expectations and accepting all of the shit in between that will determine your fate. All three things I just mentioned are down to you.

So, enough talking about it; how do we actually cope with being out of work? Everyone is different and every day varies. On Monday I may feel like the world is draining everything that I am out of me, making the struggle too hard to bear, but by Thursday I will feel that elevating sense of determination, and a rush of creativity will allow me to achieve something that may have seemed too ludicrous to even contemplate on Monday. The important thing, the thing we're dealing with here, is what one does between Monday and Thursday. There's no one way of coping; you'll be pleased to know that there are many! I cannot instruct you how to achieve contentment nor can I map out your coping mechanisms for you. All I intend is for you to have access to some options and ideas that are proven and that may help; and hopefully even if they fail to help they may, at the very least make you feel less shitty about feeling shitty. You must spend time listening to your heart and feeding your mind; these are completely necessary for your sanity and strength (two things you will need to call upon when the next audition comes along!)

Frustration, desperation, confusion, misery, worthlessness, incompetence, and depression are all words we can associate with being 'Out of Work'. They have varying degrees and manifest themselves in different ways, with no two people ever experiencing them in exactly the same way. A variety of reasons can trigger them and there are a number of ways to deal with them. We're gonna go straight for the jugular, with this debilitating turd…

REJECTION

Take it, process it, tell it to go fuck itself and then assess how to move on.

'Well, you chose this path and that's all part of the job.' This is true. It is also one of the most irritating and bloody unhelpful things you can hear as an actor – like we took a GNVQ in repeatedly getting your heart broken and your confidence slashed in between voice classes? Just because it is part of the job and we know it to be such, doesn't mean it hurts any less! We know that fire burns but when we put our hand into it it's still sodding painful despite the fact that we accepted the inevitability that it would be. The truth of it is that you have a right for it to affect you; you're human! (I'd be rather concerned about your choice of career if not doing it didn't have a negative effect upon you!) The difference is that as an actor you also have a responsibility, to yourself and your career, to monitor how debilitating the effects are for you personally and to manage them accordingly. Dealing with this is no easy task, and just when you think you've mastered it something will take the rug from under you. Acknowledging that this may happen is the first part of dealing with it.

'It doesn't matter how you get knocked down in life because that's going to happen. All that matters is you gotta get up'...
Ben Affleck's speech, Oscars 2013

Too true Ben. Both of the following cause rejection, both of the following will be a part of your life as an actor; neither need get the better of you.

NOT GETTING ANY AUDITIONS

Ever thought…

> 'I think I'm really rather good; if only people,
> no, the right people would notice.'

Of course, we all have! Probably 67 times a day. It's so bloody infuriating too as most of the time there is no one to directly 'blame' for this. Obviously if you have an agent they will bear the brunt of it. Even if you don't have the necessary evidence to justifiably direct frustrations at them, you will! Careful here. Cry and shriek and stamp and pout in private and in your own time, and always save an arsy email in your drafts folder and have a cup of tea and a word with yourself before pressing send! Your agent's job is not to be your emotional punch bag, nor is it to be your therapist. Keep a healthy line of communication open with them, of course, but remember that they are professional confidantes, who just so happen to deal with issues that affect you personally and emotionally. They are not your 'mates', or your wet-nurse. Strike a balance. The relationship between actor and agent is such a peculiar and complex one; varying hugely depending on the size and temperament of the agent in question, and on the levels of endurance of the actor. Some matches work, and some are disastrous! You must gauge them; try to understand their point of view and game plan, but always make sure your voice is heard. Never forget that an agent has seen potential in you, which is why they took you on in the first place! Finding people who have faith in you can be a bloody difficult task, so take care not to attack them unduly or let your frustrations mar your interpersonal skills.

Your agent might deserve your backchat, I dunno, they may be neglecting you, or not doing enough; they may not have the contacts they claimed to have, or they may simply have lost interest in you and haven't bothered to say so. These are not the attributes of a good agent, and instead of wasting your energy trying to teach a crap dog new tricks, that energy would be better spent trying to get the attention of new agents. Don't sit in a problem and piss and moan about it, just take your time to assess the pros and cons of any action before following through with it.

If you are in control of your own representation then not getting auditions is not only more likely, but more soul-destroying because there is less opportunity and therefore less hope. When there is literally no one you can blame, the finger may begin to point towards yourself, which is not only unfair but also not constructive. Tormenting yourself will not create an audition; what it will do though is get you into a state and ruin your chances should one come along. As I've said, keep writing letters, keep your CV on exposure sites and continue to search for opportunities. You must have enough faith in yourself to equal the amount that agents, publicists, PAs and shrinks would have – all put together! I've always thought that expressing my unwavering faith in myself loudly enough for long enough would eventually result in somebody listening! Energy must be your best friend and inertia your archenemy. (See Chapters 4 and 5 for ongoing productivity; self-promotion and marketing.)

Knowing you have potential that isn't being seen or noticed is an enormous part of the unfairness of our job. The frustration it causes is a feeling that's kept me awake many a night and one that I simply cannot put into words…it makes me want to storm the stages of the West End or throw my television out of the window. And no matter how many solutions I offer here for you to combat it, you will still feel it. It's what you do with feeling it that counts; I don't storm the stages (or haven't yet) and couldn't fit my television through my window if I tried. So, instead, when an explosion of frustration is about to ignite, I get a grip, probably have a cigarillo and then smirk and say to myself 'at least I have the potential, even if no fucker ever knows about it… One day they'll know.' … Useful? Probably not, but it amuses me! It's about holding your nerve; believing that your chances will come, and being ready for them when they do.

'Get a grip' and 'stay positive' are all so pissing easy to say, I know, and during the next few pages I will stop with generic motivational mantras and get down to the practical steps you can take to achieve them.

NOT GETTING THE JOB

Ah, look, it's not-getting-any-auditions' evil twin! They're both cows, and the upset one causes can only be equalled by the pain that the other one inflicts. Not getting the job is like being dumped, or even worse (if it's a killer job) stood up at the altar! It's utterly hideous, especially, if like me you have an enormous mouth and end up telling everyone and his gerbil about yet another audition that you intended to keep to yourself! And when the phone doesn't ring and you start eating carbohydrates by the truck load, you then have to answer sixty seven 'Have you heard anything yet!' Hell. Even if you don't particularly want the job, it smarts. We all want a guy to call, right? Whether we want to have his babies or whether we spent the entire date fantasizing about the barman behind him. (Of course I've never done that… I'm usually far more interested in the wine in the barman's hand than the barman himself; fit barmen are ten a penny but a good wine is hard to find.) Point is we all want to be wanted!

Anyone outside of the business who chances upon this book is going to laugh and sneer at what about I'm about to say (mainly because it's melodramatic, but perhaps also because most people wouldn't know emotional investment in their work if it climbed down the chimney and rogered their spaniel). When you go up for a part you must apply yourself totally, forming a bond and an attachment to the role you are being considered for; you must do all of this on the premise that you may eventually be told to walk away from it. (Wait, it gets more dramatic…) It's like fostering a child, hoping for adoption and in the end the child is taken from you, kicking and screaming… (C/UP on your teary face, pan out to reveal a solitary empty swing blowing in the wind, the deserted playground symbolising the emptiness in your heart…) Yeah, deep shit huh? I've never fostered a kid… Pah! Like they'd let me…but I have invested my emotions in auditions, only to be shat on LOADS of times! Your emotional investment will both serve you and slay you; it is your gift and your curse, the thing that makes you good and the thing that near-kills you when you're not given the opportunity to be.

If you love stories and characters as much as you profess to, you will know that losing a job is a sort of grieving process which includes shock, disbelief, regret, devastation, anger…certain amounts of scotch, and then, eventually reason and perspective…and finally (I think) acceptance. It's a pretty exhausting process to go through, and to keep going through; eventually though, the pay-off comes – you get one of the buggers and when that happens it feels phenomenal; so phenomenal that we quite willingly risk experiencing the grieving process all over again as soon as we possibly can. Without taking that risk, we have no career.

I'm not going to say that losing out on a part gets easier, because it doesn't, they all kick the shit out of you (differing amounts of shit of course and some kickings take longer than others) but I can promise that those of you who stick at it will become more philosophical about the whole thing, you must; if you don't, or at least try to, then you may as well do yourself and everyone else a favour and fish that WH Smiths application form out of the bin.

No? Still with me? Ok…

Not getting a job is one thing, but the harsh reality (mentioned in Chapter 4) is that you may never hear either way, you will simply have to assume that you haven't got it. This is awful and we are one of the only industries where this is deemed the norm! If I were Queen (could still happen Harry if we work together) I would make it LAW that a decision has to be made within 4 days and that everyone who auditioned received an answer. So let's imagine me as Queen for a moment…terrifying. Though at least if Harry and I were on the throne the end of the British Empire would have one hell of a wrap party! … I digress.

On a practical level there are just too many of us for my law to work; it is a fact I have accepted most unwillingly, but I do accept it. Ish. Occasionally you will receive a 'no thank you', or more likely 'it didn't work out', and very occasionally you may even get feedback (warranted or not). I have found that the more you work and the better you get to know the casting directors, the less just never hearing happens; but, it can and it does and you have to make peace with that by organising your thoughts around it and by knowing that taking offence from it is utterly pointless. Instead of seeking feedback, assess the thing for yourself:

- Did you feel that the audition went well?
- Were you pleased with your performance?
- Did you do as much work beforehand as was needed?
- Did you take direction well if any was given?
- What was said in the interview?

If the answer to those three top questions is yes, then you seriously can do no more, and must release yourself from any 'blame' if the phone doesn't ring. A director in a meeting recently told me that a previous audition I did for her a few months before was the best audition she'd ever seen. Didn't get the part though. Don't think I've got the one I went in for that day either. Sometimes there's no sense, no rhyme, no reason and no fucking point in agonising that there might be. Do what you do and let them do the same; I make it my business to impress or at least do my best to impress anyone who encounters my work, what they do with that is then up to them and beyond my control.

One thing that always slightly improves my state of mind following a disappointment is to remember all the jobs that I did get. Sparing a thought for all of the actresses who were going through hell when I was celebrating, somehow makes it easier to compute; it's a sort of swings and roundabouts deal, sometimes it's our turn and sometimes it's not. Another good one is to think 'well, I'll be available for other, better jobs'. It may not work out quite like that, but it is true that something else will usually be around the corner. Whatever rationale you use, you cannot let a knock from one blow have any kind of effect on the next opportunity and when I say you cannot, I mean it. You may as well quit now if you allow that to happen (and yes I am using the word allow, intending to indicate that you do have a choice; it is mind over matter and nothing else). This is harder for some than others, but achievable for all if the determination to get what you want is rigid. To let negativity or self-flagellation get the better of you is artistic suicide; you must go in with an 'I'm gonna get this' attitude, you must believe that you can and that you will get the job, otherwise what is the point? Admittedly this is going to set you up for one hell of a fall if it doesn't work out, but like I said earlier these are necessary risks. You can't reach for the stars if you're afraid of heights. If you're in this then you must believe in yourself, because if you don't then no one else will.

Something I make myself do is watch the job I didn't get. I do this for a few reasons; firstly that it acts as some sort of closure because if the actress is totally different to me I can say to myself 'Oh well, they went for a completely different look, that's why'; if she's shit then I can sneer and say 'Fucked that up didn't you', and if she's really really bloody good I can (almost sincerely) say 'Good job. You deserved it'. Apart from the 'self' part of this plan of action, it is also very useful when the director who didn't give you the part (because they thought you were great but just not right) brings you in for another audition – you can talk about how much you liked it. This shows initiative, intelligence, commitment, professionalism and courage. It's also really interesting to see how someone else approached the part in comparison to the way you did; it sounds like an activity on a par with sticking pins in your eyes I know, but trust me, if you have the stomach for it, it's useful. Lessons are there if you dare learn them.

Whatever lessons you end up learning, there is no flowering it up, 'losing' or 'missing out' on a job is devastating, but the devastation will pass quickly if you rationalise and philosophise. Allowing perspective to kick in is a wise choice and it will aid you to get straight back on that horse. Are you a victim or a fighter? If you've read to this chapter, then you're probably the latter.

MY AUDITION TORMENT

– (Looser's Lament)

Though a lovely BBC gig of mine aired recently, I haven't actually been paid to act since I finished filming aforementioned lovely BBC gig eight months, 1 week and six days ago. I've been 'out of work'…

I had a recall audition today. I really want it. Though it went well I haven't got the foggiest whether it went well enough. Now, at 2.46am I am starting this 'out of work' chapter, my aria of empathy to you. (I fully intend to edit most of this tomorrow and wipe the tears and snot from my Mac.)

Before bed I made the grave mistake of watching a phenomenal TV series in an attempt to escape the pain and confusion of 'waiting for the verdict' (which, I might add begins the second you step out of the audition room and doesn't end until either the phone rings or you finally, two months later, stop expecting it to). Whilst the objective of distracting and inspiring oneself was a good one, and one that was accomplished, the aftermath was not so kind. Suddenly in the post-distracted lull I dipped from inspired to desolate quicker than Usain Bolt with his arse on fire. That quick.

The phenomenal programme I speak of is *Breaking Bad*…

IF YOU HAVEN'T WATCHED BREAKING BAD **DO IT. DO IT NOW...**

I guarantee that in years to come, having missed this series will be one of the most popular deathbed regrets of our time. Slightly dramatic? You'd know it wasn't if you'd WATCHED IT!

So I had effectively absorbed myself into that for all of around five hours, only to reach the shit part of the night, when supposedly one should be asleep, as most rested, sane people are; the DVD has gone back to the main menu, and I stare at it with debilitating levels of alcohol and caffeine swishing around a tender and fragile mind, a mind racing with ins and outs of the day's events. Suddenly I am replaying the audition to myself in the bathroom mirror. (I seriously hope at least a few of you do this weird shit that I'm admitting to, because if not, instead of a nice write-up following this book's publication I may just be 'removed' from society!) So I replay it. The comments (both mine and the director's), the amused grunts they let slip as I read the scene, the strength of the handshake on the way out; decoding begins on whether or not 'Thanks for coming in' meant 'piss off you talentless twat', 'oh my god you're an acting genius', or whether it in fact meant 'thanks for coming in'… However stupid it sounds, and however much I am attempting to make you chuckle, this is the audition aftermath analysing arse ache. I love a bit of midnight assonance, I'm gonna put that in a text box…

AUDITION AFTERMATH ANALYSATION ARSE ACHE.

Remember the 'Cycle of Doom' from Chapter 4? Well, I'm in it! Now in the midst of panic and frustration I then go from analysing the audition to questioning (and basically hyperventilating about) not only my whole career but MY ENTIRE LIFE!!! Comparing myself to the *Breaking Bad* actors and conjuring up philosophical questions like 'What is the purpose of any of it?', 'Why do I do it?', 'Why do I love it, if it causes this unbearable level of pain, frustration and confusion?' 'WHY OH WHY'... Admittedly, I think it'd be fair to put a large amount of that down to the cheeky Rioja I picked up from Mr Marks & Mr Spencer earlier, but even without their input the questions would be there as the ocean of self-doubt drags me under.

I didn't get the job. I found out this morning.

Cue 'He ain't heavy, he's my brother' by the Hollies...

> 'The road is long
> With many winding turns,
> That leads us to
> Who knows where
> Who knows where
> But I'm strong'

Ugh... I'm strong. Yes. I. Am. I am... Am I? Yep... YES, I am.

So, following some serious self-flagellation, some tantrum throwing and some throwing of other household objects, I have done what I always do which is to get over it. There are two choices, and not getting over it looks like a bleak and joyless option. One thing that helps to 'get over it' is to:

FIND AN OUTLET FOR FRUSTRATION

Mine's writing, hence why I started this particular chapter ahead of schedule at a time when I knew there was venting to be done! It feels fitting and appropriate to share the above story with you in the hope that the admission of my own anguish can go some way to proving the information I provide here is far from hypothetical. We're all in the same boat. It's a crowded boat and her name is Joy.

Why is an outlet important? Naturally, within you already, you have creativity, expressiveness, energy, adrenaline and a need to play. When you experience a blow it is not only important to exercise those attributes (in order to remind yourself that you are ace) but also to exorcise the feelings of frustration, disappointment, anger, upset and desperation that are lingering.

An outlet is needed for this; a hobby or activity, whatever; a system of coping that allows you to release and cleanse (whilst bringing a bit of the old faithful displacement trick into play).

If I cry I find a reason to dry the tears, if I get angry I find a way to calm down and if I question everything I'm sacrificing in pursuit of this silly career, I always conclude that no matter how hard and silly it is, in the end I know it is worth it. The demons you'll fight are devious and dangerous; you must arm yourself well and have mass reserves of energy in order to defeat them. Carrying anger and frustration around with you reeks, and if burying them instead of dealing with them becomes habit, the industry will smell you a mile off. Find a way to offload the bad luggage to make way for the new challenges. Your outlet could be exercise (boxing being a particularly effective one), painting, swearing – whatever, just find one, or several. By noticing patterns in your behaviour following a disappointment, you will be able to fashion a strategy, tailor-made for you to be able to rise above future ones. Hopefully the rest of this chapter will help you to do so.

Enough about how we 'feel'. Let's get onto what we can 'DO'.

FINE LINES

When we want something really, really badly it can blur reason and cloud judgment making us look, well, pathetic, needy and desperate. This is not a good look and it feels pretty shite too. With almost every piece of advice that I've offered in this book there is a fine line between what I meant and what I would advise against. You, however, are the only one present when making your decisions and managing your professional life, so I hope that the next few points may clarify how to stay on the right side of these fine lines.

Ambition and Desperation – We're all ambitious and we all want to do well. If you're an actor people assume this of you, so why actors insist on 'proving' this in every conversation they have with anyone is beyond me (slight exaggeration). Know what you want and by all means discuss it, but beware of banging on about yourself in some pitiful plea to be accepted by those around you, or even worse in an attempt to convince yourself that you're worthy of being. Why try to get into a club you're already a member of? Desperation never sold anything.

Persistence and Nuisance – Persistence is needed in this industry. You need to be able to get back up when you've been put down and have the balls to knock again when a door's been slammed in your face. What you don't need or want is a reputation for being a pain in the arse. Use connections that you have, but cleverly; space out the times you ask for help or advice and be intelligent about how and why you seek their advice in the first place. It's a game and you need to be canny about which card you play and when.

Do you really think that when a 27-year-old unknown actress announced that she'd like to write her first book, everyone stopped in their tracks to listen? Nope! If what you have is as good as you say it is, have faith that this, coupled with a good amount of persistence and determination, will make people listen eventually. But be patient, keep a hold of your self-respect at all times, stay calm and be rigidly focused on what it is that you hope to achieve without letting emotions cloud and/or dictate your professional decisions.

Self-Assessment and Self-Flagellation – Self-assessment is essential in our job and we must be deeply perceptive when looking at our own abilities and the ways in which we work. I fully encourage assessment and a healthy amount of awareness in whatever we do as I believe they are essential learning tools. In doing so one must always be careful not to turn something that should be constructive into something very destructive; we have to develop an alarm bell that will notify us when self-assessment crosses over into self-flagellation. Learning from something is great, but beating ourselves up over things will only exacerbate the situation and possibly cause us to make future unnecessary errors.

Cheeky and Stupid – A very, very fine line and one that is difficult to call hypothetically. Only you, in a given circumstance, will know whether there is room for cheek or not. We've all heard the stories of cocky actors turning up to closed auditions and getting the part, but I guarantee there are so many more stories about stupid actors who tried and failed miserably (whilst damaging their reputation in the process). I am becoming better at using my natural cheek more and more these days, having adopted an 'if you don't ask, you don't get' attitude, but I am continually assessing specific situations and relationships with the people in question before doing so. Being over-familiar with industry professionals and asking inappropriate questions of people in positions of power are what the word cringe was invented for. Once you have built foundations and formed liaisons, then you may be able to get away with a sprinkling of cheek – at you own peril!

Confident and Cockhead – Fairly self-explanatory. Think you're good, know you're good even, but always know that you can be better and that someone else probably is. Take care of how you radiate your belief in yourself, you neither want to be forever blowing your own trumpet, nor forcing people to compliment you hourly; both are tedious to be around and ugly to witness. Self-awareness.

There is a significant difference between all of these; and in your darkest moments it can be hard to see the very fine line that distinguishes them. Look harder and identify those lines right now! It matters.

Ok, you're out of work, you're feeling shitty (but are mildly entertained by my book), you now understand that not getting auditions hurts, as does not getting the jobs, and you have a handle on a bunch of fine lines. Fab. I think (before this book becomes longer than the *Lord of the Rings* trilogy) we should perhaps move onto some pragmatics behind the subject.

CONTINUED PRODUCTIVITY & MAINTAINING POSITIVITY

(One feeds the other.)

HEALTH & WELLBEING

Depression

Ok. Let's jump straight in at the deep end. Not literally. (The first of only a few distasteful jokes, I promise.) I really battled with myself over including this section for two reasons. Firstly because I am no Doctor; depression is an illness and I would never want to give the impression that I am qualified or willing to attempt to diagnose or cure with what I write here. Secondly because it is a subject that I do have a personal connection to and I was therefore concerned that whatever I wrote could not be objective enough to be of any help to you. These things still concern me as I write this, but already I feel easier about the fact that I've levelled with you about them. I am not going to tell you whether you are suffering from depression. I am not going to tell you what you should and shouldn't do if you are. All I can ask is that by touching on this vast and complex issue I may perhaps make a taboo subject feel a tad less lonely, a confused mind an ounce less confused, and a desperate person know that there is help and hope.

Why is this subject relevant in this book?

If you have to ask that question then I am really envious of you, it means that you are fortunate enough not to have had it affect you. If you look around you, really look and listen to the actors you meet and work with, you will see a pattern and that pattern is that most of us have had, live with or will experience a form of depression at some point. Why? Because being an actor is hard. It takes tons of emotional investment, and the extremities we experience along the way (often at the hands of others) are bound to take their toll.

Irritability   Low self-esteem   Unpredictability
        Pressure   Stress   Sleep deprivation
              Sorrow   Frustration   Worthlessness   Confusion
Guilt   Exhaustion   Headaches   Hopelessness
        Disappointment   Inertia   Boredom   Anger
Bitterness   Discontentment Doubt   Shame   Debt

Ring any bells? These will be familiar to any actor, whether the label
of depression has been suggested or not. Actors' emotions are messed with
continually and are expected to be easily accessible most of the time, so it's
no wonder that we're susceptible to them getting the better of us every now
and again. To me depression isn't about ticking off symptoms, it's about
recognizing patterns; when you're low, what makes you low and what tends
to lift you out of it? People can be depressed without having 'depression' and
others can function daily with their treated or untreated illness remaining
undetectable to the outside world. Whether medical advice is sought or
required, it is important to remember that your feelings matter and that
there are people around you, and organizations available, whose main aim is
to help you understand them. No one should accept unhappiness as a state
of mind, or have to stagnate inside of discontentment. If you are low then
the only way out is change; change of lifestyle, change of thought processes,
change of scenery, change of tack – however and whatever the change, it is
the key to improvement and betterment.

1. Admitting that change is needed.
2. Identifying what that change might/could/should be.
3. Trying to see how the change is achievable.
4. Having the strength to make the changes.

These changes might be massive, and they might be minor; a change in
diet, a change in attitude, a change in career (see Chapter 10), a change in
accommodation, a change in your support network, a change in habits. To
be honest I think the most difficult part is admitting (to yourself, let alone
others) that you are struggling with the contents of your own mind – not
exactly a thrilling prospect is it? Thrilling it is not, but in my opinion it is the
only way to move forward. Whilst there is no blame and should be no guilt
for feeling the way you do, I do want to proffer that you can and must try
everything and anything to help yourself change things.

**'The secret to change is to focus all of your energy
not on fighting the old but on building the new.'
Socrates**

Sometimes things will have gone too far and control is a ship that will have sailed (in which case, go to see your GP). However, if you do have the strength to fight, you must use it; wallowing in and ignoring a low will only push you deeper which may then lead to a time when self-help is not enough.

Though it is slightly less of a taboo subject than it was, disappointingly depression now seems to have a sort of clichéd coating, where one needs to almost convince (hopefully not those closest, but possibly 'society') that a problem is genuine and that one is not some charlatan claiming to suffer from something that cannot be 'proven' and therefore argued with. Focus on your own problem, not on the ignorant issues that everyone else has with your problem. No one's opinions or prejudices matter and you must use the people who know and care about you to help and support you, treating any ignorance you encounter with indifference and contempt. It's no one else's business. If you feel low and want to tell people do, sharing can be wonderfully useful in diluting, and even eradicating, some of the feelings I mentioned earlier; but never feel pressured to talk if you don't want to. Sometimes talking to someone less emotionally invested in you can be useful as it frees you from any sense of duty towards them and releases you from editing to save their feelings. Whether medical intervention is warranted or wanted, confiding in someone about your feelings and worries is a step in the right direction and hearing that others feel or have felt similarly can be a comfort. (Having said that, your mind and situation are unique to you and you must find your own way of getting through what you're experiencing.) It comes in so many forms, in so many shades, and no one has the right to measure one person's experience up against another; if life is a struggle, it's a struggle, and there are no prizes for who gets the most symptoms or who covers it up the best.

Don't suffer in silence.

Don't blame yourself.

Don't accept that this is the way you are and the way you feel.

Do cherish life and do everything within your power to make yours everything you want it to be. You're worth that.

Options?

A psychiatrist, St John's Wort (herbal supplement thought to help depression), anti-depressants, Cognitive Behavioural Therapy, The Samaritans, help from friends and family. Change.

Whichever you do for whatever size or type of problem you have, do something.

I'm not going to delve any further into this, as I don't feel qualified to do so, as I said. What I do know about are the things that have aided me and the things I've chosen to change in order to help myself. I can recommend them and am keen for you to adopt them as healthy lifestyle choices, regardless of whether or not you're low!

Diet – This is not advice on 'dieting', or a section that suggests for a minute that there isn't a place for fat in the entertainment industry because there most certainly is! (Perhaps not in LA, but we're not in LA.) I have included a section on diet because the types of food we eat directly affect our mood and mindset. Whatever your relationship with food is, you must acknowledge this to be true and accept it as one of the easiest and simplest ways to help yourself to be happy and healthy.

Rant one: I'd like to point out that it is an absolute outrage that it seems cheaper to eat unhealthily than healthily in this country. This is appalling and something that I hope will change. Perhaps when Harry and I wed… No, let's stay off that, it was distracting enough last time.

Listen, I am no organic, eat well freak so please don't assume that I am, far from it. Throughout the years of wading through this life choice of mine I have identified important parts of everyday life that directly affect me, and therefore my work. Bad mental and physical health are detrimental to your abilities and therefore to your possible or probable success. Diet affects your mental and physical state, so recognize that it's important and make good decisions a priority. You will feel the difference.

- If you are overweight or unhappy with your weight, change it. But do so steadily, healthily and only because you want to.

- *Don't 'diet'.* If you are overweight then you should couple a healthier (not just smaller) menu with exercise (next on the list). This ain't rocket science and you already know this.

- Don't totally 'ban' things that you enjoy. Coping with our turbulent lifestyle will mean that you need and deserve little rewards; grant yourself these. Incentive and reward is a good tactic. Incentive suggests that you'll have to achieve something to get a treat (which is always good) and treat suggests that it is something you don't allow yourself to indulge in too regularly.

- Do eat fresh veg, fruit and salad and buy from a market – the prices are SO much cheaper!

- Always have breakfast. Keep it light if you're not a breakfast person but have something. Not only is it a good idea to give your body energy at the start of the day, but also if you have eaten at breakfast you are less likely to gorge at lunch! You'll make healthier choices.

- Food on the run is a healthy diet disaster. Not only does it mean that you will not be digesting your food properly but it also means that whatever you end up grabbing will contain probably about 300 more calories than the package admits (and will cost a bomb; a bomb that you most likely do not have). So, try as much as possible to plan ahead by taking a pack-up, allowing yourself time in the day to enjoy it. (Pack-up? What am I some cheerleader in Idaho?)

- Eat dinner with flatmates and friends, make sure mealtime is a sociable and fun thing as well as a necessity. Also, avoid always eating on your lap; sitting at the table is far better for your digestion. Plus it's just more bloody civilised.

- Most of the 'value' stuff at the supermarket is actually more or less the same as the branded stuff inside. For god sake don't feel any sort of ridiculous shame for buying this stuff, save money wherever you can! (Most of you reading this will have been students for the past three years so I am perhaps preaching to the converted!) For most people graduating means an end to student life; for actors, it's just the beginning. Wonder why Peter didn't use that as his happy thought…

N.B The food you eat affects not only your insides and your mind, but also (if we want to get shallow) your hair, skin, teeth and nails – all of which are the packaging for your product.

Exercise – Oh, what a bloody cliché right? Clichéd or not, there's a reason why many actors consider this a good idea, and why so many brand it as a lifesaver. It improves mood, productivity, alertness, and stamina and can combat a myriad of feelings mentioned earlier. Exercise is of course good for everyone; I won't go into the scientific explanation of why because, I can't… (be bothered) and besides you already know it to be true. Exercising is good for your body (both inside and out) and has an excellent effect on your mind. Plus, acting is a physical job and we must ensure that we are able to leap and throw ourselves around (whilst making it look easy/pretty), eight times a week!

Looking after yourself is a very important part of being an actor, from a health and fitness point of view as much as from an aesthetic one; which in no way means that I think that every actor should look like Brad Pitt and every actress like Natalie Portman (my lady crush). What I am saying is that aesthetics are important, they are our calling cards whether we like it or not, and whatever your 'look' is, keeping as trim as you're comfortable with and taking care of your appearance are to be expected. The way we feel about ourselves radiates out of us and alters the way that we think, feel, behave and come across too; whether the impression we give off is one of self-confidence or of self-consciousness matters. No one wants to watch a self-conscious actor and there is certainly no place for it in an audition room, so we must try and stay in good physical condition with a look that we are content with. We are constantly judged, cast and pigeonholed because of our looks; the more you engineer yours to work for you and make friends with the result, the easier these shallow parts of the industry will be for you to swallow. Being attractive is, of course, about so much more than being pretty or slim, or buff or chiseled; it's about charisma, an unfathomable pull that entices and intrigues. You as an actor are supposed to create that pull and if you are happy within yourself and with what you radiate to the world then you stand a far better chance of doing so.

Despite all of that vanity stuff, it is the effect that exercise can have on your mind and general outlook that will be invaluable to your survival, especially during the downtimes. I am not suggesting you can cure depression with a jog and a grape, but I do know that both can help the condition, and go a long way to preventing relapses.

You don't have to join an expensive gym. You don't have to join a gym at all. Sure, if you have the funds and wish to do so then do, it can be a great place to focus and reflect, and the facilities will undoubtedly be of use in your pursuit for physical and mental fitness.

Don't forget that you can claim gym fees as expenses when doing your tax!

For most of you the added expense of a gym will not be practical, and the ludicrous contracts that tie you into them certainly won't be. Running outdoors is free, as is jogging, skipping (bit weird), walking, cycling and having sex – Yay! You can easily do cardio without any mechanical apparatus and even though you may feel daft doing work-out DVDs (especially in communal areas in shared accommodation) they all accomplish the same thing and that is to keep you in shape, keep you active and keep you motivated.

Other ideas to keep active are classes; either yoga or dance, whatever floats your boat – get on a Boris bike on a Sunday and see the sights! It is not the activity of choice that matters; it is the doing of the act itself. If you are down, or bored, or inertia is getting the better of you (and especially if all three of those apply) then seriously take my advice on this one. It is your job to maintain health and wellbeing in between work and by doing so you massively increase your chances of being employed once an opportunity does arrive. I joined the gym five months ago and it was literally like a switch had been flicked. Exercise doesn't solve all or any of our problems, but it does make you far better equipped to deal with them.

Fun and Relaxation – Sounds like a bit of daft thing to remind someone to do doesn't it? Work and life can become all-consuming in quite an unhealthy way when you're going hell to leather towards a goal, and you can (quite unknowingly and certainly unintentionally) become dull, insular and unappreciative of the things and people around you. Don't let this be you! Hopefully if this is relevant to you, reading this will have triggered some alarm bells. It is so important that you identify how you are able to relax; it may be activities like yoga, long baths, walks or listening to certain types of music, or it may be cooking, reading or playing air guitar. Taking time to identify and indulge in other interests that calm and fulfil you is so important for both mind and soul.

You simply must have fun or what is the point in anything? Pursuing something that means the world to you is one thing, but letting it take over your whole existence is another. Please don't focus so much on the future that you forget to enjoy the present; as dramatic as this may sound I've heard many actors say that they've regretted not having lived 'in the present' and that they'd missed out as a result.

Are most of your friends actors? Mine are, or were. It's obviously fairly normal to have friendship groups in the same line of business, common interests bind people; just be careful it doesn't become all you talk about. We all need to be just human beings as well as actors every now and again, and I would encourage, not necessarily going out and purchasing new friends from five different walks of life, but certainly monitoring how 'submerged' in work you allow yourself to be.

Vices – Hmmm. Ok. You know I said have fun? Well, I meant it…just be careful how much! Most actors drink (certainly most if not all old school actors). And why? Because it tastes nice and feels great. AND because it numbs pain and feigns merriment for a suspended period of time, which are both useful if you are utterly hacked off with the world and its contents. Loads of actors (especially the old school ones) smoke. And why? Because it is a sociable thing to do, and because it calms and looks cool… I mean, crap, it looks crap. Plenty of actors also take drugs. Legal or illegal activity is not my concern here, I just want to make the observation that in all three things I've mentioned the effects gleaned are those of escapism; things that make us feel 'better', that make us forget, that make us not care, that make us calm, that help us sleep, that make us fun, that make us numb, that make us feel alive and allow us to feel in control of something. But are we in control if we need something else to make us feel as if we are? Given our turbulent lifestyles it is no wonder that we (and I am certainly including myself in this) reach for crutches every now and again. But harking back to the discussion about fine lines I will point out (with no hint of righteousness in my voice) that you must acknowledge the line between indulgence and addiction.

What can be or seem like an innocent habit can quickly turn into a problem, a problem for your health, a problem for your finances, a problem for your lifestyle, a problem for your behavior and ultimately, a problem for your work. Be aware of what affects you and how and also how not indulging affects you too. If I'm low I know not to drink to excess, not because I'll get emotional or morbid, Christ no, I'll still be the life and soul of the party, but the next day when I'm alone and have come down, I'll pay for it in a way that can take days to recover from. We are venerable and vices feed on that.

I have included this section not to preach or lecture (like I could and like all of my friends aren't laughing whilst reading this sensible sermon of mine), I am mentioning it so that it has been acknowledged as a potential issue and so that you are clear that it is your responsibility to monitor it. Look after your ability to do your job, look after your reputation and look after your overall wellbeing. Be informed instead of blindly weak.

Now, pause on that thought as I pour my 7pm scotch…

What? It's got a dash of water in it and water is good for you.

Other things in life – As I've said, it can be all too easy to make your work your whole world, sometimes without even noticing you have. Our job is to imitate life, or at least elements of life within a chosen structure or style; it is therefore useless if an actor has no experience of said life. I find it very difficult to put much above acting on my list of priorities, but sometimes, frequently in fact, it should be done. There are three reasons supporting this argument. One is, like I've said, about not having enough experience of the world, of people, of life to accurately articulate through characters what the story requires them to have experienced and know. The second is that you will be dull, so very dull, if you make this your ENTIRE life; and finally I think there is a huge amount of truth in how holding on too tightly can be counterproductive (relating back to the ambition versus desperation chat earlier); being ambitious and dedicated is an absolute requirement but being obsessive can trigger all sorts of ugly and unhealthy things. To avoid this I recommend filling your life with additional loves, passions and fun. Allowing yourself to let go will reenergize and enrich the work you do when you return to it and will make you a far more interesting, rounded human being in the meantime. And who doesn't want to be that?!

There is so much emphasis (certainly at drama school) on 'how much you want it', 'how far you'll go' and 'what you'll put yourself through' that it can become ridiculously difficult to focus on or enjoy anything else without guilt creeping into the equation. I hope this section may give you license to perfect the skill of letting go. However letting go happens for you, doing so will provide some psychological distance and therefore, clarity of thought. We all need a little rest bite from the intense and demanding job we do and we must allow ourselves to take it for our sanity's sake! (I'm working on it, which is sort of perfect irony for you.)

OUT OF WORK, WORK

**'The only problem with being out of work,
is that you have to work.'**
Kenneth Tynan

It is a huge cliché that 95% of actors are waiters and one that I used to nervously laugh along with so as not to seem bitter or stuck-up. Nowadays I tend to stay po-faced, before eventually admitting that my lack of amusement is because of the boredom I feel when hearing this tired cliché yet again. There is some truth in the cliché of course! But why people get satisfaction from announcing it at you, I will never understand; it's like me going up to an old person and saying 'Huh, 95% of your friends must be ill, dying or dead. Ha, ha, ha, ha, ha'… Well, not exactly like that, but you get my point. You will find your own way of dealing with the rest of society's inability to compute the words 'freelance' and 'artistic'!

Most people's lives are built within a rigid structure. Those in positions above them set the majority of the boundaries in which they are required to operate, and the rules by which they blissfully comply. We are outside of this 'system' and therefore have to endure the bewilderment of others who are inside of it. It is unfair to say it's only people who are outside of the business who are dense about these things, if only it were; we could have actor and civvie sections in pubs! (What a vile prospect.) I had my costume fitting for my first film and arrived wearing a suit, looking rather smart. When a costume person said how smart I looked and enquired as to where I'd come from, I answered truthfully that I had been doing some temp promotions work. She looked at me and said 'Oh.' She then paused (reducing my self-esteem to nothing with her look of disgust) and eventually said, 'How long have you been out?' (of drama school). I answered and she said cheerfully 'Well, it's alright to still be temping in between then.' After I'd picked my jaw up off the floor I muttered to myself 'I know. Bitch.'

When you are 'out of' acting work you will never be more aware of the fact than when you have to take up a temp job to pay the bills. Not only will you have to deal with the fact that you're out of acting work, you will also have to endure hours of doing mind-numbingly boring/soul-destroying types of work. Cheerful little book I'm writing here huh? I really don't mean to bum you out, but in order to advise you how to cope with obstacles that may trip you up, I have to explain what the obstacles are.

The people you will work for/with while you are temping, the nature of the work you'll be asked to do, the minimal amount of funds you will be offered for doing so, the nagging guilt and debilitating misery that goes along with not doing your actual job and the complete lack of knowledge of how long you will have to endure it all for will take its toll on you. I know, it's taken its toll on me and will do again.

You must remember and keep repeating to yourself:

Definition of 'Temporary':
Lasting for only a limited period of time; not permanent.

Temp work is a stepping-stone, a means to an end and a path we all have to wander down in order to arrive at the destination we wish to reach.

Sigh. Ok, let's talk temp work.

TYPES OF TEMP JOBS

Ooh, this varies hugely. The obvious ones are waitressing, ushering at the theatre, bar work, promotions, role-play, call centre and teaching. The less obvious ones are perhaps medical experiment volunteering, selling LED signs, escorting, lifeguarding and unraveling wires. Only one of those I haven't done; I'll leave it up to your imagination to guess which. So it seems that there's plenty of opportunity to earn money outside of acting? If only. All work of the temp variety (which, by the way I've decided stands for)…

Terrifically
Excruciatingly
Mundane
Profession

…comes with issues and problems:

Is there enough work available and will it pay me enough or will it have to be one of three jobs that I juggle?
Being hired for an undisclosed amount of time and having flexible hours is good, right? Well, not if you don't know how much work you are likely to have and when. If you are financially ok, then this could work nicely for you, as shifts will be picked up and dropped by both you and your employer in a relaxed way that suits both parties. However, if you are like me (and the majority of actors out there), you will be pretty much living month to month, hand to mouth at various times. Unpredictable amounts of work make it desperately hard to budget and plan, and can and do screw you. So,

look for jobs that will ideally book you for chunks of intense work and/or will pay you within a relatively short period of time. You may not manage to get a job that is absolutely ideal, but knowing what you should be looking for is a good start. Anywhere that pays by the week is great and having a temp job that understands and supports your situation is a (rare) luxury. These jobs are out there and you can job hop until you land somewhere that fits your situation.

You may have to juggle more than one job. If you get in with a place that needs you two days a week and offers some of the attributes mentioned above, then you are probably better to take it and try to find other work around it rather than lose money searching for something more suitable (especially as that 'more suitable' job may never come along!) Juggling work can be good for one's sanity too as it provides some variety and breaks up your time – always find a positive!

The answer to the question 'Will it pay enough?' will invariably be no! (Sad but true.) As a temp you are either an add-on to the regular staff, or someone hired to do something no one else wanted to do – this in itself does not suggest huge financial rewards. You will be paid the minimal legal amount in most places and will be treated as 'disposable'. Try and make peace with this and take comfort from the fact that you are using them as much as they are you. Don't take umbrage; it wastes energy that will be better spent elsewhere. Other people at that company only have that work, that is their life; relish the fact that it is not yours and take pride in the knowledge that you are sacrificing the security they cling to in order to pursue something you adore. Even if that assumption is wildly inaccurate, pretend that it's not to make yourself smile, I do! (Quite often it is accurate!)

As I mentioned at the start of the chapter, you may do more temping than acting in the early days of your career and this means that you will really have to budget around your circumstances as pay will be low and sporadic, and more often that not – late. (See Chapter 8 for more information on this side of things.) You'll become a master at balancing the books and your diary will look like a small child's scribble pad.

What is my humiliation-ometre like?

This has probably been my biggest downfall as an actor. When acting, I'm not self-conscious and I welcome looking silly; I take great joy in the fact that vanity and ego go out of the window when I become somebody else. But when I am 'just being me' I will fully admit that I'd probably rather not look like a tit (in a professional environment that is, at home I almost always look like a tit).

Many actors are hired to do temp work that requires them to be excessively extroverted; to be blah where others would be shy, and many actors accomplish this beautifully. I find the clichéd assumption that all actors are born with tendencies to attention seek and be 'over the top' irritating to say the least, and though I can be outgoing, I am not someone who isn't satisfied unless the whole world sees, hears and likes them. So that, coupled with the fact that I don't respond that well to authority (especially when it's being exerted unnecessarily by people I have no time or respect for), along with the fact that I've never been very good at doing things I don't want to be doing does not make me an ideal candidate for BLAH-style temping! I realized this was a slight issue early on when doing some promotions work for Barlcays bank. I was required to dress in a skimpy garment made up solely of Barclay cards, many of which, over the course of the day, were dislodged by members of the public and 'swiped' in places... The other girls seemed to laugh this off. I feigned cystitis so I could keep going to the ladies to cry. Whether I am unable or unwilling is debatable, but I knew then and know now that if I love what I do enough I will find a way to stand it. Remember that when you see me handing out condoms or Nutella or something outside Waterloo station next month.

If you are one of these brave/strong/daft people who can just do the job, whatever it is, then I salute you; even better if you're one of these types who actually quite enjoys it and uses it to somehow release 'artistic' frustration. For the rest of you who, like me, are devastated by the prospect of kissing ass or smiling for nine hours a day (whilst being treated like shit), if I can do it, so can you! You have to set your own boundaries and deal with the consequences that those boundaries create. If you will not do certain types of work, you have to be ok with the fact that you may have to search longer and harder for something else (whilst others around you earn a packet). It is about assessing your overall happiness and weighing up what is endurable for you personally. You will be continually tested and it's been a real case of trial and error with me to find what I will and won't do and where I draw the line. Of course in the early days I started and quit more jobs than I care to remember; when rent was due I had no choice but to at least try to grin and bare it – (hence why I have some of the temp stories I have, including working at Pizza Express for all of 36 minutes, and another which involves me making an inappropriate joke in front of Mohammed Al Fayed).

It can be heart-breaking and desperate when we're forced to do something we dislike, but I promise that if you try enough areas you will find what you can and can't cope with and there will be something that works out. (The hope always being that acting work comes along and solves the issue – for a while at least!) At the end of the day, we love our job and every shit temp job we do proves what we are willing to go through to make the idea a reality. I will not supposedly 'prostitute my artistic ability', but I cleaned toilets at drama school – you have to work out your own tolerance levels and stick to them for the sake of your own sanity and self-respect, in the hope that one day you will be able to look back and laugh at it all.

Is the temp job flexible and will they allow me to go to/prep for auditions?

This is the most important element of temp work and possibly the most difficult to crack. You must have flexibility and acting must come first. You may be promised flexibility and then be made to feel guilty when you need to utilise it, which apart from being highly unfair, forces you into having to make difficult decisions between what you need to do for your career and what you need to do to make money. You may be lucky and stumble upon a temp workplace with a really convenient set up that fits around the demands your career makes. Most places that are used to taking on actors will understand this (or at least profess to) and many of them even use this as their own USP when trying to recruit actors. Sacrifice your dignity, your time, even your bank balance but never let temping get in the way of work; you have to go to auditions or else there is no point in temping; you may as well just go and get a full-time job, flush the dream and earn some money.

I have been immovable on this and as a result I have lost many temp jobs and pissed many people off along the way; but I have never not been able to make an audition, or even switched a time slot. Don't get me wrong, this has by no means been easy and I have really suffered financially because of such a fierce stance, but I thoroughly believe that it has had a direct impact on the way my career has progressed. If you are to make a stand, you must learn how to survive having made it. If you jeopardize an opportunity linked to your career because of a temp job there may not always be other opportunities; there will always be other temp jobs.

How regularly do they pay and will I get paid on time?

Jobs that pay weekly are fab. Monthly is fine, but only if you know what specific day of the month you will receive the funds (otherwise you are left not knowing how much you will have in your account on what day which makes direct debits impossible unless you have a float – as discussed in Chapter 8). In my experience, especially where invoicing is required (i.e. me invoicing a company for pay I'm owed by them for work I've done), they will wait as long as they can before paying you, better that it's in their account than yours right? Yeah, FOR THEM!

Be clear on payment etiquette when you work for a company; you are perfectly within your rights to enquire as to what will be paid and when, and if there is any sort of option be clear about what would be best for you. This is your livelihood; you are not doing them a favour, and you should be assertive when it comes to money. Check their payment etiquette and always know what they owe and when it is expected; there's nothing more crippling and distracting than having outgoings due to leave your account when you have no idea when the money you've earned will reach you.

I only have acting credits on my CV, how will I get a temp job?

You are an actor, it should be no surprise that your CV is full of acting! Having said that, someone hiring for an admin role will not give a flying crap that you've played Hamlet at Regent's Park. They may care that you got A* in English at school and that you archived for a company during your bout of unemployment before playing Hamlet though. I have my acting CV and my 'other' CV, which simply lists what experience I have in different things, the jobs I've done over the years and skills I've picked up or noticed that I seem to have. Include any work you did whilst you were a student and any qualifications you have from school or otherwise. It is assumed that as an 'actor' you have bags of confidence, excellent communication skills, are good in a team and will be grateful of the work. If any of those are true then use them. Our core skills as actors are very useful in many normal workplaces, so be sure to list them (though Gold award in Double Rapier, may not need to be included for working in Greggs on a Saturday).

Can I sign a contract if it's part time?

NO!!!! Never sign a contract for anything that is not acting work. You cannot and should not be tied to anything that isn't your career. If a temp job won't let you be there commitment free, then walk. There is no compromise here. I am so adamant about this not only because a contract is a legally binding document and I would hate for you to be trapped or get into a legal dispute, but also because I know it can be a slippery slope to accidentally waking up one day with a new career you never asked for.

RULES OF A TEMP JOB

- Dip your toe into their world but remember that you are not a part of it. Be polite and friendly but remember that you are only there because they're paying you.

- Talk shop with the other actors (if there are any) but beware of not bumming each other out or repeatedly justifying yourselves to one another. It'll make you feel like shit. If others do it, let them, and then take the high road.

- Be on time and do the job to an adequate standard or they will get rid of you.

- If you really enjoy it and feel that you might prefer it to the life you're living then listen to yourself (Chapter 10).

- If you are earning money doing something you hate, make sure that you allow yourself some treats!

- As tempting as it will be to delay finding temp work after finishing an acting gig, don't wait until the money has run out completely – this will make the whole thing ten times more stressful than it already is.

- Realise that most of us are in the same boat, you are not alone, nor are you the only actor ever to get pissed off with the situation. Cut yourself some slack.

- Try and find the positives in it; whether that be that you're learning about a subject you never would have chosen to learn about, or whether it's simply eyeing up the talent whilst glass collecting.

JOBSWORTHS

Good god they're everywhere! It doesn't matter that I have a first class BA Hons or that I have worked for the BBC, when I am a temp everyone appears to be or behaves as if they are my superiors, and as if I am the thickest person ever to walk the earth. This has been and continues to be highly annoying and fairly insulting. Though at times mildly amusing (you gotta laugh). I have been 'shown' how to put a leaflet into an envelope, I have been lectured on the health and safety guidelines surrounding the use of a shredder and I have been monitored whilst speaking on a telephone. Whether my frustration clouds my vision, or whether these individuals are in fact as petty and sad as I suspect they are, it is a certainty that you will come across those who would like to make out that their role and responsibilities are of an inflated amount of importance. In many cases it's not malicious and in almost all cases it will be a subconscious style of working, but regardless of where the tendency comes from, it is there and you must (as much as possible) learn to stomach it.

STAYING SANE

Having read all of that I felt that I needed to insert this last heading!!

In my life some days this is easy and other days I'm not entirely sure it's achievable; or ever will be again. Whilst being forced to temp and to deal with the palava that it involves, remember that you are only doing it because you are pursuing something that you consider to be worth it. Make enough money to survive and look after your physical and mental health by filling your life with good and nice things. The more solvent you can be and the healthier you are, both in body and mind, the more likely you are to shine when the industry asks you to.

**'Success is the ability to go from failure to failure
without losing your enthusiasm.'
Sir Winston Churchill**

10. DOUBT

Addressing the un-addressable with balls and no guilt.

So what in the name of Belinda Carlisle and the orphans am I doing including a section that addresses contemplating leaving the business inside of a book that is designed to assist and encourage longevity and progression? Well, from the conception of this book I intended to support and nurture the actors of our generation, hoping not only to motivate and enthuse you, promoting the positive wherever possible, but also, and maybe more importantly, to deal with the negatives head-on, instead of shying away from them. Doubt is one of those negatives; one that slyly breathes down all of our necks at some point with varying degrees of intensity.

I'd feel like I'd let you down if I didn't address this, and I'd feel like an absolute hypocrite if I were to encourage you to simply sweep niggling doubts under the carpet, or worse still deny that they're there at all. Just this week I was huddled in a little heap of snot and tears because I didn't get a part, and six months ago I couldn't enjoy much at all because I was so frustrated with the lack of work. So now I'll what, tell you you're gonna rise above it, ride the wave, that it'll be fine and that it happens to us all? No. I'm gonna level with you and admit that sometimes I despise the fact that my life is so turbulent; it's like being in an abusive relationship with a lover you cannot get enough of, no matter how they treat you, and no matter how many times they slap you in the face you go back for more because you love them and feel that you were destined to have them in your life. I am not going to tell you that everything will be fine, I am not going to presume to know whether this is the best life for you or not, how the hell do I know whether you've made the right choices? It would be irresponsible and idiotic of me to be so generic with something that is so intrinsically personal.

What I aim to achieve within this chapter is a safe forum; I want to make it ok for you to wonder, for you to question everything and anything, and for you to admit that at times, our industry's an absolute twat. But know that ditching your career is very different to spitting your dummy out, so you must learn to assess the difference! Every time I've fallen down so far I've managed to get back up fighting, but it is ok not to, not to know how to, and not to know whether you want to. Bailing out of a nose-diving plane you suspect might crash and burn is an intelligent decision and is brave, not cowardly; I hope the information here will help you to figure out if the plane still has wings and can fly, and whether or not you wish to sit it out. A chapter that confronts this is needed, for all our sakes; and those of you who know, or have known these demons, will welcome the openness I offer here.

You may be thinking of leaving the business, you may be exhausted by the life you lead, you may be flirting with the idea of another career or you may just be having an off day/week/month – year? All are understandable, and whatever your circumstances I hope that you will appreciate the opportunity to think and feel freely here, without judgment or pressure of any kind. Analysing how and what you feel takes an unnerving amount of self-assessment, and the strength to act on that assessment can be incredibly hard to muster. The findings from any such assessment are personal and private and certainly never a sign of weakness or lack of dedication; they are the truth, your truth.

What's the point? Why do I bother? What the fuck do they want from me? Is it all worth it? How can I keep this up? Can I live like this? I don't know what to do and how to make sense of anything. Do I enjoy this anymore? Am I good enough? What am I aiming for exactly? What am I missing out on by sticking to this? Is this what I thought it would be like?

… These are just a handful of the questions and thoughts that flit through the minds of actors throughout our careers (sometimes throughout the day). Most of the time they will be fleeting and usually triggered by a momentous blow of sorts (or will be the result of some sort of substance-induced moan). Whatever the source or trigger I believe that these thoughts are always worth paying attention to, especially if they arise with any sort of frequency, or if there's a pattern to their reoccurrence. *Really* asking yourself these questions and not just saying them may be difficult, as what may unfold within the answers might be hard to swallow. However, whether you are in real doubt or not I believe that it is always a healthy choice to check in with oneself. Most of the time digging of this sort will simply reconfirm your ongoing passion, determination and drive; if not, the answers will be telling in a different way; a way you must listen to and eventually, when you're ready, act on.

There's so much talk about actors having to be driven to a ridiculous degree, about us having to have nerves of steel and skin as thick as it comes; no superhuman powers are bestowed at birth, there is no magic coat of armour purchased upon enrolment or any binding contract of dedication signed when we enter the business! We are who we are and we do what we do, with no real grasp of how any of it is going to pan out. You deal with it or you get out, right? Wrong. There are a million colours of 'dealing' with it and a billion shades of not and unfortunately there is seemingly no question, no discussion, and certainly no support for anyone who is trying to figure out where the hell on the colour chart they are. From happy to sad, from determined to desperate, from content to lost are huge leaps; areas littered with an array of stages, questions and decisions. No matter whether you're in one of these extremes or if you've fallen into one of the gaps, doubt will be present in some form at some time, whether it waves and leaves, or sets up camp. We wouldn't be human if we didn't doubt; who is absolutely certain of everything? Liars are. Let's not lie, let's be honest, at least with ourselves.

ASSESSING THE SITUATION

– weighing up the options

Whatever happens in this book stays in this book if that is your wish; any feelings stirred, or realizations made are nobody's business but yours and it's important to me that you have such a resource in times of need. I know that one of the most agonizing parts of experiencing a phase of doubt can be admitting it, whether to yourself or others. Here you have the license to doubt privately, ponder privately and decide privately, with no interference or lasting reminder that the thoughts were ever present. If you are contemplating chatting it over with a mate then great, that would suggest to me that you have already taken a huge step in admitting your doubt to yourself and sharing can be a wonderful way to make sense of what you're feeling; hearing yourself say something out loud can be ever so revealing. By all means seek support from the people you trust (they can cuddle; with the best will in the world I can't get a book to do that!) but in doing so, do be wary of others' opinions clouding your own. It is fairly easy for friends (especially if they are also actors) to unintentionally merge their state of mind with your plight, or their plight with your doubt; or to accidentally push their emotional investment in the subject onto you. In no way am I suggesting that you shouldn't confide in someone, but maybe give yourself time to organize your thoughts a little before letting others in on the decision-making process.

I am not able or willing to tell you what to do with your doubt, or how to feel about it; how can I know what course of action is best for you personally? How can I know to what extent you're struggling? I can't. All I can hope to do is pose questions that I feel are relevant, useful and revealing.

THERE ARE ABSOLUTELY NO RIGHT OR WRONG ANSWERS HERE

Over the page is a collection of questions that I feel may help to clarify your conscious and subconscious thought processes. Each one will have a profoundly unique response, followed by an equally unique course of action, personal to you.

Some of these might be a bit deep, or even harsh, but I think asking them is essential if you are to be truly honest and clued up about your career, life and future.

Ok, I'll stop dithering and just ask 'em…

Are you enjoying your life?

How does being out of acting work affect the rest of your life?

When you do work do you feel satisfied and fulfilled?

What is your ratio of being in work and out of work? How does this impact on your day-to-day well-being?

Realistically speaking what are your goals and do you have a tactical plan of how you might achieve them?

What is your financial situation and is it bothering you? To what extent?

As time goes on are your priorities changing? I.e. relationships and the thought of starting a family? If so, have you thought about how it will be possible and whether you want to/can juggle everything?

Do you sleep?

Do you enjoy things outside of acting?

Is there anything else you'd like to/are interested in pursuing as a career?

Are you under pressure from family members to 'succeed'?

What levels of 'success' are you seeking?

When you get an audition are you excited or full of dread?

Do you get auditions and are you likely to?

Are you interested in training further or taking any add-on courses?

Was drama school more stressful or more fun for you?

Are most of your friends actors? And is this at all tiresome?

How deeply does it affect you when you don't get a job?

How would you feel if someone told you that you could never act again professionally?

Have any of your friends expressed doubt about being an actor? How did it make you feel?

Are you depressed or think you might be?

Do those around you think you should continue – what's their consensus of opinion and how does it make you feel when and if they express it?

Did you decide to be an actor as an adult or was it a childhood dream you stuck to?

Do you want to travel?

How much are you willing to sacrifice for the job, should you need to?

Is there another area of the industry you're interested in? I.e. Directing, Writing, Casting Director, Design etc?

Have you put a time frame on how long you'll 'try' for? If so, what is it?

Do you like living in London? Would you live here if you weren't an actor?

How often do you get to the theatre/cinema? Do you enjoy it when you do go?

Have you had a holiday recently? Do you get time and space away from your career? And do you need it/want it/crave time out?

Do you envy your friends who are acting more regularly than you?

Do you envy your friends who are outside of the business who have cars, families, mortgages, holidays etc.?

Do you envy your friends who were actors and are now not?

Do you think you're a good enough actor when you compare yourself to others?

How do you spend your spare time?

Can you imagine not being an actor? You may not want to, but can you? What does your life look like if so?

Is your doubt erased when you get a job? Does it return straight away once unemployed?

Why do you actually like acting? What is that want/need to do it actually about?

That is a shitload to think about, I know. The idea certainly isn't to bombard you, or indeed to create doubt! These questions are designed to encourage you to assess your life (on a grander scale than just work) and to enable you to see what your heart thinks when your head isn't butting in. I feel that these are important questions that we all should have the balls to ask ourselves. How can we know if we're happy without asking? Profound? (Ish).

Which questions will be most relevant to you will depend on your age and the stage of your career, but as no one follows one strict code of thinking in life, by any specific timescale, I'm not sure it does any harm to ponder all of them, for a second at least, whatever age and stage you are in when you pick up this book. Try to listen to your gut feeling first before rationalizing or 'fluffing up' the answers; and whilst you're perfectly within your rights to do 'fluff', know that admitting to yourself that you have done so is progress in itself. You may come back to this set of questions many times and your answers may or may not change, and if that is useful to you then by all means do it; but don't neglect to notice that you do keep returning.

The questions circle round a few points, I guess.

Are you happy? If not why? Also if not, what can be done?

Are you still sure that you want the job, now that you really know what life comes with it?

Is your love for this business deep-routed and do you spend most of your time living and breathing it, or could you enjoy it on a more part-time basis?

What is your priority list in life? Where does acting come on that list?

And most importantly, a question that I think unlocks all kinds of untold secrets about you and what drives you, is the last question from the initial list:

Why do you like acting? What is the want/need to do it actually about?

Is it cathartic? Is it the admiration and adoration that goes with it when you're on top? Is it the attention? Is it the hope of a wealthy life and the dream of grand scale recognition? Is it to do with acceptance? Is it a need to tell stories? Is it to escape reality? Is it to avoid structure and routine? Is it a weird obsession you've never really made sense of?

What is it for you? Again, there is no right, wrong or preferred answers, no one but you is going to know the outcome anyway and we all have our reasons and objectives for doing what we do; yours are for you to know and you alone. I have asked myself these questions, of course I have, and I think I have a handful of answers now which help me make sense of my life and inform my choices. I honestly don't know how you can chase something if you aren't sure what it is that you're chasing and why.

Drama school focuses on delivering the goods once the order has been made; a lifelong order made, in many cases, by eighteen-year-olds (and younger!) It seems barbaric in a way that so many youngsters enter themselves into a raffle without being absolutely sure of what the prize is, what the odds of winning are, or how to walk away when they no longer wish to play. In my opinion these questions should be popping up throughout the syllabus; if they were I feel that we'd have possibly fewer actors (no bad thing), and the remaining ones would be far happier, contented, informed and stable than the majority of us are today. To me, drama school and the first few years of being an actor should be as much about observing whether one is able to succeed as it should be about whether one wants to and why.

How did it start for you? A school play? A village pantomine? A drama club or class? No doubt it was an innocent hobby that adorned a future far more complex than a child with dreams could have attempted to comprehend? Suddenly the drafty village hall where it all began becomes a distant memory as agents, overdrafts, commercial castings and tax take over, leaving limited time for contemplation and little allowance for uncertainty. Continuing is not always about being good enough, or even about being fortunate enough to be working; it's about accepting the all-consuming life that goes with it, and making a well informed CHOICE for that to be your path, every day for the rest of your life. That ain't no decision to be taken lightly, or to feel stuck with. Christ, if I'd have obeyed my first career choice I'd be a purple-haired rock-chick touring Britain's holiday parks in a band named 'Zeus'. (Actual truth, ask my mum. She may have preferred that to be honest, at least it was a regular income during the summer…) I don't see why anything has to be a lifelong decision unless we consciously make it so and even then the only person withholding the get-out clause is you. Be aware, don't be lumbered. We now live in a world where change is embraced and freedom of choice is, well, better than it was. People stand in front of God and promise to be together until they die; ten months later they're signing divorce papers and arguing over the marble soap dish. People change, minds change, life happens and we're all allowed to admit something isn't what we thought it would be.

All of you will take something very different from this chapter. A few of you might be able to challenge and cure momentary defeatism (repackaging it as a meaningless wobble), whilst the majority of you will use it to reawaken your ambition and reconfirm your determination. But for those of you who, having read this chapter, are now feeling a huge amount of anxiety, or even a huge sense of relief, read on and allow yourself to take the first steps towards shaping the life you actually want to live – we only get one. (I assume? I'm an agnostic atheist, so in my mind we certainly do! But even if we don't, try not to bugger this one up by wasting time being too stubborn or chickenshit to take control of it.)

CONTEMPLATING A DECISION

– ripping off the plaster

Ripping off the plaster is intended to symbolise admitting doubt and assessing it, no more. Coming to a conclusion would be far nearer the 'biting the bullet' phase. (See later.) For now, acknowledging that you are less than chuffed with the way things are going and making the link between your career and the knock-on effect it has to your whole being is a huge step. Be gentle with yourself, whilst being as honest as you can stand, in doses that are constructive and manageable – only you can judge this.

Hopefully you will have answered the questions earlier and have gone back to them several times to recognise what your true answers are. Just because you said 'Yes, I can imagine myself doing something else' or 'Yes, I do want children, sooner rather than later' does not mean than I intend you to jack it all in; as I said there was no hidden agenda behind the questions and certainly no leading pattern to them; it wasn't a flow chart in disguise. I need not dwell on my reasoning for the questions, they are ones I've asked myself and ones that people around me have admitted to asking themselves; your use for them is up to you, but if you're still reading this I suspect they've been enlightening in some way?

So, assuming that this doubt you may feel is a little more than a wobble, we need to think seriously and sensibly about what's to be done about it? This will not happen overnight and you cannot compare yourself, your situation or your reaction to anyone else; as I've said, this is fundamentally private and specific to you as an individual. To what extent do your doubts reach? Are we talking danger point or a niggling doubt that comes and goes? Some people stay at danger point for years and others allow the niggle to be enough to tip the scales very rapidly. As I said, this is about you. So, what do you think? Can you see how things go for a while or have you been doing that and nothing's improved? Don't let the hope of something happening be the only reason to stay in the game. There needs to be more justification than that. You need to back that up with more passion, more determination and more pragmatics for that to sound like a good plan.

It's worth noting than many people keep the bunting in the box and stand a safe distance away from the mega phone when this decision is made; it's not something many feel the need to yell about or celebrate, in fact many slip out of the business undetected, and others wake up one morning and realise that they're doing a different job and enjoying a new life without much anguish or debate having preceded it. These are the lucky ones and this chapter caters mainly for those of you who are somewhere in between camp pissed off and camp admission; some of you will be battling with yourselves regarding the course of your future and others of you will be too devastated and confused to contemplate doing so. The stages are sensitive, non-linear and not to be rushed through.

Talking it out can help, and I only advised you to assess things privately earlier to prevent you from being swayed or pressured by well-meaning colleagues or friends. It can be easy to sweep things under the carpet for fear of being the odd one out; there can be a pack mentality among actors, a club, a community, and facing leaving this can be a very daunting prospect. At this stage, if your unhappiness is demanding change, do confide in someone, someone who can be objective and sensitive. On hearing yourself saying it out loud, you may realize that you can't realistically step away from what you love, at least not right now. On the other hand, hearing yourself say it, may confirm the need for change.

Take the pressure off of yourself. There is no ticking time bomb and there is nothing to say that any decision is final, if you don't want it to be. You are the only one who has to suffer the uncertainty of the decision-making process and you are also the only one in control of how long you endure it for. A decision may come organically; or, you may need to be assertive and accept responsibility for moving things along. The course of action and pace of change depend solely on what kind of person you are, what you need and what process is best for you. Trust your instincts, listen to your heart and your head in equal measure and be realistic. Stripped bare, all that actually counts in this life is a happiness that you create for yourself and some sort of a sustainable contentment. I'm giving you a safe place to say that you've changed your mind. I'm also forcing you to test your own endurance. Which of these applies to you, only you know.

BITING THE BULLET

– Brave

I designed this chapter to act as a filter, losing readers as it progressed. If this has worked then those of you still with me will be having serious doubts about whether you want to be an actor anymore. This is an ordeal and only those who have loved a career as we have could possibly understand what it is to face letting it go.

Firstly, if at all possible, I think you should go on holiday. If you're anything like me you won't have dared leave the country much whilst you've been actor for fear of missing anything, (and any trips you have taken have involved a couple of ounces of guilt and mobile phone glued to your hand.) GIVE YOURSELF A BREAK. Not only will the space and change of scene do you good, but also the relaxation will provide clarity of thought and an infusion of calm. I don't mean you have to swan off to the Carribean for a fortnight (though nice if you can) but a weekend, a city break, a camping trip, even a bloody drive somewhere – anything, whatever form it takes the principles are the same; give yourself the time and space to make peace with your doubts and, ultimately, your decision.

Like I've said, there is no rush and you must not allow yourself to be rushed; though at the same time the temptation to stagnate and sit in what is familiar will quite probably override the prospect of facing crunch-time so be careful of that too! Banish unhelpful phrases such as quitting, or throwing in the towel, or failing. None of these are useful or accurate; it's changing.

By this point, after all I've said and everything you are likely to have considered, you will probably know the answer to the next question.

WHAT NEXT

– the future's yours

Once the decision is made a huge part of coping with it will be to look at what's next. What do you want to do? For many of you it might be glaringly obvious, and for others the search may become a bit of a full-time job in itself. How exciting to be at the foot of a new journey though?

The great news, brilliant news in fact, is that the skills you possess as an actor are really useful in most, if not all, walks of life. Your people skills, communicative abilities, confidence and energy will stand you in very good stead for new areas of work; you just have to have a good long think about what that new area might be. Maybe it's something within the industry (though be careful not to exchange one set of problems for a whole new load if freelance is something you're trying to be rid of!), or it may be something vaguely connected, like teaching. Or perhaps it's something completely random that you've always wondered about. Do you fancy retraining in something? You may wish to go back and study a new subject? Or you may quite simply want to earn a living doing whatever and have a bit of fun the rest of the time! Whatever path you choose, take your time and enjoy giving yourself a chance to be good at something else.

Intense chat over. Well done, you ok? Answer me or I'll worry!

Hey, most bouts of doubt are twitches and nothing more. We live in extremes and making rash decisions when in an extreme state is never a great plan; always let the dust settle first. We don't split up with a guy every time he leaves the toilet seat up, do we? You do? Wow, high maintenance…

Whatever decision you come to or don't come to, whether you revisit this chapter a million times and never need to make the decision, know at least that questioning is not only allowed but also encouraged.

Now, either go and watch a film and remember why you do this crazy job, or if you're still confused, pour a generous helping of your favourite alcoholic beverage, take a large swig, a deep breath…and go back to the questions list.

11. CONVERSATIONS WITH THE PEOPLE OF TOMORROW

Watch their space!

This chapter was the loveliest part of the process of writing this book. I got to sit down for a few hours with a selection of exciting, tenacious young professionals, without any other agenda than to pick their brains and drink some tea! (It's hard being an actress-turned-author-turned-Parky!) To be fair, I was a bit shite with the question planning, but as I had hoped, when enthusiastic people start talking shop the rest seems to flow rather effortlessly and before you know it you've put the world (or the industry) to rights and it's kicking out time in the bar (coffee shop).

My idea behind this chapter is rather simple; firstly I thought it might be very useful to hear opinions and experiences from a handful of people who are representing some of the key roles that you will be meeting, working and collaborating with throughout your career; the very people that can and will have a direct effect on your work, and possibly lack thereof. Secondly, in the spirit of the whole ethos of this book, it is important to me that you encounter some fellow ambitious, skilled and dedicated professionals who are either in, or not far from an age and/or stage that is relevant to you. These are not 'success stories' with some tacky 'if they can then you can' slogan attached; they are simply examples of how to do the thing you love well, whilst making a living from it. I could think of no better way to demonstrate how the formula of hard work + ability + attitude = achievement and respect. What they all have in common with each other (whether these attributes are known to them or not) is gumption, and what you have in common with them all is the love you have for what you do and your determination to spend your days doing it.

Throughout your career you will be working alongside and collaborating with a myriad of different people, all of whom will have differing jobs; many of which have a direct effect on your own career. The professional collision of our roles is inevitable, and therefore our understanding of what each other does is, in my mind, imperative.

I hope that this informal little peep into their side of this crazy industry will not only provide some clarity for you about what it is that their jobs entail, but that it will also allow you to notice the links between all of the roles; especially yours and theirs.

So, here they are, a handful of skilled young professionals, including a director, a casting director, an agent and an actor, who have kindly agreed to offer their thoughts and opinions of the business you are in. I hope that you will take their advice and feed on their enthusiasm. (Also enjoy the break from my voice; chapters 1-11 may have worn you out and after this chapter it's back to me again so savour the articulate wisdom whilst you have it)... Ha, no pressure then guys... Don't fuck it up...

I'd like to thank Bruce, Alice, James, Sean (and Mark and Brogan from the other chapters) for giving your time, energy and knowledge so willingly; your support, sense of fun and generosity were a pleasure to behold. Thank you so much for taking part in this insane quest to inspire and motivate the next batch of actors; your words have helped to make sense of it all.

... God help you all if I ever win a BAFTA, my acceptance speech would run right into the ten o'clock news.

A CONVERSATION WITH
DIRECTOR BRUCE GUTHRIE

Bruce is a British Theatre Director. Throughout eight years in the business he has moved from fringe productions to working in the West End and the National Theatre. Though he was teching his production of *Othello* for the Singapore Repertory Theatre, he very kindly set an hour aside to Skype me so we could chew the fat about work. *(Nat's dialogue is in italics, Bruce's dialogue is in regular type.)*

Bruce, you were an actor first, you trained as an actor, so how did directing arrive on the agenda for you?

I trained as an actor for three years at GSA and directed my first play just before I left. A friend of mine who was in the same year thought that I would be quite good at directing and wanted to play the lead in a specific play so asked me if I would be interested in taking up the project. I was and we decided to give it a shot. I knew that if I wanted to do it then I wanted to do it for more than just a couple of nights, so I thought we could take it to the Edinburgh festival. So I used money that I had saved up from my part-time job at Tesco and worked double shifts on Sundays in order to raise the budget. GSA were running a fringe scheme that enabled third years to submit proposals for productions they wanted to stage in the studio, which was great as it gave people the opportunity to explore different roles; to give producing or directing a go. I talked to the school a lot about our project, and the plan to take it to the Fringe. No one else who was submitting ideas was attempting to do what we were – however, when the list of who had been successful went up, we weren't on it and I was...a bit annoyed about this.

(I laugh.)

So I went over to the production office and sat waiting until somebody would see me. Eventually I got in to see the Head of Production, and after I'd calmed down and stopped ranting I asked why we didn't get it. He said 'because I wasn't passionate enough in my application'. Now, the application was as basic and non-exploratory as you can get, I had just followed it. It was a hard lesson but a very good one; sometimes just giving people what they ask for is not always the best course of action. It also taught me that if you really want to do something you have to be prepared to follow through on it no matter what, so if there's an obstacle put in your way, find a way round it. I turned round and said to them 'This is happening; one way or another, this is happening'. To their credit, the Head of Production was incredibly supportive and took me through what it would take to make it happen. Eventually we did it in a studio space in Guildford. I had no idea whether it was any good or not before we put it in front of an audience!

But you were pleased with it?

Yes, well, I thought it was really good; I'd enjoyed it and I thought that the guys had given some of their best work to date. I don't think it was necessarily down to me as a director, it was the whole atmosphere; it was a great play, the production was interesting and the actors all really wanted to do it. They put so much into that production. We took it to Edinburgh and made a profit. The actors were only being paid limited expenses and we agreed to use the profits to put it on for one night in London. It took almost a year for that to happen. I'd never done this before and was lucky enough to find a mentor in Ashley Herman who was Chairman of the Board at GSA. He helped an awful lot. I honestly believe that the reason he helped is because we had something that was already going, past the idea stage. If you ask someone to create an opportunity for you, nine times out of ten they won't, but if you have something already on its feet and you ask for advice then I think that they're much more likely to help.

It's not simply investing in an idea then is it, not just trusting someone's whim, it's actually seeing potential in motion and choosing to assist.

Indeed. Time is very precious. I think that's a really important thing to remember; people in the industry don't ignore you for sport, it'll be all about time. Everyone wants a piece of influential people and the reality is that there can never be enough time for them to listen to or help everyone.

Exactly. It's not a personal issue.

And do you think that that ability you had, to be able to ask for help, to be confident enough to feel that you could and should ask, has been quite a factor in your 'journey', as it were?

I think so.

Do you think this is an attribute that young ambitious people should have, should dare to have?

I'm not adverse to picking up the phone and asking people who are where I want to be if we can have a chat. I've been very lucky that I've worked with some amazing people in my career. Their support and guidance has helped me to visualize how I'm going to realise what I want, both long-term and short.

And do you think that actors or directors, professionals, should have aims and goals, not set in stone necessarily but aspirations certainly, with a clear view of how they're going to get there?

I think everyone should have a strategy, and by nature ambitious people are always looking ahead aren't they? Rupert Goold always says (of directors) that you should have the play that you're working on, the play that you're working on next, and then something else sitting on the periphery that you'd like to do in the future. Then strategies can be formed around those goals. But understand your own strategies – Say an actor wants to work for the RSC, well why do you want to work for the RSC? Who casts? How are you going to get seen? Do they do workshops? What productions of theirs can I see? If there's a goal in sight, there are all sorts of things that can be done in order to achieve it, and the one thing that does not help, in any way, is doing nothing. People who wait for the phone to ring are

*Ridiculous/*idiots *(we say in unison).*

Inertia is one of the biggest killers of careers I think. And it's something we let happen.

A recurring theme throughout my life has been that people have said that I've wanted too much, that I've aimed too big. But how else are you going to get anywhere?

(I laugh knowingly.) It's quite a hard balance to strike sometimes I think, between allowing yourself to aim high but also being practical about how the hell you're going to get there. Everyone can say 'I want to'. Plus it's all too easy to concentrate on what everyone else is doing and measuring our own efforts and aims against theirs.

Competition can breed results sure, but it should be about wanting the best for your career, or your production, instead of wanting others to fail.

So after that first show that you directed, then what.

I directed another play on the fringe and then one at Trafalgar Studios. After that I had to sit down and think about things. It didn't go quite the way I wanted it to. With that project I was unable to transfer what I had in my head onto the stage, to create my vision properly. I felt I didn't have enough experience to take myself to the next level, I'd just reached the limits of my knowledge at the time.

Do you think that you learnt as much, if not more, from that production?

It's a cliché isn't it that you learn more from your failures than you do from your successes, and yes I did probably learn more from that 'failure'… but I preferred the successes!

Ha, of course.

So, I licked my wounds for a bit and then I decided there were two ways of dealing with it; I could figure out how to get better at it, or stop and do something else; so I decided to do a bit of assisting, to see how somebody else directs. Up until that point, I'd been trying to be the director that 'I would want in the room if I were acting'. I didn't have the knowledge and the information to change that and I didn't want to get it from books, I wanted to get it through experience. So I went and assisted. I did an unpaid job at Southwark Playhouse and then, through the recommendation of friend and fellow director Ruth Carney, I had a meeting to be Resident Director on *Shadowlands* in the West End. I went and did that and did a good job so that led to more work, and more work. I kept writing to the National Theatre Studio; I knew that they had a young directors course and I knew that would be an ideal place to do it. I wrote to them six times. Eventually, I got a meeting there.

Persistence is another attribute that ambitious people must possess; they go hand in hand. You mentioned earlier that you took unpaid work, and that you wrote several letters before being acknowledged etc. Those trials and knock-backs obviously relate to the life and job of an actor too. So, when one is building and climbing, do you think that unpaid work is something that actors, certainly new actors should consider?

Oh yes, I think it's a necessity for most, because theatre is an expensive thing to do and the wonderful thing about the fringe, whether in London or Edinburgh, is that you can put on a piece of work just with a bunch of people and a script, anywhere. And there's no substitute for practical experience.

And experience outside of the comfort of drama school as well.

Absolutely, it's a real test. The only thing that I would say to anyone who is considering doing unpaid work is that you have to know, before you say yes to the job, that you're actually OK with not getting paid for it! Because the second that you start resenting that fact, is the second that the job is over, and it'll end in disaster. The same goes for low-paid jobs.

(I laugh.)

One might assume that those actors have their priorities all to cock; any actor worth their salt who truly loves their craft would quite happily do it from dawn until dusk if the director and the project required them to.

I'm a director twenty-four hours a day, my life kind of revolves around it. Obviously people can do what works for them, but it should always be a want not a chore. The thing that mystifies me is when actors graduate and never do a class or set up a script-reading session – everyone waits for everyone else to do stuff.

I've mentioned this a lot, not only what we said earlier about inertia being basically professional suicide, but also how unattractive being passive is. I think being productive and making your own luck is what it's all about these days. Lyn Gardner wrote an article about it a few years ago where she said 'Actors can't just act anymore. If they want to work they have to be entrepreneurial: they have to make work'.

People have to be prepared to put everything they've got into something, in the knowledge that it may fail. If it does fail, they must be prepared to start the process all over again and ask 'what did I learn'. (By failure I mean that we can all reach the limits of our expertise; we can all need to know more and can and should always attempt to improve.)

And that's the reality of becoming good. Reality is something I'm focusing on rather heavily in this book, for obvious reasons, but mainly because I think fantasizing about things is dangerous. I don't want my goals to be dreams, I want them to happen for real. I think for many people there's almost more joy (and certainly more safety) in the imagining of something, rather than the actual experiencing of it. Like you said, it's a twenty-four-hour-thing, that's the reality, and it's certainly a lifestyle choice and not just a job.

It's a gift and it's a curse. The thing that you love to do, your passion, hobby, is also your job, your living. And that is quite an odd thing I guess. During my second show when I was basically living on about £1 a day (as most of my money was tied up in the show), someone close to me turned round and said to me 'yeah but it's a hobby, you don't get paid for it, so it's a hobby'. I went ballistic.

I bet!

I was like, 'don't you get why I'm doing this, I'm investing in this way so that one day someone will pay me!' I was hardly doing it for the good of my health; it was killing me!

If I can sort of shift onto auditions and casting a little bit? I think it's really useful for actors to have a bit of an idea what happens on the other side of the table. One of the most valuable experiences I had as a young actress, about five or six years ago, was when I had been cast ahead of other people and was asked to come in and read with the auditioning actresses in the recalls. It was such an eye-opener. It was not only pretty cool to be totally relaxed and nonchalant in an audition environment (because I already had the part) but it was also utterly fascinating to observe the other actresses' behaviour. I was asked to stay and discuss the candidates with the director and casting director, and I watched in amazement; decisions made in a heartbeat, two actresses equally talented and right for the part so their hair colour was the deciding factor – it was a real turning point for me; I started to think about the world beyond what I do, and the roles and decisions that directly impact my job… I want to try and imitate that lesson as best as I can at various junctures throughout this book. So, I know this must differ and vary depending on the project, but do you generally go through agents/casting directors to find actors or do you trawl Spotlight when you cast a show?

It's kind of evolved over the last few years. I used to look at Spotlight a lot and still do in certain instances, but the more experience I've had and the more I've worked with people, the more I've formed a sort of mental catalogue. But then also, in the last few years I've been lucky enough to have a casting director, which makes life so much easier because they put together lists etc. It depends on the size of the project and what your requirements are. Casting directors are really useful for directors; the best ones will find actors who are accurate to your breakdown and who you will get on with. They are vital to the accuracy of the casting. Now though, chances are, after having had eight years' experience as a director, that I'll have seen the actors in something, or I'll spot someone on their CV that I know, in which case I can pick up the phone and ask them what they've been like.

Very important point.

Very. Reputation is just…hugely important. Key. Your reputation as an actor is priceless and people who mar theirs or take it lightly are daft. Both in terms of the personal and professional reputation – those things aren't separate. You can be the most talented actor in the world but if you get a rep for being difficult, and I don't mean in terms of quirky performance things, I mean difficult as in disruptive to the process, then people aren't going to want you in the room.

And if a director called you and asked your opinion, what would be some of the things that might make you not recommend an actor?

I'd have to try and consider what type of director they were and wait for them to lead it. They might ask 'How did they get on with the other actors', 'Did they contribute ideas', etc. … An actor has to work out how a director works just as much as a director works out how an actor works in order to be able to get the best out of them. I do a lot of watching in the room; I watch how people interact with each other, I watch what they're doing when they're not working and when they are. Key things for me: are they prepared, do they work hard, do they listen, do they take direction well, do they interact well with other actors, do they give, do they look after each other. Being a good person helps enormously too. It's a 60/40 split, or maybe 70/30 – 70% being about what you can do on stage and 30% being who you are offstage.

Reputation is so important, from the first job onwards and it never stops being important; each job that you get allows people to form opinions of you.

It takes a lifetime to build and a second to destroy… Lateness is one of the worst bad habits. There's a casting director I know who puts it rather well: 'If someone is late then it tells me that they think their time is more important than mine.'

Would not want to be on the receiving end of that comment in a casting!

Our work is informal a lot of the time and I think the lines can get blurred; although it's playing, you're being paid to play, it's also work and business! Professionalism has to be a given. If we're talking auditions as well, actors should be rigorous in their preparation. If you want to work for, let's say the National or the RSC, my main question is 'Why. Why do you want to work with them? Name five productions of theirs that you've seen' – most actors can't. 'What director do you like there?'…they say 'I dunno'. Why the hell would you want to go and work in Stratford for a year when you don't know what they do there?! And the amount of actors that I meet who don't go to the theatre and don't watch movies – they call themselves actors! When I'm at home and not working nights I'm in the theatre maybe three or four times a week and I'm not flush, I haven't got money to burn. You can go and see a show at the National for £5 if you stand, £12 if you want to sit.

There are ways to see theatre on a budget.

It's a myth that there aren't. There's masses of stuff. And if you're really hard up you can go to the National Theatre Studio and go to the archives and watch things for free. There's always a way if you want to do something. There's always a solution.

… You touched on professionalism a bit earlier and we were sort of edging towards rehearsal etiquette, which I know is something that you think should possibly be focused on more in drama school? That, and marketing?

Absolutely. You need a rounded, informed view of the business you're going into. There should be a class on how much it costs to put on a show, on how businesses market themselves. Actors are their own business. Getting through the door is one thing and then being good when you do is another. In auditions, some directors know within about twenty seconds whether or not the person has something that we want to see more of, that we can work with; then the rest of the audition is just confirming or denying the instinct you had at the beginning. Which is why some auditions can be brutal. Some of the best auditions that I've seen are when the person has totally prepared and when they're very excited and enthusiastic about the project; it's not just about them wanting the job. When an actor walks in the room as if it's the first day of rehearsals it makes you want to make that happen for real.

I have banged on about preparation in this book a lot and explained how it's certainly my own work ethic and the only way that I can function. When I've prepared thoroughly it makes me excited to go into the room and it also means that I can leave knowing that I've done all I can; I've kept my side of the bargain, what fate deals me and what decisions are made are then beyond my control. I can only relinquish control because I know that I have done all I can. That attitude is also what enables me to move on if I don't get it. I simply couldn't cope with rejection if I knew it was my 'fault'; that I could have done more.

And some people can't cope because it's not their 'fault'. Because there are so many other things at play, they feel powerless over their own destiny, which is very very difficult. It's the curse of the actor and I really feel for them; it was one of the things that I hated the most when I was an actor. I hated auditioning.

I think the more we know about the way casting works and the more stories we hear, the more sense we can make of it, or the more accepting we can be of the fact that there isn't always (what we'd class as) 'a reason'! Decisions are subjective and sometimes, only about a whim or a feeling. Or politics. We aren't, with the best will in the world, able to 'create' or 'manipulate' that.

It's a fine balance between being able to say to yourself, 'I just wasn't right for it' and being truly honest and saying 'did I prepare well?' And, if you don't get it, can you learn anything or take anything from it?

I think there's always something to be taken from observations and experiences, especially where auditions are concerned, that's why I always have a debrief (pint) afterwards, so I can properly process what happened, what was said, how I performed, how they reacted… And also I think it's important to assess the decisions and assumptions that I've made about them, and the way that they work, and whether I think it's a way that I would enjoy and respond to.

Definitely, definitely… Auditions are never a 'waste of time', they're practice if nothing else and certainly, it's a two-way process.

Of course, and it's about planting seeds. Yes, you aim to get the job, but if you do good work in the audition then you've bought yourself twenty minutes of good exposure with an industry professional or two. Not getting jobs might feel like you're not getting anywhere, but as long as good foundations are being made, something will come up that has your name on it.

Absolutely and this is where business thinking comes in. If you've 'impressed', then suddenly you have a 'relationship', or a connection with those people and can write to them and talk to them if you bump into them at press nights etc.… There should also be classes in networking. I think a lot of people see networking as selling out, which is total idiocy.

Of course, and this is something else I've mentioned in the graduation chapter.

Networking is sort of making friends, you are essentially becoming acquainted with, or attempting to make contact with someone who will be useful to you, so that in turn you can be useful to them. If you approach it from a cynical point of view of 'I want a job from you and you should give me one', then you've fundamentally misunderstood what networking is; it's about getting to know people.

I think the key, or one of the keys, for actors certainly, is knowing your own worth; not having to 'project' what you are or what you supposedly 'have'… not gobbing off, I guess!

Exactly, and actually the best tip about networking is to make the person talk about themselves. Ask them questions because you are interested in them and who they are.

(I nod.)

Be interested and interesting.

Oh, so important. Being interested in what they do and what they're saying and not just attempting to use or go through the motions for the sake of a connection is incredibly important. It's transparent if not and ultimately, completely ineffective, actually it's then counterproductive and potentially damaging.

And to be 'interesting', you've got to be doing something towards work, even when you're out of it.

Athletes train and practise regularly, being a performer is no different; you have to look your best and every ability you have must be on form at any given time. People assuming that they can access their skills after having had no practice for six months are in for a shock.

Well yes, I'm not a class-goer, I'll admit; seventeen years of 'classes' at school was enough for me. However, I do practise, and my mind is almost always in a creative mode of sorts. You've constantly got to be on the edge of being brilliant. And that's tiring… It's tiring being brilliant is what I'm sayin'!

(Laughter.)

Existing in that state doesn't just mean staying fit and psychologically healthy, it doesn't just mean practising your craft; it also means knowing what's going on, who is working where, what's opening, what's closing, which producers have been nominated for things etc.

Exactly, exactly. I think that's very true.

There's another important point about being in a constant state of 'readiness'. In those quiet periods, being in that state of readiness provides hope and alertness; knowing what's going on makes you feel part of things, even when you're 'technically' not. You aren't only an actor when you're acting… One of the things that I do think stumps actors, which is directly related to how you function when you're 'out of it', is that oh so familiar audition question 'What have you been up to lately?' It absolutely crushes people. I've seen it happen in social situations, let alone when it's a producer asking! It's ridiculous to me that there's any shame in being out of work, what we do is freelance, who says how many weeks, months are acceptable – and based upon what?! There are bound to be gaps, Robert De Niro has gaps. However, how you fill those gaps has a direct impact on how well you do when the next opportunity does come along.

I couldn't agree more. Be honest about your situation and don't be ashamed. A director can see when you last worked; they can't see how you've been using your initiative in the meantime, so tell them. Anyone who is worth their salt will know what the business is like and there won't be the 'judgment' you fear there will be.

I went into an audition a month ago and was asked 'the' question. I said 'Things were a bit crap last year, and this year I'm writing a book'. I wasn't showing off and it's not like I decided to write a book so that I had something to say in auditions, but suddenly not only did I become this intriguing human being (outside of being an actor) but I also injected some energy and enthusiasm into what could have been quite a bleak chat. Because this happened I went into the scenes with a spring in my step instead of a tear in my eye. I think we can and should (with judgment) manipulate the chat in auditions to best suit what we want to put across. Just because they're technically asking the questions, doesn't mean we're powerless to steer the answers towards other questions!

(He laughs.) Very true, sneaky… Something else I get from actors is that 'they're too busy with their temp jobs'. It's hard to hold one down and

manage your career, of course it is, but in my mind finishing a ten-hour shift and then going to the theatre afterwards should be a reward, not a chore, and if it is the latter I'm not sure why actors insist on remaining so. I'm not saying you have to be in the theatre seven times a week and kill yourself doing it, but you've got to find ways of staying in. People can fall into routines and ruts and forget why they were there in the first place. But if it's that easy to slip into that way of living, maybe it should become a more permanent plan? There are so many people who want it and I think you either have to factor into your own head that you want this more than anybody, or admit that you maybe don't… It's what you do to get what you want that counts. Wanting it is not enough; the most successful people eat, sleep and breathe it.

And will have probably sacrificed and paid a price in order to do so… I don't think that drama school should be the thing that necessarily decides whether you're up to it or not; it simply isn't a good enough replica of the life and the job of an actor. You should be able and allowed to make up your own mind once you're in it, once you're doing (or not doing) it; it's not for everyone…

To go full circle with you Bruce, before we wrap it up, I wanted to go back to mentors, people you've learnt from and look up to. Who have been your main influences and why?

I've been very lucky to work with quite a few of my 'idols'. When I was a staff director The National for a year, I worked with Howard Davies, Richard Eyre and Deborah Warner. It was the most fantastic experience, I was working with three powerhouses of British theatre and I learnt so much from all of them. I then did the Bridge Project with Sam Mendes who is one of the most successful/respected directors of theatre and film in the UK right now.

It was *Richard III* starring Kevin Spacey, one of the biggest world tours that's been done, around twelve different cities, across four continents; it was a big deal, an incredible job. It taught me so much, it got me to the point where I needed to be to say, 'right, I'm ready now'…

And Ashley (who I mentioned earlier) who gave me all that guidance and time in the beginning and pulled many strings to get those early shows up and running… I said to him after that first show 'How can I ever thank you, I literally don't know how to thank you' and he said 'Well, the only way you can ever really truly thank someone who does you a favour is by making the most of it'.

Brilliant.

And I've kind of lived by that and hope very much to be able to pass that onto people in the future.

I think that's a rather wonderful place to leave it Bruce, thank you so much. Best of luck with the show and let me know when you're back so that I can buy you a keg of beer.

A keg? How wonderful, I'll look forward to it.

A Q&A WITH CASTING DIRECTOR ALICE PURSER

Alice has been involved in casting for nearly 10 years, first in fringe and regional theatre, and is now Andy Pryor's Associate. She assists on long-running shows such as the BBC's *Doctor Who, Call the Midwife*, and also worked on the television film *United* and Stephen Polikoff's feature *Glorious 39*. Some of the questions here were answered via email and then I caught up with Alice for lunch to probe a bit further! Below are a mixture of the answers.

Q. *What made you want to be a casting director?*

A. I love the excitement that comes with the beginning of a project; the different possibilities there are in creating a whole world from some words on a page.

Q. *You've been a part of some very exciting work already. How did you come to work with Andy (Pryor)?*

A. I went to University with a now well-respected agent, who Andy works with a lot and whose opinion he trusts. I was coming to the end of a fixed-term contract at a regional theatre where I'd been assistant to the Artistic Director. A big part of my job had been casting, which I enjoyed immensely – but hadn't realised at the time. Andy had sent an e-mail putting feelers out for a new assistant and my agent friend suggested I get in touch.

Q. *How much say in the final casting decision does a casting director get?*

A. The choice is obviously down to the team; the director, producers and network. But we put a selection of choices in front of them that we feel are suitable and will do a great job.

Q. *You must have so many submissions for the roles you cast – how do you get the final list of actors to audition?*

A. It's a mixture of ours and the team's preferences; people who producers or directors will have already worked with and feel are right for a part. I would say that for most parts, only 10% of the suggestions will be right. Not that the rest won't be good actors, but you get to know a network or producer's taste…and the rest is instinct (or possibly luck)!

Q. And when you are creating that list of choices, what numbers are we talking?

A. Gosh, well it varies. For an example, we put out a breakdown for *Call the Midwife* Series 3 twenty-four hours ago and we've had 382 submissions for one female role in an episode.

Q. Right, and how many will you and the director decide to meet?

A. Again it varies, but possibly 5 or 6.

Q. And the reasons behind those choices? I know, again, they must vary.

A. It can be about many different things; the look of an actor, if they've worked with the director before, if we or one of the team have seen them in something or previously auditioned them and been impressed, or there might just be something about them that fits. But everyone that we bring into the room we believe in; they have the potential to get and play that part.

Q. It must be quite a task to whittle down that many applications?!

A. Yes it is, and decisions are rapid and instinctive a lot of the time, they have to be. That's why it's so important to have a strong and striking headshot; it's the calling card we go on a lot of the time.

Q. What might make you want to use an actor again? Apart from them being able to act...

A. They need to act well yes, but they also need to audition well; making it clear they will be someone who will get on with the rest of the cast and crew and that they'll support the process and not get in its way. Be a good egg, really.

Q. So reputation of an actor would be considered?

A. I'm not saying having a good reputation would get you the part, because it wouldn't, but having a bad one might prevent you from getting it!

Q. Is it worth writing letters to casting directors? Are they read?!

A. Yes of course. I can't say I relish going through lots of post and filing e-mails when there are a million things going on, but it's important for actors to feel like they're keeping their hand in what can feel like a pretty powerless position. Just don't make a nuisance of yourself – or send a silly present to make you stand out, it seldom goes down as intended!

Q. *What are the worst/silliest things you've seen written in a letter or happen in an audition?*

A. The misspelling of Andy's surname is never a good start – make sure the basics are correct before you start telling us why you'd be a better Doctor than Matt Smith! Amongst the silliest things in auditions would probably be trying to recreate fantasy worlds and creatures on *Doctor Who* – always fun. I think it is fair to say that a host of actors, Andy and myself included, have got the giggles at one stage or another, which is fine as long as it's between takes!

Q. *Does it matter whether actors send a CV designed by themselves or their Spotlight CV?*

A. It won't make an actor any more right for whatever we're casting at the time no. It's the accompanying letter or e-mail that really represents you (see what makes you use an actor again…), the same principles apply; give off a good vibe. And know that we're not the enemy!

Q. *I'm glad that's come up because I think that drama schools and the industry on the whole almost wreck and certainly confuse what should be a really strong and healthy relationship between casting directors and actors. We're somehow taught to fear you or bow down to you or be intimidated by you. I think we should surely view you as allies rather than enemies – What are your thoughts?*

A. I couldn't agree more; it's teamwork. We get you into the room and you wow whoever's in it. When actors do that, we look good, they get work and we trust them to do the same time and time again. Andy puts it very well – casting directors are a bridge, not a block between actor and gig.

Q. *Is it useful for actors to have a variety of 'looks' on their Spotlight page? If so, what kind of looks?*

A. Having a few pictures is helpful, but not putting yourself too much in a particular box. For a woman; both hair up/hair down for example. For a man with and without facial hair. And a colour photo is always important if the main headshot is black and white.

Q. *Does it matter whether the pictures actors send are 10x8, 7x5, 6x4?*

A. Economise where you can, pictures in the body of a CV rather than separate hard copies are more than adequate. We know it's costly.

Q. *Is it useful for an actor to 'dress like' their character in an audition? (Subtly)?!*

A. Yes, if you are auditioning for a period project, I always think it's best to come in styled with a nod to that era – but not to go completely over the top.

Q. What is the most common acting blunder you see in auditions?

A. People not delivering the lines that are on the page. You don't have to be off book to have checked pronunciation or looked up a word you don't know. Also, another obvious one, but it happens – read the script! We can tell if you haven't. I love it when someone comes in to audition for only a few lines and they've not only read the script but have obviously submerged themselves in the world of the story – it's magical. Never think 'well it's only a few lines', because the actors who are thorough usually get the offers.

In screen auditions you must understand the genre and what it requires from your skillset. Self-awareness is a must, self-obsession is not; there's a big difference between vanity and self-assurance. I know it sounds silly but you can tell the actors who are familiar with how they look up close from the ones who aren't. How you manage yourself in front of the camera matters. Also, try not to make too many decisions in terms of the character and the text, or, don't be too stuck on the decisions you do make. It's about playing and reacting.

Q. What do you think makes a good showreel?

A. Less montage – more acting.

What a lovely chat with a lovely person on a lovely sunny day. Lunchtime rooftop picnics rock.
Thanks Alice!

A CONVERSATION WITH ACTOR SEAN BIGGERSTAFF

Sean is an actor of stage and screen and was born and raised in Glasgow. You may know him best as Oliver Wood from *Harry Potter (The Philosopher's Stone* and *The Chamber of Secrets)*. Though still young, his career has spanned two decades already, and I caught up with him for a cuppa and a chat about it. *(Nat's dialogue is in italics, Sean's dialogue is in regular type.)*

So, we'll start off gently, with a nice clichéd question....

(Uncertain, suddenly regretting agreeing to this.)

Uh huh...

...(Nervous laughter.) When did you first think that you might want to be an actor?

I was about seven or eight when I started going to drama class and thought 'Ah, well, I'll do this then'... I remember saying to my parents 'Can you, like, do this, as a job? When you're a big man?' (Not that I'd ever actually end up being a big man.) ... Seemed the answer was yeah, so I thought I'd do it. And then I just didn't stop doing it. I started working when I was ten.

That was your first professional job?

Yep. I was ten… My career started off spectacularly. I was in Michael Boyd's production of *Macbeth* at the Tron theatre in Glasgow with Iain Glen as Macbeth and Peter Mullen as Macduff and the fine Jimmy Chisholm as the Porter. Then I did my first film when I was thirteen, *The Winter Guest,* directed by Alan Rickman… And it's been downhill ever since *(laughs)*.

Behave! So how did these jobs come about? What happened between going to drama class aged ten and filming with the wonder that is Mr Rickman?

I went to the local youth theatre. My Dad saw on the telly that they were having auditions for the Tron theatre…and I didn't realise this but he told me recently, that he didn't in any way have to hold my hand or pressure me into it, he just casually mentioned to me 'Oh, they're having auditions at the Tron', and the next thing he knew I had already phoned them and arranged the audition… I mean I would never do that now; I'm not nearly bold enough – wish I was! I got it and then a guy who was in that production told me that he went to the Scottish youth theatre and that it was really fun and so I went down there, and that was around the same time as Alan Rickman was looking to cast kids for the play version of *The Winter Guest*… so he came in to observe some classes…and everyone was screaming 'the bad guy from *Die Hard*'s here!' (I was ten, I hadn't seen *Die Hard* so I wasn't screaming…) I auditioned for the play and was too young, but by the time he made the film version the boys who had done the play were too old…

Cue Sean.

Indeed. Then almost as soon as I left school I got an agent (ICM, now Independent Talent), which was thanks to Alan Rickman's help.

Do you remember if you were scared or nervous auditioning for him or did you just take it in your stride at that age? Kids often do don't they?

Yeah, and I mean, if I'd never had an encounter like that and now had to go in and audition for Alan Rickman for the first time I would probably shit myself! My experiences of auditions as a teenager were much more positive than they have been since!… There wasn't as much competition then, and generally, when I went for things, I got them… For me it's been the complete opposite to people's perception of 'getting that one break and then you're off to the races'. My run of almost perfect success with auditions stopped at *Harry Potter*. And since then I've just been exactly the same as most actors where you have ten total failures for every one glimmer of interest.

Sometimes there is no rhyme or reason to most things that happen during an actor's career is there? Which I think is a very hard thing to grasp and be at peace with… There aren't always 'answers' or 'reasons' for what happens and I suppose it's learning to function without those answers – quite a skill.

I saw an interview with Stewart Lee recently and he kind of expressed a good way of thinking about it; it's far too easy for people to think when you fail and when you don't get anywhere, that you're the victim of this horrible machine, that it's just the whim of some idiot and that it's not fair; but when you succeed then you're a hard-working and talented individual who has earned and deserves whatever bone gets thrown to you! Your successes are just as much a product of chance and the whims of whoever happens to be in the seat of power at that moment as your failures are.

But it's important not to adopt the attitude of 'well if it's down to chance I won't try' or 'what's the point in trying', don't you think? You have to continuously deliver to a high standard to stay in the doorway, always proving one's worth and ability but having the realistic view that the final decision is a complex one. We can do nothing other than try our best at all times…

Yeah, of course, I'm sure that most jobs I've done there was someone who auditioned better than me…and I am also sure that I've auditioned better than lots of people who have gotten the jobs I went for. ('Cause I've then seen the finished article!) We can but do our best whilst knowing that the decision-making process sometimes has nothing to do with our performance.

And do you find that one of the most difficult parts of being an actor? … Or are there many others?! (We'll do the depressing questions first.)

That is difficult yes, like 'what more can I do?'… A couple of years ago I almost quit. I applied for Uni and I got in. I ended up not going but I wouldn't rule it out.

What were you looking at doing?

Philosophy, Politics and Economics.

Ooh (wondering if I can even spell those).

And I think the reason (apart from the interest I have in the topics), was that after so many years of acting, you do start to crave involvement in something where there is some correlation between what you put into it and what you get out!… I'm always amazed when people come into it later having had a secure and stable life… I'd be terrified going from secure salary and paid holidays to this!

God yeah…on the flip side, I think that's what causes many actors to leave the business; the seductive power of stability! Especially when it creeps in gradually, when perhaps a temp job slowly morphs into a permanent one and before you know it a regular income has set the precedent for the lifestyle you're living and the prospect of losing it becomes terrifying.

Exactly, you could easily get used to that…and also, for most of us there comes a point when you start to realise that there are other things in life…

Ah, the old changing of the priorities!

Yeah, if you want to set up a home, or…

Have a holiday?!

Yeah, a holiday… I mean everyone's like 'Oh, what do you mean you need a holiday, you've got all this time off…'

(In unison.) *It's not a fucking holiday!*
Like it's a sodding holiday!

I'm not in Barbados, I'm at a Jobcentre! There's jack shit that's 'restful' about it… It should be called tensing. 'Are you working?', 'No, no I'm tensing at the minute'… I hardly ever have holidays. You can't plan ahead. And if you're not working very much then it's hard to afford a 'normal life' and if you are working a lot then you don't have time to have a normal life… Um… Yeah, I'm not really sure why people do it!

(We laugh/cry in agreement.)

I know why the seven people at the top doing so well that they can just pick and choose and play and plan, I know why they are doing it.

And do you think that ultimately, if we were all honest, that's what everyone's after really? If so, that's a bloody lot of people for only seven top spots!

Maybe… I think people seriously overestimate what portion of actors are actually able to do that, it's not much of an exaggeration to say that you can count them on your fingers. And even then it's not all simple.

Fame comes with a whole host of its own problems I imagine? Experiencing it yourself at such a young age must have been weird?

Yeah, but I've been quite lucky in that I've always very much been in the shallow end of that; it's never taken over my life. I've obviously had a few strange experiences, but…I have friends that have had ridiculous things happen… Your anonymity and ability to lead a 'normal life' are things that you only fully appreciate when they're absent. I don't think you can fully understand what a headfuck that is until…

And people who say that fame is an actor's job; to be bugged and harassed, and followed are…well…idiots in my opinion. The people who seek or have fame as their profession deserve no sympathy but the people who get it as an add-on to doing the thing they love – it must be tough for them.

(Sean nods in agreement.)

I think the fame thing can be a novelty but it's certainly not what most talented individuals crave.

Most 'famous' actors I know are quite gracious about it.

It's actually ludicrous though isn't it, if you really think about it!

Yes! What is it?! And the idea that if you are famous you sort of 'owe it' to the people because they're 'supporting' your career is stupid as well because most of the people that do the autograph hunting/lurking in doorways stuff aren't the real people who are enjoying and appreciating your work anyway; most people standing outside the stage door waiting for 'famous people' haven't even seen the show!… When you say to a 'fan' (as you're about to do an autograph) 'Who's it to? What's your name'…and they say 'Oh, don't put my name'… I'm like 'NO! What is your name'…because you know it's going straight on eBay if it's left blank! …

Ha, so true… So, you started working when you were ten and then went straight into films so drama school and 'studying' acting wasn't really on the cards for you?

Er, I intended to go to the RSAMD (now RS conservatoire). That was always the plan but by the time I left school at sixteen I was getting more and more acting work (more than my friends who were graduating from there). I guess I was aware of how hard it is to maintain any kind of momentum in this business and thought well, if I can work, I should keep on doing it… And training…people can be really polarised about training. There are extremes of opinion; some people think if you didn't go to RADA then you're not going to be good enough to ever work or reach the top…

I think the amount of times that it's helped and the amount of times that it's hindered is probably even. Of the actors that I really look up to, it's probably quite an even split… I mean, if you get to school-leaving age and you have no acting experience and no contacts…go to drama school! Don't think you can just phone Duncan Heath and expect that anything's gonna happen!

I am a big advocator of drama school, I really am, but I think there's a lot that they get wrong, or a hell of a lot that could be improved upon. I learnt so much during my first few years as a professional, but I guess those seeds were sewn at school… There's a lot to be said for simply watching pros at work, being around them. Obviously you've worked with some gems…

Yes, and that's luck. I've worked with some amazing people but I was lucky to get the gigs and that they happened to be working on them too. I've witnessed a huge range of people all with differing ways of working, so in that sense I've had a very varied education. But then I think that there are some actors who really limit themselves, and the choice is theirs, it is to themselves they do this. If you stay at the same place for four years, working with the same people on a soap or whatever then it's not going to be quite as rich an experience as I've been lucky enough to have. Depends what you choose and what's 'right' at the time.

So, would you dissuade anyone?

(Not even a milli-second pause.) Yes.

Ok. (Laughs.)

It's not that… I wouldn't say don't do it…just make the decision to do it with your eyes open. Be real about what it is. I'm quite a good example of how all the things that you think it takes to 'make it' are just not true. 'Get your foot in the door and then you're flying'? No. It's not a straight line or a fair game; I got my foot in the door twenty fucking years ago.

(I nearly choke on my tea.)

… And I still don't know where the next job's coming from. You know? I still can't say with any degree of confidence that I'm going to be able to pay the mortgage in six months' time. Even if the tick boxes are ticked, you are still being rejected and disheartened on a daily basis. The reality is probably going to be working in a bar and struggling and occasionally getting little bits of work (that sometimes only serve to tantalise you and give false hope)… If you're willing to risk that, if you want it enough that you're willing to risk that, then yes, absolutely, go for it…but only if you're ready for that reality to become yours.

Do you have a cut-off after auditions when you decide you haven't got it? For my own sanity I try and cap it at 48 hours; I try to let go after that and then anything I hear is a bonus!

No. I leave the audition and forget about it straight away (as much as possible), because you just never really know when it's gone well and when it hasn't. Sometimes even now I'll dare to think 'Oh that went well, I may have done better than the other people there'…and then you don't even get a response…not even a no!

That's one of the most horrible elements of the business, don't you think?
Oh god yes.

Ah, so my next question is, if you could put one thing from the acting industry into a room 101 what would it be? Would it be that?

Yeah, it's quite despicable really – it might be that. There are a lot of things to pick for room 101 but that would certainly be one of them.

You mentioned earlier that you thought of going to Uni and I know you have a real interest in music too. Do you think that it's important that actors have skills, interests, ambitions, or hobbies outside of acting?

I do a lot of other things with my time, which is hugely important to me, for my own sanity. It's probably been the reason I've been able to stick at it. And I've been lucky that when I do get a job it tends to be well-paid enough that I can afford the quiet periods without having to work in a bar…so if I have time I can afford to use that time well, which is a luxury that most actors don't have… And I think to be honest if I hadn't been able to do that I might have quit long ago. … Any skill you develop, any experience you have can obviously be useful for the job that we do. I've done a lot of martial arts training in the last few years and I play guitar, both of which could be of use in terms of work; anything that may be relevant to the character, or that you can make relevant to the character can be nothing but a plus. Or just doing shit that you just enjoy doing for no other reason than selfish enjoyment, is very important.

Do you have a preference between working on stage or working on screen?
Erm…

I always think it's a bit like having a wife and a mistress – loving and wanting them both for different reasons but always feeling like you're slightly cheating on one of them when you're enjoying the other!

Yeah, yeah, absolutely… I'm just trying to think which one would be the wife and which one the mistress…. Er. *(Sigh.)* Both have such huge pros and cons; film has nothing to offer you that is in any way comparable to an opening night going well, but it also never gets as breathtakingly tedious as the 55th performance of the same show. Plus it's virtually impossible (unless you're at the National or in the West End all the time), to make a decent living, or certainly to sustain a decent living from working in the theatre alone.

So what would be your process when (and if) you choose jobs? Is it about the role, is it the need to pay the mortgage, do these vary?

I've always been of the view (and I'm aware that I'm quite an extremist in this) that if I need money, if I need to put food on the table, then I'll get a job, any normal, temp, whatever – job. But when it comes to acting work, if the only reason I'd be doing it is for the payday then no, I won't do it. Some actors are much 'better' at making the best of something but for me, if the dialogue's not there then neither am I, I just can't work with bad dialogue and make it anything, and it feels so awful trying to.

I think there's a danger that, where a good job can make you better, a bad job can make you worse and give you/enhance your bad habits and can possibly put you on a certain track that is difficult and sometimes nigh on impossible to deviate from. We all must experience in order to learn, but I think one should be wise to the pros and cons of any decision.

It used to be (and maybe this is just nostalgia) that you'd be judged by your record and it was necessary for all the stuff on your CV to be of a high quality if you wanted the good jobs, whereas now it seems that if you're in a thing on the telly then you'll be put in another thing on the telly, even if the thing you were in originally was bloody terrible… But, bearing that in mind, it's quite possible that a lot of things I didn't do (because they were so terrible), wouldn't have done me any harm, in fact I'd probably be in a better position to get a lot of the jobs that I do now want if I'd taken some of them!

I always use the analogy for my life and situation of a gambler in a casino – I don't know whether the decisions I'm betting on are right, if they're going to pay off in some way, probably not, but if my gut tells me at the time that they might, and my gut is being advised by my knowledge and understanding of the industry, along with my agent's opinion, then that's all I can use to indicate what may be a good choice and what could be a bad one.

It's even more fucked up and frustrating than a casino, because if acting was just totally random and in the lap of the gods then I think it would be easier to accept that's how things were meant to be – but there are people making these decisions, choosing our hand for us… It's a rigged casino!

But you're still betting? We all are.

Indeed.

A Q&A WITH AGENT
JAMES PENFORD

James studied English and Drama at university and started as an assistant with Hatton McEwan in 2004. Since then he has become a very successful agent in his own right, representing actors across all areas of the industry. He works alongside two other agents and has recently been made a partner in the company which has been renamed Hatton McEwan Penford.

Drama school

Q. What do you look for in an actor's headshot?

Nothing overly fancy, a good, clear, in-focus shot that not only shows how the actor looks at their realistic best but somehow also captures something about them. It's all in the expression of the eyes.

Q. What things are useful to include on a CV and what aren't?

A well-thought through selection of acting credits and related skills. I think actors sometimes think that having a page full of credits makes them look like they work non-stop but it means the key credits are often lost amongst other less impressive ones. Skills should be those that are genuinely of use to a performing career and accents should be the actor's native accent and those they can genuinely do to a proven native standard. An acting CV is different to a standard job CV so an agent only needs to see your acting credits and not your exam results, or non-acting employment history.

Q. Should drama students invite you to third-year shows, prior to showcase?

Yes, we do try and cover as many as we can and always like to see as much of the students' work outside of a showcase as possible. It's preferable for a cast to organize themselves and send one letter or email so we're not inundated with 20 letters for the same production.

Q. What are the most common 'mistakes' or blunders you see in letters that actors write when seeking representation?

The biggest mistake is to send out a blanket letter to all agencies – we do get them addressed to 'Dear Agents' rather than us by name and making no reference to the fact they are interested in joining us rather than one of the hundreds of other agencies. We receive thousands of representation requests every month so approaches should be to the point, clearly stating if an actor is in something we can see and pointing us to personal websites, Spotlight and online showreels etc. We often get letters telling us about a show an actor has just been in, which is pointless as we can't see them in it. If a letter runs to more than a few short paragraphs we simply do not have time to read it all so could overlook important information. The letter, headshot and CV should gain our attention and interest and we will then want to find out more.

Q. What do you think a graduate should be looking for in an agency?

Someone they feel they can work with and talk to. Leaving drama school and entering the industry is a daunting time and graduates need supporting through this. Coupled with this they need to do their research on the agency and be sure they hold the same values and aims in mind. (See also Q.3 in 'A Working Relationship'.)

Q. Is it worth university students contacting you in regards to shows or showcases?

Yes. We consider invites from all courses. If a performance is outside of London it's less likely that we'll see it from a practical point of view.

Showcase

Q. How do you decide which showcases to attend?

Usually from our past experiences of that drama school and if we have had success with previous graduates of that school, any school that is a member of Drama UK (formally the Conference of Drama Schools) is a good start for us. It's not possible to attend every showcase as our main objective and responsibility is to look after the current list of actors and we have to balance the time we spend in the office or watching current clients' work with that spent looking for new signings. We also talk to a lot of casting directors each day who will recommend seeing a particular showcase or group of students if they have enjoyed their previous work.

Q. When you go to showcases do you have a specific agenda of what you're looking for to 'fill a gap in your books' or are you open to be surprised?

We are extremely open and don't operate a 'shopping list' of casting brackets we need to fill. That being said there is no point in us taking on numerous graduates who look the same or have an identical feel as that would split our focus and reduce opportunities for the clients.

Q. What would you consider to be the biggest and most common showcase mistakes?

Trying to shock the audience through excessive swearing or risqué pieces, it usually gets boring very quickly and I can see the industry professionals around me tuning out. Comedy is also really hard to pull off and you have to be sure you can nail it – we want you to do well but won't laugh if something doesn't amuse us and that silence can feel huge as you struggle through a comedy piece.

Q. What are your three top tips for a successful showcase piece?

1) Find something that suits you as an actor, that is age- and casting-appropriate and uses your natural accent. 2) Choose a piece that is not overdone or from a play everyone in the audience has seen a hundred times – you will inevitably be compared to a more experienced actor we have seen perform it. 3) Enjoy your time on stage and entertain us.

Signing

Q. In interviews with new clients, what are you looking for?

Confidence and focus, someone who is passionate about an acting career and everything it entails. We see this meeting as an indicator or how an actor will treat an audition. If they're overly nervous, low energy, turn up late or call five minutes beforehand asking for the address we can only imagine they will do the same with a meeting for an acting role. We ask a lot of questions to try and assess how well we will work together and actors should always have questions prepared to ask an agent – it shows interest and seriousness about their career.

Q. When you are 'signed' to an agent does that mean that they are your only agent or can you sign with more than one?

Most agencies have an exclusive agreement with their clients so actors can only sign to one agency. Some have voiceover, modeling, or occasionally commercial agents on top of this but they should always discuss and agree these with their acting agent first. We co-represent some of our clients with American agents or managers but again this is discussed and agreed between us first.

Q. What should a client consider when choosing/signing?

How well they get on with the agent and how comfortable they feel talking to them. They should do research into who else and how many the agent represents, what contacts they have and what work they value. Asking for personal opinions is worthwhile but you could get completely different points of view from other people as the actor/agent relationship is so personal. I would always recommend checking an agent is a member of The

PMA (http://thepma.com) which is a group of agencies who agree to a code of practice which includes provisions to ensure actors are protected.

Q. What do you as an agent consider when taking on new clients?

Whether we believe we can make work with them to start and maintain a long-term career in acting. This is a combination of the talent they bring to the table, an intuition on how well we would work together, whether they express a plan for a long-term career that marries with ours and where we feel we could get them opportunities.

Q. Financially there's no payment to have or get an agent. When do you get paid, how and how much?

Actors should never pay a joining fee to join an agency. Agents get their income from taking commission on their client's work for which the industry standard ranges from 10% - 15% of the actor's gross fee. The actor's fee is paid to us and then processed by our bookkeeper who deducts our commission (and the VAT we must charge) and then pays the remainder out to the client.

A working relationship

Q. What are your feelings about actors getting their own work?

Everything should be done in conjunction with the agent. Part of an agent's role is to act as a buffer between the actor and the creative team to ensure that the business side of things is handled and doesn't cloud the creative process. Inevitably over the course of a career an actor will develop close connections with people they work with who will offer them work directly and they should always direct the person offering to their agent. Agents also act as a safeguard checking a project is paying the correct money and has the right contract in place. There are some individuals out there who will try and exploit an actor's desire to work and an agent can help to weed these out.

Q. What are your feelings about non-paid/profit share and fringe work?

Mixed – it has to be worthwhile in a good venue and with a production team aiming for high standards and (for want of a better word, as it's not paid) a professional production. Agents and other industry professionals do attend fringe work but we limit it to a small number of venues.

Q. How would you describe a healthy relationship between agent and client?

One where they work together to build and progress an actor's career, it should be honest, open, productive and respectful.

Q. How would you describe an unhealthy relationship?

One that slides into all the opposites of those qualities detailed above and becomes a culture of each blaming the other one for a lack of progress.

Q. What do you think about clients contacting directors directly?

I think that writing to a director is productive if you have seen their work and genuinely enjoyed it and would like to work with them. It's also worth keeping in touch with directors you have worked with and/or met and making sure you are up to date with their current projects. Never be a nuisance obviously, and write with a purpose.

Q. Should a client 'check in' with their agent regularly or trust that the work is being done? How does an actor strike a balance?

I think they should trust the work is being done – if they don't they're with the wrong agent. We are always open to a client calling if they have something to say or ask us but would much rather be focusing on getting them work so we can call them with something rather than discussing with them the fact 'they want to work'. We take that for granted.

Q. What might make you 'let go' of a client?

Usually when the trust has gone and the relationship is no longer productive. It can be because of an irreconcilable difference of opinion or when we feel an actor has lost focus on their career.

Q. If things are not working out, how best should an actor or agent handle this?

In the first place by talking to each other and airing their opinions and feelings on the matter. It is a relationship and like any other relationship can break down and ultimately a parting of the ways may be the best option for both.

General

Q. How many clients per agent do you think is manageable?

This is a really hard question to answer as different clients in different places in their career take up different amounts of an agent's time. Agents also work very differently from one another and so what is too much for one may be too little for the next.

Q. What's the most annoying/irritating/frustrating thing about being an agent?

We can be doing our job wonderfully – getting in all the right meetings, on great projects but ultimately the moment you give the meeting details to a client whether we see any pay off from our work is out of our hands. There's also a feeling of frustration amongst many agents at the moment about a decreasing number of opportunities for actors and a downsizing of budgets, maybe even a growing lack of respect for actors from some areas of the industry.

Q. What made you want to be an agent?

I was always fascinated by the theatre but at a fairly young age knew I didn't want to act. I applied for an agent's assistant job not really knowing what it would entail and almost instantly I was hooked. You get to work with some wonderful people, not only clients but also colleagues and other industry professionals; it's always a challenge and can be extremely rewarding.

Q. It must be very satisfying when a client gets a job and is doing well? I presume it's also the opposite for you when things aren't so good?

Absolutely – that really hits the nail on the head. We can have days where we constantly give out bad news to clients and we do share their feelings – the good as well as the bad.

Q. There's a lot of work that you do that actors aren't aware of; we only get the news when we're required to hear it. What are an agent's main responsibilities and what does a typical day include for you?

Our main responsibility is to create and handle opportunities for our clients. A typical day in the office starts by going through emails that have been sent overnight before the phone starts ringing. We make suggestions to projects for our clients, handle the meetings coming in, negotiate deals and check contracts, read scripts and ensure we are covering our client's work. We talk about the clients constantly – with each other, to casting directors and producers.

Q. What do you think makes a good agent?

A passion for working with actors and for the industry as a whole, empathy, patience, a sharp eye for detail, enthusiasm, thick-skin and the toughness to negotiate a good deal.

Q. What makes a good client?

All of those qualities above plus a desire every morning to get out of bed and be an actor.

Q. Being a member of Spotlight is a given, but do you think it is important to be a member of IMDb? And if so, why?

It's increasingly becoming so. IMDb is used more and more by the industry but I don't believe it will ever replace Spotlight as the main casting resource. With Spotlight you have full control over your profile whereas all sorts of people contribute to IMDb.

Q. Is it an ok tactic when writing to agents to use recommendations from industry professionals and/or to mention mutual colleagues? i.e. this casting director has agreed to vouch for me or I was in so and so with your client etc.

Definitely. Casting directors know us and our taste in actors so if they are willing to recommend an actor to us it's a good first step. If you have been in a show with clients of ours there's a good chance we'll have seen it and already have an idea of your work. We will rarely sign an actor without seeing their work though, so a recommendation supports an application but we won't rely solely upon it.

Q. What attributes does a 'good' showreel have?

Short (no more than 6 mins usually), showing good quality, recent work and preferably professional work. Like many agents and casting directors I don't like montages during a showreel where you get clips of the actor, usually accompanied by music, and will skip past these. We want to see you act – not see how skilled your editor is.

Q. There seems to be a bit of a trend for actors to 'go to the US' at the minute – what are your thoughts about actors doing this?

I think actors need something to go to the US with – a project they have been involved with that will open the right doors and be of interest to industry professionals in the US. Increasingly there is a crossover with projects casting both sides of the Atlantic and a number of casting directors in the UK work on US projects, putting actors over here onto tape. Actors should think carefully before they jet off to the US about what they want to achieve over there and whether they could achieve it here – otherwise it becomes a very expensive holiday. Actors should bear in mind that to work in the US they will need a particular type of VISA and the process of obtaining this is expensive and tough and usually relies on a producer in the US sponsoring it.

Q. What's the difference between an agent and a manager?

There are very few managers working in the UK as agents over here tend to fulfill a number of roles that are separated out in the States. In the US agents would do the deals for a client and source them opportunities and meetings and scripts whereas a manager is traditionally more concerned with the development of the actor's career and its day-to-day running.

Q. What are the most helpful and productive things an actor can be doing whilst out of work?

Watching TV, film, going to the theatre, attending classes, reading scripts, practising self-taping, going to the gym – anything that keeps them focused and thinking about their career as an actor. The least productive thing is to sit at home staring at the telephone and willing it to ring.

Cheers James – I think we've covered everything there!

12. TIPS & QUIPS
Catchy.

This chapter is a mish mash of tips (both silly and not) and funny little stories I've collected over the years, with a few bits of industry lingo thrown in at the end. The tips are pretty random, but are things that I feel are worth flagging up; it might even be suggested that they're things I thought of late in the day and then couldn't fit into the main bulk of the book…stupid suggestion (possibly true). Let's start with the most important things…

Foundation

If, you're anything like me, no matter how poor you are there is one thing that will always take priority over bread and central heating – a good (usually meaning expensive) foundation. (I know, I know, I'm a girly girl masquerading as a strong, modern woman.) Sometimes it is not always possible to pluck £30 plus from your account to purchase this item of phenomenal necessity, so to tide you over until payday (if you have shaken and scraped the last drops from your bottle), go into one of the big department stores, over to your brand and start to 'browse' (with intent). When they pounce on you (and they will) express your interest in a particular foundation (yours) but be a little unsure as to whether it will suit your 'allergies'. When they suggest that they plaster you in it to find out, say that you are already made up and are on your way somewhere but a sample would be ideal. The sample they give should last you a few weeks (unless you cake it on like Katie Price). I don't feel bad advising you to do this as I have temped for a couple of these lovely beauty brands over the years and consider now that they deserve everything coming to them!!!

Prep one more scene than is asked of you

For an audition, if they ask you to prep one scene, prep two; if they ask you to prep seven, look at an eighth, just in case. It would be awful if they asked for more scenes having enjoyed what you've done and then you had to cold read. I'm not saying learn the whole film or prep the whole play but do your best to have at least familiarized yourself with a variety of material. So, if they have asked you to prep two scenes but when you arrive the director says 'So, what have you got for us today?' You can confidently suggest either what was initially asked of you, or what you most enjoy doing/what you think represents the character best. However, if you only have 24 hours' notice (regular occurrence) then sod 'em and do what you can!

Eating on tour

In your digs it is likely that you will be sharing a kitchen with a family of six and won't be on a salary that allows you to eat out every day. Though you may get into the kitchen, it isn't your own and it can feel, well, weird. So, here are the options: there are some fairly mega microwave meals now that are not only fairly healthy but tasty too. Your theatre will/SHOULD always have a microwave in the Green Room providing a calm and welcoming sanctuary in which you are able to enjoy a meal without feeling as if you are intruding. Alternatively, if your landlords are out during the day it can be an idea to cook and eat your main meal at lunchtime and then take healthy snack-type nibbles/cold dinner to eat at the theatre for before/during/after the show. This will work well with your timings too (during performance) – not many actors I know want to be eating a main meal less than an hour before the half anyway, so a bigger lunch and then add-on food could be a plan Stan.

What to do with a day off on tour

Explore, find cafes and read books (perhaps mine…?), meet up with the cast, do touristy things. DO something. It can become very lonely and terribly boring if you don't. Use the paid spare time wisely.

Joining gyms on tour

A friend of mine, who's on tour, recently told me that when she attempted to get access to a gym for the week it was nigh on impossible; they all demanded that she sign up for 3 months or whatever. Many gyms offer free day passes as a 'trial' for the gym. So, rather cleverly (sneakily) she obtained trial passes for all four gyms in the town on different days and boom, problem sorted and no money spent. Genius.

Amazon for cheap books and DVDs

Why pay full price for anything if you don't have to? I like to have the actual book in my hand rather than sides when I'm working on a play, and sometimes even when I am just auditioning for one. This can get expensive. So, I go onto Amazon where nine times out of ten I will be able to purchase whatever I need for a matter of pence. These will probably be second-hand but as long as there are no notes, who cares! (The condition of the item is always described by the seller.) This is also a great way of getting DVDs etc. at a cut-down price. Should I, as an author, just have advised you how to buy books on the cheap… Methinks no, oops.

Furniture

Whilst we're on finding stuff cheaply, it is likely that you will be moving around like some sort of gypsy for a number of years; flatmates change, piss off and get married and/or leave the business and get a mortgage etc.

etc. Moving twelve times a year is not only irritating (sorry to all the dads of actors who are now professional removal men – yes Dad, you), it's also damn expensive. You may be moving from furnished to unfurnished to part-furnished blah blah yawn. If you manage to buy the stuff you need cheaply, then that ceremonious trip to the tip when you find you're moving to a furnished place is a lot easier if the stuff you're ditching cost you next to nothing. Freecycle is a great website where people advertise things they no longer want or need; sofas, dining tables, desks, bikes, doll's houses – whatever you need, it is likely you can get it on there for nothing. Sign up and attach yourself to different locations so the stuff that comes up on your feed isn't over the other side of London, but local to you. Good huh? And if you don't find what you're looking for on there, the British Heart Foundation is a great source of cheap stuff. I've found all sorts of furniture in there for about £20. And they deliver to you! (Little tip – don't buy a sofa that's so pissing large that the delivery men (two years after they got it into the lounge) shrug, say it's impossible to remove and exit the property without said humongous sofa – this just happened to me and WAS NOT FUNNY. That sofa was then involved in a sort of chainsaw massacre and dumped at the tip. No sofa deserves that.

Funny skit time…

POTENTIAL

Courtesy of actress Sarah.

42-year-old actress SARAH had been teaching this particular class of Monkey Music intermittently for about a year.

A MUM: Sarah, you're wonderful with the children.

SARAH: Ah, thank you.

A MUM: And you're so good – You know you should go on the stage.

Beat.

SARAH: Well actually…

A MUM: I'm sure you'd be good enough for the local Am Dram.

Pause.

SARAH: Me? Don't be daft.

(Wipes a tear and continues tapping her tambourine.)

Buses are cheaper

If you can get somewhere by bus rather than by tube in London, do (if you have the time). Not only is it cheaper, it will also allow you to get a better understanding of the layout of the city. Plus, if you take the right bus it's like a sightseeing tour that only costs a quid instead of twenty!

Put named drivers on your car insurance, it lowers the cost!

Many people think I am insane to run a car in the city, but my family live two hours away and I need to be able to get to them. Plus, having my car gives me a sense of control and freedom that is important to me. I have no idea why having named drivers on your insurance lowers the amount you pay, but it does, and every penny helps! So add your mum, your girlfriend, your hairdresser and get saving. (Obviously you may want to check if your hairdresser has any past driving offences, or, you could add your mum and dad and realise that the last suggestion may not have been an altogether serious one.)

Wash up your bloody mug

Why would you not? A Green Room or rehearsal space is not your lounge, and though it is not stage management's responsibility to wash up it will be them who end up doing it if you don't. You don't want stage management to be your enemies! This is common courtesy.

Ooh and hang up your bloody clothes

Same principle, at the end of a show, no matter how elated with your own brilliance/desperate to get to the bar you are, hang up your costume. Your stage manager is not your mum.

'I'm a bit under the weather.' Fail.

Never say at the start of an audition (especially musical theatre) 'I've got a bit of a cold'. Don't excuse yourself before you've begun; it makes you look shit, gives the impression that you're not good enough or that you are attempting to justify your own incompetence. Any producer and director (in theatre especially) wants to know that you will work through illness and that the only excuse not to is that you are in fact dead.

Loo stop

Always (if possible) find a toilet when you arrive at an audition; do this to refocus yourself after the journey, check your face for tube dirt smudges and toothpaste stains and to empty your bladder of all the Evian you've been manically guzzling. Wriggling through a soliloquy is not advised.

Buy a programme (if you can afford it).

By making a habit of this you will build up a catalogue of productions you've seen which can be a great go-to source in order for you to recap your theatre viewing. It's also a good way to keep track of the actors/directors you've seen and liked. (If you're a real geek you might even make the odd note of the post-it variety?)

Cheap drink

Always go and have a pint in the pub next to the theatre instead of in the theatre bar if you're brassic. (I'm sorry theatres but you charge obnoxious amounts for things, beverages in particular!) Better still, do as my dear old Nanna always did and never leave the house without a whiskey miniature… Buy a bottle of coke from co-op and Bob's your uncle. Well done Nanna, well done.

You rub my back…

I would be surprised if anyone was brazen enough to actually use this phrase, but the meaning behind it is widely used throughout the business and you'll do well to remember it. Think carefully before you say no to someone and always do so with care – this is an industry that sits on a bed of favours and just as someone may need you, you may need them back at some point!

Gift Vouchers

Theatres, cinemas, Raindance, Samuel French's etc. all have gift card/voucher systems – tell your loved ones and get something at Christmas that is more useful to you than a bright pink colander or faux suede lamp.

Blatant theft

Borrow (steal) stationary from office temp jobs. You must do this cleverly, gradually and in moderation but trust me, it will make working there feel an ounce less soul-destroying. (Especially if stationary turns you on as it does me.)

Happy hours

Maxwell's Covent Garden every day and at Café de Paris Fridays 5-8pm
There are loads more. Do your research. Nothing more to add.

Per diems

This is the money given to you when you arrive on set or at your hotel when filming. It is an allowance for your food/other needs when you are away from the set during your time with the production. Usually about £40/£50 a day.

+ 1

If you are invited to a screening of your work, or an after party you'll probably be entitled to bring someone with you, but you may have to ask, as they may not offer!

Look after your teeth

Apparently you're not supposed to drink red wine...sod that! Just brush them, go to the dentist regularly and bleach them if you need to when you have the cash! Do look after them though, there is a real shortage of toothless characters.

Ink Cartridges

I told you I have an obsession with stationary...

Buy ink cartridges from Tesco not Ryman's – there's about £6 difference, you could buy three scarves in Covent Garden or a large glass of Rioja for that!

My mantra

If you have to buy cheap everything, do; except make-up and wine and lingerie.

Audition exits

Shake hands in auditions but if there are loads of them on the panel, maybe thank them collectively with a slight wave (that was a *slight* wave) and a smile – shaking eighteen people's hands can't half go on and becomes very cringe! (N.B. Always leave through the exit and not the cupboard – Chloe.)

10x8s

When you restock your photographs, I would replace your 10x8s with 7x5s; they're cheaper to order in bulk and do exactly the same thing. Almost everything is online now anyway but hard copies are still useful when sending letters etc. Spielberg won't overlook you for downsizing.

Chit chat

Talk to other actors whilst in the waiting room for an audition – an atmosphere is unhelpful and uncalled for. Plus, other actors seem far less intimidating once you've found out their name and identified the same nervous quiver in their voice that is present in yours. (But, a hello is sufficient – if someone is running lines be sensitive to everyone's 'run up' technique and try not to distract. Sabotage ain't cool.)

THE TAXI THESP

Courtesy of actress Katie

TAXI DRIVER: Going somewhere nice?

KATIE: Er…an audition actually.

TAXI DRIVER: Ooh, an auditon…

Pause.

What are you then, some sort of actress?

KATIE: *(Smiling.)* Some sort, yes.

TAXI DRIVER: I did all that, back in the day, acting and that.

KATIE: Really?

TAXI DRIVER: Yeah yeah, oh yeah. Played all the main roles; God, Rumpelstiltskin…

Passport

Always have your passport ready, in date and valid for travel at a moment's notice (and remember where you keep it – not in that VERY safe place that's so god damn hard to find!)

Social networking suicide

Don't ever update Facebook or Twitter with stuff regarding work…

a) If it's classified information about plots/characters that haven't been aired yet.

b) Naming any people in the industry.

c) When drunk.

If you must comment on your professional life, be cryptic and always remember who could see it/pass it on! My advice is keep Facebook for friends and Twitter for business, but still never comment on scripts or auditions etc. as there are BIG and SERIOUS secrecy clauses around these things and you will piss people off; a one-way ticket to unemployment!! By all means use social media to advertise and promote yourself but be very clear what is personal and what is professional. I keep Facebook for personal/trivial use (have every privacy setting activated and a select group of 'Friends') and Twitter for shamelessly promoting work i.e. air dates, opening nights…book sales…

Status rant

Whilst we're on the subject, think before you post a bloody status. Don't do it drunk (unless you are highly humorous and very self-aware even when inebriated). Don't assume that anyone is interested in the food on your plate or the contents of your womb and most importantly for us, be a little bit sensitive to your 'friends'. If you have 86 friends who are out-of-work actors, it may not be that clever an idea to brag 24/7 about how wonderful your career is… Just a thought.

Ooh, and if you're paranoid and arrogant like me I'd be careful what pictures you upload too; get a high-profile job and *The Sun* will be all over that shit. A shot of you face down on a lawn in a pile of kebab and vomit with your pimply arse hanging out might be funny to your mates but probably wouldn't do much for the public's perception of you.

Saving

Organise a direct debit of £10 a month to go from one of your accounts into a savings account. Start this in October (if you are male) and April (if you are female) and throughout the year, without even noticing, you will have saved up the majority of your Spotlight renewal fee without having to agonise over a chunk of money you don't have. Even though we all know when it's coming, it still stings like a mother when it does.

Entertainment on the cheap

With cost in mind you may want to check out cheap nights for things. For instance, you should take full advantage of The Royal Court's Cheaper Mondays, The Arcola's Pay What You Can Tuesdays and The National's Travelex tickets. It's also an idea to queue for day tickets or returns if you have a free morning and fancy bagging a cheap West End ticket.

If you'd rather a cinema trip then there are cheaper options here too; I am with Orange Mobile so get 241 Wednesdays, and I also go to The Coronet cinema in Notting Hill on a Tuesday for £3.50 cinema. Most (indie) cinemas like Prince Charles, The Ritzy and The Curzon Soho do cheaper day tickets, so take advantage of the fact that you don't work 9-5! Check out what's on at the BFI too.

If watching something isn't floating your boat on a certain day, why not go to a gallery – most are free! And if you don't wish to be cultured or intellectual but want to have a good time there are Happy Hours all over town as mentioned!

This is a good website I found: http://brokelondonlife.wordpress.com/

Aside from leaving the house you can quite easily stay in and be entertained, steady… I meant, that there is a wealth of cracking homegrown dramas and comedies on the television (if you dodge the reality shit) that you should be informed about. There is also a huge variety of ways to access entertainment online – for more details check out the Appendix.

Make sure you do step away though; every now and again, watch a B movie just because you fancy the guy in it or use money you've allocated for a theatre trip on a gig ticket or a go-karting day. We're human too.

Baggage

I know it sounds trivial but try to arrange your stuff (bags, coat, umbrella, folder etc.) before you go into an audition. If you are fiddling with your coat, fighting with your zip and searching for your script at the start it looks awkward, feels awkward and will put you in the wrong place to begin the audition. Not only that but once you've wowed them with your talents, you wanna get out of there looking as smooth as possible!

Lube – (not like that)

By all means 'lubricate the vocal folds' (or whatever tosh you're told to do at drama school), but don't overdo it before an audition – if you do all you will be able to think about during the meeting is needing a wee.

Minty fresh

This tip is two-fold. I always have an extra strong mint before I go on stage or enter an audition (especially if I'm required to sing). It'll give you something to do in those horrific minutes before being 'called in'. (At a funeral once I asked a friend's wonderful Nanna if she was ok and she nodded and said 'Oh yeah, take a deep breath and suck on a mint and you can get through anything' – priceless.) Not only will it calm you and give you something to do, it will also make your throat feel like it's expanding, like it's very clear and ready for use.

Also, on the mint front, if you know you have to snog someone in performance, or even in audition, be kind and have a mint; sharing fluids with a complete stranger is an immense amount of fun on a Friday night when you're too pissed to taste their dinner, but at work, let's at least pretend that we're being professional about it!

Who's doing what

Keep a notebook by the television or by your bed and note down programs that you've enjoyed and who cast them. The result is a great go-to resource of who's doing what.

The Equity diary

Getting a free diary with your Equity membership is lovely, but I always felt like a total actor-twat pulling it out every five seconds, it looking like some pathetic attempt to confirm my actor status to those around me. Self-conscious much? You know the sort though…

'Oh yeah, yeah, well I'm artistic, I'm an actor, an artistic actor being artistic a lot – look I have the diary, I'm in Equity, I'm an actor.'

Plus it's tiny and I am FAR too busy to fit all of my engagements etc. into it (obviously I have a file-o-fax, OBVIOUSLY). I keep the Equity diary (at home) and use it to log my auditions/meetings/introductions – this means that I have an easily accessible log of who I've met that year including producers, writers, directors, the date I met them and the projects they've been involved with. Anything professionally significant goes into that bad boy and the information is all there if and when I need to access it/pull it out to prove myself.

Talking shit

Try not to gabble in auditions. (Easier said than done.) Listen to any question asked (don't just nod), take your time to assimilate what they've said and only then open your mouth to answer, editing as you speak (and FYI they only need to know the bare essentials).

Know about the world

Watch the news; it is current and relevant and theatre, especially, is often put on because it is relevant to what's happening in the world around us. You should be able to make the connections.

Inter-thespian-relations

By all means date people in the industry, sleep with the world and his dog (not literally, that's sick) but always bear in mind that it is a SMALL WORLD and if you blush easily perhaps rethink dipping your nib into the company ink. Don't really know why I've put this tip in because everyone is shagging everyone; it's one of the few perks to the job and completely inevitable when pretty people get paid to touch each other.

So, what did you think?

The sentence dreaded by all loyal friends and colleagues who go to watch productions that may not hit the dizzy heights of greatness. A classic line to use on company members of a production that you HATED is 'It was interesting, intriguing yeah, I haven't quite processed it yet, it's going to take a while to settle... But well done... Drink?' Shit, now I've admitted that I'll have to think of a new one...

Comps

Always tap up mates working in the theatre for comps or discounted tickets. Production companies want bums on seats and if there's anyone who knows of cheapies available it'll be the cast as they are often given house seats. But always repay the favour when you can!

Spotlight

Don't ever look in the mirror at the top of the stairs at Spotlight, it's a fat mirror; you'll go up the stairs feeling like Jennifer Aniston and into your audition feeling like Ann Widdecombe.

Play it cool Trig…

If a director or casting director comes to see you in something don't come bounding out of stage door like a puppy on acid and scream at them 'Did you enjoy it? Was I good?' Let them tell you what they thought. (And how you can hold your head up high if you don't already know the answer to the second question I just typed, is beyond me!!)

Teamwork

Look out for your fellow actors. If you see a role that may suit a friend TELL THEM. We must look out for each other. (Plus, they may repay the favour one day – score.)

Three last tips, and probably the most important ones…

1. Heal the world, make it a better place.

2. A dog is for life, not just for Christmas.

3. Don't be a Cun…ctator.

(Yes, an actual word; my iPhone dictionary's definition: a procrastinator; delayer).

Now a little list to finish off, designed to give you a heads-up on words, phrases and such like that may crop up throughout your career. Many, if not most, you will know but I thought I'd mention them, just in case.

- Sides – Pages of script, usually at an audition.
- Cold Read – A reading of a script when the actor hasn't seen the text before.
- The half – Half an hour before curtain up.
- The boards – The stage upon which we tread.
- Cans – Earphones to the main system of communication for the crew backstage.
- Penciled in – Provisionally booked for a job but not confirmed.

- Recall – a second, third, fourth round of an audition.
- Making the day – Crew on set having achieved the schedule for that day.
- Day player – An actor who is on set for one day/a couple of days filming only.
- Curtain up/down – Start/end of a theatre performance.
- The dailies/rushes – The unedited footage shot that day.
- Reverse shot – The reverse shot of the angle just filmed.
- Two shot – A shot of two people.
- Wildtrack – Sound recorded separately from the action (for editing use).
- ADR – Additional Dialogue Recording or Automated Dialogue Replacement. Going to a studio during post-production to record some dialogue.
- Theatre is dark – Theatre is closed, there are no shows in it.
- Press – The night allocated for reviewers to come to a show. Followed usually by a party.
- *Macbeth*/The Scottish play – Meant to be bad luck to say in the theatre. Ask an old(er) actor why.
- Method – Method acting.
- Masking – getting in between the audience and another actor for any length of time.
- Rake – The angle of the stage; to what degree it is tilted from US.
- US – Upstage! (Furthest away from the audience.)
- DS – Downstage. (Nearest the audience.)
- Previews – Shows that happen before the press night.
- 'Business' – Activity on stage i.e. June makes a sandwich, Peter polishes his shoes.
- Dry – To forget a line and pause in horror until one remembers it.
- Cutting room floor – When a scene or line is not included into the final edit.
- 'It's gone the another way' – You ain't got the job.
- Off book – All of your lines are learnt.

Arse over tit

My first film. Filming in Newcastle. Am now chatty acquaintance/practically bosom buddies with high-profile actress in said film. We wrap at the same time; hugs…

ME: Are you getting the 7.20 train back to town?

HER: No, I was gonna rush for the 7.

(It's about 6.50.)

Reckon we can make it if we hurry?

ME: *(Panic.)* Ok!

I sprint to my trailer, rip off my hairnet; gather my masses of luggage (having not quite yet gotten the hang of packing for location) and leap into the car. We scream through town, pull up at the station, and gleefully run together, laughing at the panic and excitement of it all. Though she is a good decade older than me she moves like the wind, her neat satchel not weighing her down at all. I sweat profusely, the droplets blurring my vision. The last announcements for the train are screaming out as we fly over the bridge and down the ramp to the platform. 'How cool is this', I'm thinking. 'Won't it be great when we're finally sat on the train, panting and laughing, ordering a beer and retelling the 'we nearly missed it' story'.

She reaches the bottom of the ramp and glances back excitedly.

HER: Doors are still open!

My mind wonders onto the train doors and off my feet for a second, my pre-emptive celebration of victory distracting me from the ramp beneath; I trip. I not only fall, I tumble down the ramp, suitcase bashing me, shoes flying off and high-profile actress looking on in horror. I land; sprawled across the tarmac, grazed, dazed and mortified, just in time to see the doors of the train close. We missed it.

Rushing over to me she didn't know whether to laugh, feel guilty or call an ambulance. Later, when we boarded the next train and sat in awkward silence over a beer I quietly said to her…

ME: When I write my book this is going in it for fucking certain.

She moved to LA where people are cool…

13. I CONCLUDE

That's a wrap – tadar!…
(admittedly that's more of a sound than a word)

Wow, can I talk or what? Imagine going on a date with me; blah, blah, drink, blah, blah, pearl of wisdom, blah, yawn, taxi, sexy time? Nope, more chat.

So, my book – How was it for you? You can be honest; I can't hear you. For me it's been pretty epic; even if I've not managed to tell you anything I've taught myself a few things. Writing a book is pretty full on, and has been the strangest mixture of delight, pride and muted panic that I've ever experienced. There's been no dramatic hat-trick of blood, sweat and tears, but only because I'm not a crier – I've lost three stones of sweat, coped with seven paper cuts and lived to tell the tale, or, write the book…. And here we are. I wrote it chronologically so this is actually a conclusion, a reflective full stop and a fond farewell. No, don't close the book, I'm not gonna get all wanky and start thanking people; to be honest it's been a desperately lonely bloody process, so actually, if I'm going to give any thanks it's to my new best friend; last name Mac, first name Apple. Apple, we've spent many an hour together, me pressing your buttons, you falling asleep on my lap, me wanting to throw you out of the patio doors when you insist on spellchecking with Americanisms – It's been special… However I'll thank Apple properly later; let's get back to you.

Jesting aside, I hope you've taken what you need from me and have already started to make informed, healthy and interesting choices in your career as a result. There are still a few words sticking in my throat that I just want to run past you before we part. The first two words, sitting at opposite ends of the earth but somehow still managing to hold hands; Success and Failure. Our perceptions of them vary and our paths veer towards and away from them as often as the wind changes direction. There is no linear line from one to the other, no one way, no right way, no certain way. Acting is not as black and white as success and failure; there are so many shades of beauty and ugliness in between, with no concrete way of predicting how long each one will last.

What is failure? What is success? The definition of failure: Lack of success. The definition of success: The accomplishment of an aim or purpose. So, by my reckoning that means we are only 'failures' if we've accomplished nothing? Which I know damn well does not apply to you; you've read this book, that's an accomplishment in itself! I think that these two little words are disconcerting, misleading and unhelpful labels; labels we put on ourselves and labels we allow others to attach to us. They suggest destination to me, conclusion of some sort, and for that reason alone they cannot be relevant to us, as we are a work in progress; we have reached and concluded nothing, and it ain't over till the fat lady sings. Cue Susan Boyle… Ooh, yep, I said it and I'm not deleting it… If we are not careful, fearing failure and chasing success can blind us to all that we are and everything that is around us in the present; not yesterday, or tomorrow, but today. There's only one sure conclusion in life, and if we don't take pleasure in the fascinating journey towards that conclusion then what the hell is the point of existing at all? Release yourself from the unnecessary pressure that comes from attempting to categorize achievement; instead, why not give enjoying the ride a go? Before I release you from my drone, I do want to flag up a word I just used – pressure.

In striving to achieve you must inevitably risk; risk self-esteem, risk finance, risk happiness. Risk causes pressure; therefore one cannot gain without enduring the anxiety it brings with it. These sound familiar?

Pressure to work
Pressure to earn
Pressure to be happy
Pressure to perform
Pressure to create
Pressure to be good
Pressure to be different
Pressure to not mind
Pressure to organize
Pressure to pursue
Pressure to know
Pressure to not be a cliché
Pressure to be there
Pressure to impress
Pressure to see work
Pressure to be noticed
Pressure to matter
Pressure to not put pressure on oneself.
Pressure to do all of the above simultaneously.

It's understandable that it can get a little much. Anxiety grows the more we feed it. So breathe, and say to yourself 'I'm good at my job. I love my job. I'm going to work hard for my job. Can I deal with today instead of worrying about tomorrow? What can I do today? How do I feel today?' We don't have enough knowledge of the future to warrant worrying about it. We can only exist for today and roll with the punches as they come; we can attempt to engineer the future, yes, but must remember in doing so that attempts can never be guarantees. Some days it will be easy to think like this and other days your capacity to cope will be like a fart in the wind.

Yes, you love your job. Will you adore it every second of the day, every day of the year? No – you'll want it to piss off, you'll want to be a schoolteacher instead; you'll want bank statements devoid of 'helplines'. But it's your job for as long as you choose it to be, inclusive of peaks and troughs, advantages and disadvantages, highs and lows – like everything in life there is light and shade. One of the peculiar things I do when I'm low or having a rant is to write it down – and bish bash bosh, the woman's got a book! By putting the thought from my head onto paper it somehow feels as if I've moved it, not erased it, but moved it from my conscious mind, clearing the decks. I guess you could say that my notepad is the dustbin of my mind. Hold on, I'm not calling my book rubbish… You know what I mean. I found a post-it note recently down the back of my bedside table. It read:

'Today I want to play mini-golf and have three children. I want a mortgage and a car and a wallet full of Tesco vouchers. I want to have a holiday booked and a dinner party to buy wine for on Tuesday; I want the phone to ring and for me to not give a shit that I miss the call; I want to buy a pair of Jimmy Choos and know that I've earned them; I want to make homemade stew and take the dog for a walk. But that's today. Tomorrow I'll want to be the next Meryl Streep again. Sometimes I just want to be normal and nothing else. And then I remember that I'm me, and that the things I'm meant to achieve, for now, outweigh any items on some shopping list of life.'

I'm not sure there's much I need to say to follow that. We must sacrifice if we want to achieve. But we must continuously monitor our willingness and contentment in doing so; lapses of faith are to be expected and should always be acknowledged but an acute awareness that cynicism erodes hope is a must for any actor. We must combat cynicism and always resist the temptation to justify ourselves to anyone who is neither able nor brave enough to walk a mile in our shoes. We fly the flag of ambition and betterment and should be damn proud of it – what the hell would the world be like without dreamers?

Please know that these 'pearls' that have been pouring out of me over the last (what I'm sure seems like 6 million pages), come from the best of places, and are given from me to you with an immense amount of respect. If my book has made one of you smile, two of you be calmer in auditions, three of you have something to wedge the kitchen door open with – then I am a happy little author.

Surround yourself with good people and keep happiness a notch above ambition on your list of priorities. Ambition won't work without it.

…130,054 words in and I suddenly realise that I may just have helped to improve my competition's chances of employment… Ah, shit. (Any fair-haired women in their mid-twenties with a Midlands lilt and a large chest, just ignore it all, I was lying.)

In all seriousness, this is a very serious conclusion, to a very serious book in these very serious times. As well as Mr Apple Mac who has kept my lap warm most nights for the last eight months, I'd also like to thank Holland & Barrett for inventing the Migrastick, my friends and family who helped to pad my room and hide all of the sharp objects, and Hendricks for providing the liquid crutch that is Gin. You've all played an integral part, not only in the writing of this book, but throughout my not-quite-there-yet career.

Oh, and biggest thanks of all goes to Jodie Dowse who bullied me in school; your relentless attention was the catalyst for my achievements. Look up catalyst you dumb fuck.

With love,
Nat x

'If toast always lands butter side down, and cats always land on their feet, what happens if you strap toast on the back of a cat and drop it...?'

I'm off to find out.

https://twitter.com/MissNatalieBurt

APPENDIX

(A small list of recommendations)

Photographers:

As I said earlier, all of the photographers I have used have been wonderful and have completely fulfilled my expectations at the time of working with them. These are the names of the photographers used by me over the years and I'd highly recommend all of them. A recommendation is of course great, but look at their websites and portfolios to see the proof in the pudding, as it were.

Chris Baker – http://www.chrisbakerphotographer.com
Catherine Shakespeare Lane – http://www.csl-art.co.uk
Faye Thomas – http://www.fayethomas.com

FYI I have recently discovered actor/photographer **Jim Creighton** and was so impressed with his work that I wanted you to know about him. Take a look at his website – www.jimcreighton.co.uk

Repro companies:

There are literally shed loads (literally?) of these companies. Refer to *Contacts* to find the many that are listed. I name these two because I have used them, been pleased with the results and can therefore recommend them as a good place to start.

Moorfields – http://www.moorfieldsphoto.com
Very nice quality, quick and efficient and reasonably priced.
I've gone back to them over the years and always been happy with the service they provide.

Image Photographic – http://www.imagephotographic.com
Used more recently and picked up an order within 24 hours from a central location in London which was most helpful.

Showreel companies:

There are also many of these companies popping up left, right and centre now as editing is becoming more accessible to the average Joe and is also becoming something that more actors are self-teaching. Actorshowreels are no different in the sense that Hugh Lee is an actor and has built this business up as a sideline. How they are different is that they are experienced and knowledgeable when it comes to both sides of the fence – editing and acting; they know about what industry professionals require from a showreel, can advise you accordingly, whilst speaking in a language that is familiar to actors and at the same time being sensitive to the wants and needs of the individual.

I have worked with them twice and have been very pleased with the results (YouTube search 'Natalie Burt showreel' and 'Natalie Burt Blandings' if you want to see them or visit their website for further footage they've created). I found the process wonderfully collaborative, done at a pace that suited me and at a price that I felt fitted the result.

Actorshowreels – http://actorshowreels.co.uk

Accountants:

Though I am not with them myself I can say that MGM (who helped with the finance section of this book) seem friendly, helpful, reasonably priced, sensitive to the complications of our industry and on the whole very approachable. I met Mark at an actors' conference where I was doing research for the book. I explained my project and mentioned that I was on the look out for an Accountant to assist me. When I bumped into him at another conference a good two months later, having had no contact with him, he remembered my name, my occupation, my project and when he last met me. I was impressed and would go so far to say that when dealing with one's finances a friendly, attentive and helpful go to person is a must.

Mark Livermore @ MGM Accountancy
http://mgmaccountancy.co.uk/

Film services:

Like most actors, I love film. But sometimes poverty gets in the way of seeing all the latest releases at the cinema so I find these services not only cheap and great providers of entertainment, but also very useful if I have to very quickly swat up on a certain director or genre. I subscribe to these two:

Lovefilm – This is a great service with no contract to tie you in and no hidden charges. Depending on what membership package you choose you will have access to thousands of films and television series by either having the discs posted to you, streaming them online or both. Packages range from roughly £5 - £14 per month and you are able to change packages whenever you please. I find this a great way not only to access thousands of films using a great search engine that allows you to find films using title, director, actor etc. but it also gives me the opportunity to always have access to film

I haven't seen, regardless of what my bank balance looks like that week. You can manage your account online easily and can list films you intend to see. This is so useful when someone references a film or a director; I go straight to my account and add it to my library of must-sees. Be careful not to clutter your lists too much though, or it may be difficult for you to receive a specific film when you want it as there will be so many for Lovefilm to choose from to send you. You can also take a payment holiday for up to three months if you wish; if you go on tour or are especially brassic you always have that option – http://www.lovefilm.com

Netflix – This is a similar idea and the two companies are in direct competition with each other. I am now a member of both as I feel that their strengths lie in slightly different areas but that they are both useful. Netflix is better for television series I find, whereas it can get annoying ordering series and seasons from Lovefilm (unless you're streaming). Netflix has no postal system, it's all done online and you can hook your laptop up to your telly. I know, I know, EVERYONE already knows this! I have been doing an HBO two-decade catch up over the last year and have found that Netflix is superior within that field. However, they don't have as good a catalogue of film. I reduced my membership to Lovefilm to the cheapest tariff and joined Netflix as well resulting in me having access to all of the desired material that I need for under a tenner a month! Happy days – http://www.netflix.com/uk

Blinkbox – This is your more Pay As You Go-type film rental. I like this one because it has latest releases that I can see really quickly if I've missed them at the cinema. You can see some 'classics' (*Jurassic Shark*) for 99p, or you can rent great titles for around £4 and then there's others for £7ish. No contracts or 'signing up', you just create an account and pay for what you watch. Some are buys and some rents. – http://www.blinkbox.com

I've heard **Sky Go** is also fairly great, but I don't have that (far too technical, haven't even worked out the green and red buttons on the remote yet). **Now TV** is the new competitor of the ones I've mentioned – have a look…

… Of course, as good as these services are, don't forget to leave the house and have infrequent contact with human beings too.

Cinemas to check out:

Prince Charles Cinema – Cheap days and tickets available. West London.

Curzon Cinema, Soho – Great venue with an interesting programme and a cool café bar filled with our 'type'!

BFI – films, workshops, Q&As, library etc. – cool café bar too.

Ritzy – Quirky half commercial, half art-house cinema in Brixton. Cheap day tickets.

Rooftop Cinema – I have only just discovered this and haven't yet been – BUT I WANT TO!

Cheaper offers available all over town and great opportunities to spend time watching brilliance there for the taking so do your research!

Books

Contacts – This really is a must have for any actor. A catalogue and a reference guide to all the available resources that an actor can and does need.

The Actors' Yearbook – An equally useful resource with listings of agents, casting directors and other 'need to know' info.

Michael Simkins' 'What's my motivation?' – Just a right laugh. I'm glad I read it more recently rather than when I was starting out though; loads of in jokes that are funny to Joe public but way funnier to those of us who are living these cringeworthy tales for real. Remember it's a compilation of drab for comedy's sake; being an actor isn't always wall-to-wall humiliation and ridicule! Well…

Acting: Cut the Crap, Cue the Truth – Great book. Couldn't put it down.

Subscriptions:

I belong to Spotlight, IMDb, Casting Call Pro (though CCP is a pointless exercise if you're not a paying member, as I am not, because you can't apply for jobs. If you do not have an agent I think the paid membership can be hugely beneficial, otherwise, perhaps not.)

As mentioned in Chapter 4, be wary of exposure sites before throwing money at them. And be aware that you can now also use sites such as Twitter, and maybe even Facebook to connect and expose too.

Conferences/Masterclasses/courses

Surviving Actors – http://www.survivingactors.com
I attended this conference to do research and found a whole plethora of information and services stuffed in one room ready for me to utilise. I would certainly recommend attending these types of events if only to see what is available to you and to talk to other people within the industry.

Perform Exhibition – http://www.performshow.co.uk
Similarly this conference/festival was really useful in terms of breadth of information. Obviously these events are designed to enable businesses to advertise to actors i.e. photographers, Equity, accountants etc. but they're also really good for networking and there are usually some really interesting Q&As with industry professionals too.

Spotlight's National Student Drama Festival – I've never attended it myself, but I'm sure if Spotlight are behind it, it will be informative and certainly worth a look-see.

Haymarket Masterclass – http://www.masterclass.org.uk
Definitely sign up for this. The Haymarket hold masterclasses throughout the year that are free and available to you simply by signing up. I have attended all sorts and think they're a fab way of doing something proactive for an hour and a half, whilst learning in the process. Playwrights, actors, directors, agents – all informative and rather informal.

National Theatre platform – These are similar to the Haymarket sessions and are basically Q&As with industry people, usually directors, writers, practitioners etc. who are working at the National at the time. There is a small fee but they're really worth going to.

Raindance – http://www.raindance.org
More for filmmakers, but possibly for actors who wish to work in film too. You pay to be a member and can then get discounted prices for their masterclasses and workshops.

The Actors Centre – http://www.actorscentre.co.uk
Offers an unrivalled programme of high calibre workshops and masterclasses for the continual professional development of emerging and established actors. They have an extensive menu of classes, workshops and courses.

The Associated Studios – http://www.associatedstudios.co.uk/
A similar idea to the Actors Centre but more focused on Musical Theatre. Masterclasses and Q&As with industry professionals. A friendly and pro-active bunch.

The Actors Guild – http://www.actorsguild.co.uk
Another great source of interest for actors. You pay a small fee to be a member and there are certain 'perks' to being one. Masterclasses and workshops etc. available.

Actors Platform – http://actorsplatform.com/
Run by two former actresses, this is an affordable membership service that provides Q&As, showcasing opportunities, casting workshops and other perks for actors looking to promote themselves and learn about their industry.

Industry Hollywood – A company who take groups of actors to LA to introduce them to what it may be like to live and work in the US. They provide information and assistance regarding visas and organise all sorts of workshops, networking opportunities and 'meetings' during the trip. I have no actual experience of this company and must admit that I think it's rather an expensive thing to do. However, I wanted you to know that it is available and it might be a really useful way of taking a break or a holiday whilst making some contacts.

My definite advice to you in regards to 're-locating' to the US would be to ask yourself why (why it isn't happening in London, why you think it'll be any different over there) and what (what you're going to do over there, what you have to offer the US market and what you might be giving up/leaving behind in the UK). By all means, go on an adventure but be careful not to be running from a hard game into an almost impossible one! Be realistic and organised about it).

Mental health

I touched briefly on this subject in Chapter 9 and want to reiterate that the information I have offered there is more empathetic than factual and must be observed in conjunction with a GP's advice in cases where self-help may not be possible.

Here are a few sources of support for anyone suffering from the debilitating illness that is depression. However severe or mild the symptoms, however embarrassed or ashamed you may feel, always, always seek advice and let people help you. The support is available and the opportunity to get better is always there.

> **Samaritans** – http://www.samaritans.org or call them on 08457 90 90 90

> **Mind** – http://www.mind.org.uk/mental_health

Acknowledgements

I'd like to very briefly acknowledge and thank all who helped with the writing of this book; your contributions have been so generously given and I feel awfully privileged that you wished to be involved (with only a small amount of physical threat and financial bribery needed). Huge thanks to:

Alice Purser, James Penford, Bruce Guthrie, Sean Biggerstaff, Brogan West, Mark Livermore, Marc Pickering, Chris Baker, Catherine Shakespeare Lane, Faye Thomas, Mark Dean, Hugh Lee, Marek Losey, Charlotte Frings at Mammoth Screen, Laura Albery, Pippa Harrison and Ben Seale at Spotlight, Richard Bean, Sam Davies, Tim Spall, Caroline Quentin, Ian Bartholomew and all of the actors I've stolen cringey stories from over the last seven years.

I'd better also acknowledge my phenomenal parents for their unwavering support and belief (cliché but they may kick my arse if I don't).

I'd also like to thank in advance all of the directors who are poised ready to employ me in the coming months and years; no need to delay, do it, do it now.

Cheers to all of you for reading/buying/borrowing/stealing this book, what a switched-on bunch you are…

'And lastly so, so many thanks to all at Oberon Books for taking a chance on me, listening to me, holding my hand and not judging me when I used the spelling of my own name for the 'gnat's fart' gag.

Natalie Burt graduated from Guildford School of Acting in 2006 with a first, a great agent and a hangover. For the first four years of her career she worked in the theatre with some fabulous directors on some wonderful texts including *Deep Blue Sea, Glass Cage, An Inspector Calls, Sugar Daddies* and *Pride and Prejudice*. She then did a *Doctors* episode and her life changed... Ok, sure, it didn't *change*, but she did realise that the screen thing could be more of a plan than she'd originally thought and an array of BBC, ITV and Channel 4 jobs including Coming up, *United, Blandings* and *Breathless* then followed. She also writes scripts and stuff, and here we are at the completion of her first book. She likes sharks and dislikes talking about herself in the third person.